Software Acquisition
Management

WILEY SERIES IN INDUSTRIAL SOFTWARE ENGINEERING PRACTICE

Fletcher J. Buckley, Editor

Software Acquisition Management

Managing the Acquisition of Custom Software Systems

JOHN J. MARCINIAK
DONALD J. REIFER

John Wiley & Sons, Inc.
New York / Chichester / Brisbane / Toronto / Singapore

Library of Congress Cataloging in Publication Data:
Marciniak, John J.
    Software acquisition management: managing the acquisition of
custom software systems / John J. Marciniak, Donald J. Reifer.
        p. cm.—(Wiley series in industrial software engineering
practice)
    Includes bibliographical references.
    1. Computer software—Development—Management.   I. Reifer, Donald
J.   II. Title. III. Series.

    QA76-76.D47M363   1980
    005.1–dc20   89-49734
    ISBN 0-471-50643-5   CIP

Printed in the United States of America

10 9 8 7 6 5 4 3 2 1

To our families:
Without their patience, support, and help
this book would not have been possible.

CONTENTS

6 Software Management—The Buyer's Model   124

7 Software Management—The Seller's Model   **158**

8 Software Management—The Team Approach   **179**

We believe that the following treatment of the acquisition of customized software systems is unique. In writing this book, we had available to us a wealth of resources including our own experiences and dialogue with our colleagues. Often books deal only with academic issues. Such books, of course, are both valuable and necessary. However, in preparing this book, we were guided by a more practical precept: to aid in solving real-world problems.

This book was designed to provide guidance on the subject of software acquisition management—the process of acquiring, via a formal agreement between the buyer and seller (for example, by contract), software that has to be developed or has an appreciable content that requires development. We were guided by our own concerns assuming that we were confronted with this management task. What are the issues? How does one deal with the contractor environment and the contracting process? How are software management requirements incorporated into the contract? How are they then managed? How is insight into the development process achieved? These and many other questions were the ones we selected to answer.

It is common knowledge that computers and software are an extremely important part of modern automated systems. Such systems affect all of us. They are used for national defense and to provide various services to improve the quality of our daily lives. They render assistance for jobs or personal tasks on an individual basis. The development of large and complex systems has always been problematic. Management and acquisition mechanisms have not matured at a pace equal to the growth of software technology. The results have often been disastrous. Developmental efforts often exceed project budgets and schedules. Delivered systems do not meet original user requirements. In extreme cases, software acquisitions have been abandoned after a huge expenditure of resources because of improper management.

Management and technical personnel are struggling to develop techniques to deal with these management issues. Corporate America is faced with many questions concerning how such acquisitions are to be managed. How to approach a procurement in terms of strategy? How to create a management environment that generates requirements for a statement of work? How to provide oversight management of the development effort? How to determine whether the delivered system meets the requirements of the contract? These are real issues facing managers in today's business world. It is this perspective that we bring to the software management discipline.

This is a book for the host of managers directly or indirectly involved in acquisition projects. It is not a book about managing the software engineering process, although it touches on subjects necessary for that task. It is intended for both the software acquisition and development manager. The book is for the manager involved in any aspect of the acquisition process—proposal managers responsible for the seller's response to a buyer's request, financial managers who plan and account for the costs of a program, contracting specialists who have to arrange the contract vehicle, adminstrative managers who have to provide services to support the acquisition, and so on.

We have tried to approach the subject on a broad scale rather than concentrating on a specific management environment. We have, however, used specific examples to explain management concepts and guidelines that can be applied to software development efforts in any management environment. Management requirements for a particular project will have to be tailored to that acquisition. Such tailoring enables applications to smaller scale projects as well. Good management is necessary for a successful software acquisition regardless of its size.

We took on this effort because of the real need for information to help managers in this area. It is our hope that the reader will find pertinent and directly usable information in the pages that follow.

JOHN J. MARCINIAK
Alexandria, Virginia

DONALD J. REIFER
Torrance, California

ACKNOWLEDGMENTS

As always there are a number of people to thank when a work of this type is undertaken. It is, however, a most pleasant task. First we would like to thank Maria Taylor of John Wiley for her early support of the proposed work. Both Jack Munson of UNISYS and Terry Straeter of General Dynamics reviewed the first outline of the work. Their positive comments were encouraging. A number of people are due appreciation for their help in reviewing the manuscript: Bernie Zempolich who reviewed early drafts, Jody Steinbacker of the Jet Propulsion Laboratories for her help with the NASA SMAP standards, and Anne Martin of Kirkpatrick and Lockhart for her help with data rights. Larry Fry of Lockheed Sanders and Fletcher Buckley of the General Electric Company spent many hours and provided excellent technical reviews. We were grateful for our graphics support provided by the Mosely team: Jan Mosely of Texas Instruments and her spouse Warren Mosely of the University of Alabama. Susan Marciniak and Mary Jo Hogan were extremely gracious with their time in editing the draft manuscript. We are grateful to Publication Services, especially David Lederman and Jennifer Hense for the fine job they did in editing and preparing the manuscript for publication. Finally, a very special thanks to our editor Diane Cerra, for her forbearance, encouragement, and tenacity.

J. J. M.
D. J. R.

LIST OF FIGURES

LIST OF TABLES

Software Acquisition
Management

CHAPTER 1

Introduction

Software acquisition management is the process of managing the acquisition of custom software systems. The key discriminators of custom software are that it cannot be developed by a small group of people (say, fewer than 10) and that it involves a set of users with direct interest in and impact on system requirements. The purpose of this book is to discuss the activities involved in managing a software acquisition. The topics are of interest to management personnel from team leaders to senior managers. We discuss the subject from the perspectives of both the buyer or acquirer of the software and the seller or developer of the software.

Effective management of software development is certainly one of the great challenges in the application of new technologies. Software (computer programs) is involved in nearly every product and transaction in the marketplace whether it is part of a system such as an automobile engine or an element of business activity such as banking. In its infancy merely 20 years ago, software was a commodity relegated mostly to a small sector of the scientific and technical community. Systems were customized for banking, military, space, and other specialized applications. Today, software is not only more important in its original applications but integral to many more. Modern software is embedded in the microchips of watches, toys, and games and guides the complex activities of global telecommunications, manned space stations, military systems, and corporate systems used for management information and production control.

With the rapid development of hardware (microchip) technology, the production or development of software has evolved from the realm of programming to other computing disciplines such as systems analysis, database design, testing and evaluation, and quality control. The size, complexity, and diversity of computer systems, and their applications, which affect the daily lives of millions of people, make proper management extremely important.

1.1   ACQUISITION MANAGEMENT

Many people think of software development as the work of a small group of programmers managed by perhaps a single leader. Indeed, many software products have been built by such groups. This may work well for a focused product such as Lotus 1-2-3™ or WordPerfect™ but it does not work for a product that will have large numbers of users and developers. Even the small-product world is changing. It was reported that Lotus 1-2-3, version 3, required 263 man-years to develop at a cost of $7 million, with another $15 million for quality control testing [Schlender, 1989].

Products such as Lotus 1-2-3 or WordPerfect are narrowly defined—they have very specific applications. They are developed in a closed community, the individual corporation. Their users are a diverse group. With custom systems the situation is more complex. They are based on a user community with a diverse set of needs. For example, a banking operation will have its own system requirements. Because most banks are not in the business of developing complex software, they will typically contract for this service. The bank then has to compile a set of requirements, select a contractor to develop the system, monitor the implementation, and assess the product's usability. To control this process, the bank must use an effective system of software acquisition management.

Some may believe that software acquisition management is necessary only for large organizations such as NASA. Government organizations of this size certainly do develop huge amounts of software (the software for the space shuttle has 25,600,000 lines of code and was developed at a cost of 1.2 billion dollars [Schlender, 1989], but in fact the development or acquisition process is widespread in the private sector as well. There are many examples: a financial system developed for an accounting firm, a legal search system developed for a law firm, a system to provide bibliographical data for a publishing company or a newspaper, and so on.

The acquisition of custom software ranges from purchasing modifications to off-the-shelf software to more complex acquisitions such as managing the development of a real-time command and control system used in military missions. The dominant considerations in acquiring complex software are that

- The requirements are diverse. That is, the system will perform a variety of functions that cannot be described in just a few pages.
- The software is not an off-the-shelf commercial product, although there may be off-the-shelf commercial products in the custom system.
- The users of the system are a diverse set performing many different tasks.
- The users or customers are different from those responsible for acquiring the system. For example, one would not expect a teller to be involved in acquiring the system for a bank. A teller might, however, be involved in testing the system.
- The developer is different from the acquirer. Normally the acquirer has a contractor develop the system.

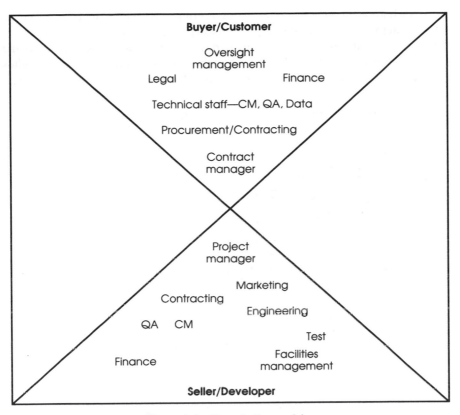

Figure 1-1 Buyer/seller model

Managing the acquisition of custom software includes the planning, budgeting, and contracting of the system. It also involves monitoring the implementation of the system, evaluating the results of development, and providing for the system's continued support. Acquisition management involves a number of organizations, including the customer or user of the system, the contracting agency or the buyer of the system, and the developer or seller of development services (Figure 1-1). Although there is a single point of control for a project, the responsibility is shared throughout the various facets of its development and implementation.

In addition, many managers exercise specific responsibilities in the execution of a contract. For example, some people buy and manage a software development contract and others supervise the development within the seller's shop.

1.2 THE SOFTWARE DEVELOPMENT ENVIRONMENT

To understand and to effectuate the process of software acquisition management, it is important to understand the process of software development. The process of software development is an engineering process akin to other engineering disciplines such as automotive or chemical engineering. Like an automobile, computer software must be designed, developed, prototyped, and tested.

Software engineering, the practice of developing software, is similar to the engineering processes of designing and building electronic products such as radios and television sets and the production process of manufacturing duplicate copies.

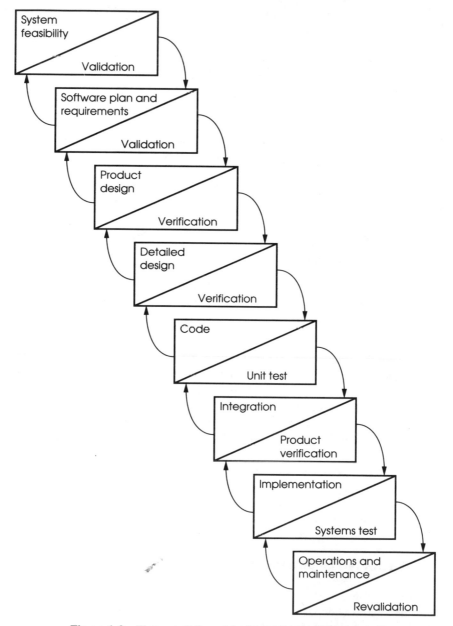

Figure 1-2   The waterfall model of the software life cycle

It begins with the identification and analysis of the requirements for a software product, which is then designed and coded, tested, integrated into the operational environment, and maintained throughout its life. This process is called the software development life cycle. A simple depiction of the process—commonly called the software life cycle waterfall process of development—is shown in Figure 1-2. It is one of the many life cycle models discussed in the software literature.

In order to automate this process and provide a production capability for software development, many organizations have established software development environments. Typically, an environment is a set of tools (for example, compilers, editors, and debuggers) that support a number of development methods. Structured analysis, structured design, and object-oriented design are a few of these methods, or specific technical procedures, that are used in the development process. In practice these environments are known by many names, such as Software Engineering Environments (SSE) or Integrated Programming Support Environments (IPSE). Many of the tools in these environments are provided in CASE (Computer Aided Software Engineering) tool sets. The tool set automates both the processes and methods used to engineer the product.

The environment is augmented by management methods and practices such as measuring and monitoring progress, judging the quality of the product, and validating the deliverable products against contract requirements. These activities provide the information managers need to control software acquisition. They provide a means of communication among all personnel involved in developing and managing the project. They also provide checkpoints, commonly called quality gates, where interim deliveries can be checked and quality assessed. These practices ensure that the product is properly built and satisfies the user's requirements.

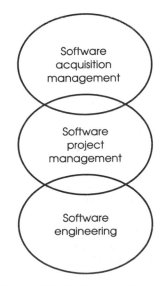

Figure 1-3   Software environment

Software management, or software project management, is the process of managing this engineering process.

To place software acquisition in context, refer to Figure 1-3. The figure shows the relationships among software acquisition, software management, and software engineering. Software engineering is the technical process of building the software product. Software project management is the process of managing the technical process. Software acquisition is the process of assembling the requirements for the system, planning the project, acquiring the development resources (usually by contract), and monitoring and controlling the implementation. The intersection between software project management and software acquisition is at the project management level because software acquisition includes this level as well as lateral and higher levels of management.

1.3 THE BUYER/SELLER MODEL

Acquisition management is performed by a buyer/seller team. The buyer is the agent for the customer acquiring the system. The seller is the contractor, or developer, who responds to the buyer's need for a specific capability. (In some cases an internal contract vehicle may be used; that is, the buyer and the seller are two separate departments within the same organization.) Figure 1-4 depicts a hierarchy of management levels in a typical contractual environment. Personnel responsible for contracting arrange for a specific contract vehicle that incorporates the requirements the software product must meet. They develop cost and schedule targets, implement management controls, and supervise the effort. Other personnel are responsible for quality assurance, configuration management (see Section 2-3), and so on. Although all these individuals have roles in the management process, the program/project managers have the most direct responsibility. As one becomes more removed from the project, the responsibility becomes more indirect, though such personnel in both the buyer and seller organizations still share responsibility.

The buyers, or clients, are interested in getting what they are paying for. They want a system that delivers expected capability within the funds budgeted and according to an agreed-upon delivery schedule. The sellers, or developers, want to deliver a system that performs well (in order to foster follow-on contractual efforts), that is completed in a timely manner, and that makes a reasonable profit.

Other issues vary with the long-term strategy of the seller and the development personnel. Sellers may do things differently if they are trying to develop a new product line or penetrate new markets. They may take a contract at a loss in order to cultivate future opportunities. Personnel will have different objectives based on their specific involvement. Technical personnel may be trying to develop new skills or move into management positions. Although these issues may not be inconsistent with the overall goals of the effort, they add cost and risk because the seller, and even the buyer, may be focusing on other matters.

The seller has primary responsibility for the software and system-engineering process. The buyer acquires the services of the seller to build a software-intensive

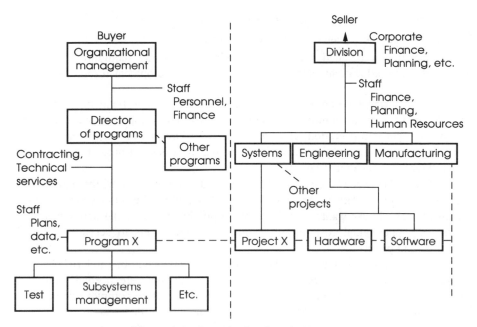

Figure 1-4 Organizational environment

system. While the sellers concern themselves with engineering, the buyers worry about contracting, performance management, procurement, finance, planning, oversight, and other functions.

The buyer must therefore plan for the acquisition by

1. Detailing the requirements that the system must satisfy.
2. Allocating resources for the development of the system.
3. Arranging for the selection of a seller to develop the system, usually through a competitive process.
4. Contracting with the selected seller.
5. Building an in-house team to manage the development process.
6. Overseeing the development (team) to ensure that it is on schedule, within resource allocation, and consistent with customer requirements.
7. Addressing support requirements, especially if the system will be maintained by a third party or user.

To the seller, the acquisition process drives many decisions. The seller must plan for the competitive selection process. The seller must

1. Decide whether the resources and capability to bid on the contract are available.
2. Decide whether to bid.

3. Develop a team to respond to the proposal.
4. Estimate the resources required to perform the effort.
5. Develop a detailed plan to accomplish the work, including schedules, resource allocations, and the organization of development resources.

After capturing the competitive award, the seller must respond to the buyer's needs in the area of contract oversight. A project development team must be organized, put into operation, and monitored to ensure that the customer's project is being implemented appropriately and that the development project is consistent with buyer's management targets.

Although the basic objectives of the buyer and seller are similar, the motivations are quite different. The buyer wants to gain a capability; the seller wants to make a profit. The buyer wants to hold down supplemental cost; the seller wants to increase supplemental cost through contract change orders to accrue additional revenue and profit.

Another level of complexity, becoming more prevalent in modern systems, involves the use of third-party suppliers. These suppliers are needed more frequently for a variety of reasons. As software becomes more complex, demanding more varied skills, few sellers have the total mix of skilled resources to apply to development efforts. The broad diversity of distributed telecommunications systems, for example, has forced many software houses to buy the communications resources they need to bid on and develop total systems. Most projects require specialty software products such as Data Base Management Systems, along with the expertise required to properly apply these products in the system. A seller who does not have all the necessary resources to apply to the development will require a supplement to the work force.

Thus the buyer faces a complicated contractual arrangement. The buyer contracts with the seller and holds the seller to the requirements of the contract, but it may be impossible to make an accurate assessment of status without looking at third-party or subcontracted efforts. The buyer needs to ensure that the third-party suppliers have the necessary management skills to complement the seller and that an effective project software acquisition management environment is provided. The balance of management skills should be consistent across the supplier mix.

1.4 PROBLEMS IN SOFTWARE ACQUISITION MANAGEMENT

The brief history of software development has been filled with problems. Projects have exceeded cost, slipped schedules, and failed to perform according to expectations. Worst of all, after years of effort and resource expenditure, some have not completed delivery at all. It is likely that many of these problems resulted from a failure to understand or apply sound software acquisition management practices.

The goal of software acquisition management is to obtain a workable system within the framework of time and resources allocated to the effort. In the final analysis, one would like the acquisition to be straightforward, like the purchase of an off-the-shelf commodity—specifying performance requirements, fitting these within a reasonable resource expectation, and detailing a schedule of delivery.

These are noble goals. Although difficult to attain, they need not be considered unrealistic. Such expectations should, however, be gauged across the spectrum of systems procured. Too often acquisition managers procure systems without a reasonable knowledge of acquisition practice. They may not understand the development processes or the time and resources necessary to engineer a product. They may be overwhelmed by the "software mystique." Acquisition managers may not understand software and may have difficulty in understanding what their subordinate or peer level managers are trying to communicate. This lack of understanding is common in software development, usually resulting in the manager's "surprise" when the true status of the development project is ultimately discovered.

It is certainly reasonable to expect solid deliveries in low-risk development efforts. The real trick is to identify the high-risk development efforts and to structure the management process accordingly—to provide control of the development and to gain timely and accurate insight into its progress. The treatment of acquisition problems is given in that context.

1.4.1 Cost

Cost overrun is probably the single biggest problem in software development because it represents time, money, and missed opportunities. When development budgets are exceeded, extreme pressure is often placed on the overall organization's resources. The budget for a project is usually projected long before software costs can be realistically estimated. In most organizations there are long lead times to get money committed. If the project is hardware intensive, such as a new aircraft, the software costs are often lost in the overall budget. In software-intensive systems, the costs projected during planning for the system and before the software requirements are known often prove wrong during or after development. Unfortunately, system planners are often haunted by poor cost projections when an insufficient allocation of dollars to software development causes the overall schedule to slip.

The difficulty in estimating costs is often due to fuzzy requirements. This problem may persist even after the project enters development. If, by some miracle, the requirements are well-defined, other risks present in the development may not be understood. When the development is precedented—for example, when an existing system is upgraded—cost projections may be quite accurate. In unprecedented (new) systems, especially when the systems development team is not experienced in the specific application, the risk of cost overrun is high. The major problem is usually creeping cost growth; projects get in trouble a little at a time, not all at once. This limits the visibility of senior-level managers and makes their controls ineffective. Often acquisition managers do not learn about the overrun until it becomes obvious. One delay in detection occurs when management does not understand the warning signals or is assured that remedial actions are under way. Cost overruns cause havoc with the organization's budget.

From a developer's point of view, senior management suffers similar difficulties, except from a different perspective. The buyer must hold down development costs while struggling to meet customer expectations. The overall cost is often fixed by contract. Therefore, when a cost disaster is first discovered, the developer attempts to implement alternative actions to protect the integrity of the contract. For example, the seller may initiate cost proposals that will reduce the scope of the effort by reducing and/or eliminating project requirements.

1.4.2 Schedule

Schedules drive most projects, and more problems are caused by an unrealistic schedule than any other reason. Changes in the schedule usually start with small, almost indiscernible alterations that go unnoticed by all but the most astute managers. For example, a slip in the delivery of a test plan may make the test program late because long lead actions were not taken. Because this usually occurs early in the development, little attention is paid to its potential impact. Slips tend to become more frequent as development progresses until it becomes obvious that there is a major developmental problem. Management suddenly admits its inability to meet schedule. All those optimists have now become pessimists, or, more accurately, realists.

Schedule changes almost always affect cost, and their impact can be severe. Software may be on the critical path of system development when slippage starts affecting the overall development process. This condition was prevalent in the development of early aircraft (avionics) software, especially when software was playing a new role and management did not clearly understand the impact of software development on the overall system. In systems such as financial networks that must be integrated into more global environments with other systems and where personnel interactions are important, the result can be equally disastrous. Management is usually presented with a number of alternative solutions to correct the problem in the hope that the overall project schedule will not be affected. Unless schedule slippage is recognized and dealt with through timely engineering and management action, the situation will worsen until a major problem has developed.

1.4.3 Performance

Even more disturbing to management than cost and schedule problems are overall changes in the performance of a system. These usually take two basic forms.

First, there is the failure to achieve system level performance requirements. This is the more serious case because it means that the system the customer bought will not perform as expected even though projected resources (and possibly more) were expended. Indeed, there are examples of system acquisitions that had to be canceled, without an effective delivery, after years of cost and schedule overrun [GAO, 1979].

The second performance problem is more prevalent and more insidious. As technical difficulties are discovered, the team tends to reduce the overall functionality of the system. This usually takes the form of reducing derived requirements, which underlie the implementation of the system, such as the retrieval time for a record. Many projects have been blatantly rationalized as examples of good software management by managers who modify requirements. As difficulties occurred in performance and schedule, requirements were reduced to maintain a balance between cost and schedule goals, resulting in reduced performance. This is unacceptable in today's environment, where management expects the engineering process to be sophisticated enough to achieve system performance based on reasonable expectations for system cost and delivery schedule.

1.5 CHAPTER OVERVIEW

The initial chapters provide an overview of the acquisition process. Chapter 2 provides an introduction to the system and software development process. It includes life cycle models and various standards used in software development. Chapter 3 deals with the processes of acquisition—the strategies and means of arriving at a contract. Chapter 4 discusses the statement of work process—how to plan for and implement a statement of work and key evaluation considerations. Chapter 5 considers contract law—types of contracts and how to administer them.

The next three chapters deal with the buyer and seller management models. Chapter 6 discusses management from the perspective of the buyer and Chapter 7 from the perspective of the seller. Chapter 8 discusses the roles of key players in the buyer/seller model and the benefits of a team approach.

The final four chapters treat special subjects. Chapter 9 deals with costing—estimating the cost of development and pricing the development. Chapter 10 provides an overview of software quality and the quality assurance program. Chapters 11 and 12 deal with a potpourri of special acquisition subjects. Chapter 11 treats special topics such as warranties and reusability. Finally, Chapter 12 explores the meaning that new directions in technology and practice have to the manager now and tries to give some advice on the treatment of these topics in software engineering projects.

Because of the diversity of people involved in the acquisition process, their interests in the various topics will differ. For this reason we have provided a guide for the reader based on these different perspectives. The guide is based on the following views:

- Oversight management—management that is somewhat removed from the development, but is in the chain of management visibility and may exercise some control over the project. Alternatively, management that may have reason to become involved in some aspect of the project, for instance solving a particular problem.

Reader	1 Introduction	2 The software acquisition environment	3 Acquisition management	4 Software statement of work issues	5 Contracts and contract law	6 Software management: buyer's model	7 Software management: seller's model	8 Software management: team approach	9 Cost issues and answers	10 Quality management	11 Special topics in acquisition management	12 Future directions in acquisition management
Oversight manager	All	2.1, 2.2, 2.3 *	3.1 *	4.1 *	5.1 *	All	*	All	9.1, 9.3, 9.4, 9.5, 9.6 *	10.1, 10.5 *	*	*
Buyer project manager	All	All	All	All	All	All	*	All	All	All	All	*
Seller project manager	All	All	All	All	All	All	All	All	All	All	All	*
Financial manager	All	2.1, 2.2, 2.3 *	All	*	All	*	*	*	All	10.5 *	*	*
Technical manager	All	All	*	4.1 *	All	All	All	8.1 *	All	All	All	All
Contracts manager	All	2.2, 2.3 *	All	All	All	*	*	*	All	10.5 *	All	*

* Optional

Figure 1-5 Chapter road map

- Buyer project manager—the manager that has the principal responsibility for managing the project from the contracting agency or buyer's viewpoint.
- Seller project manager—the manager who has primary responsibility for the management of the project in the seller or development organization.
- Financial management—those managers interested in the budgeting, costing, and resource expenditure of the project from either a buyer or seller perspective.
- Technical—those principal persons who have lead technical responsibility for the project, for example, the chief engineer.
- Contracting—those personnel who are predominantly involved in the software project contracting process.

Based on these views, a road map through the book is provided (Figure 1-5). The table of contents can be used to digress from the road map based on individual interests. The road map is only a guide—the reader may choose what is important based on personal and professional needs and interests. It is intended that everyone read Chapter 1. Where an entry for a chapter is listed "all," the bulk of the material is appropriate and it was not worth providing a subchapter directory. In some cases the material may be oriented specifically toward interests of people in government. A reader not interested in this material may choose to skip over it, although much in these sections may be of interest to commercial managers.

Others who will benefit from this book include personnel in areas of support, configuration management, quality assurance, and testing. These subjects are not covered in detail. They are important to acquisition management, however, and are discussed throughout the book in relation to various topics. For specific areas of interest, a road map (Appendix A) is provided which guides the reader through an area such as quality assurance. This will afford a convenient method for concentrating on one subject.

1.6 SUMMARY

Although it would be desirable to have definitive guidelines for projects where the principles of this book apply, it is simply unrealistic to attempt a strictly formulaic approach. Both large and small projects succeed or fail for many of the same reasons. In smaller efforts the degree of management applied will depend on the nature of the product and the risks associated with its development. A development project that produces a necessary product for a larger effort will impact overall system resources. Management will therefore have to judge the appropriate degree and form of management controls to be applied. Although this book is oriented toward projects of medium-to-large size (over two levels of management), the guidelines may be selectively applied, or tailored, to smaller projects. Certainly the principles covered will be of use to management personnel in general.

This is not a nuts-and-bolts book. That is, it does not teach how to develop or engineer software or manage a project. It discusses software management only in the context of the real subject: managing the software acquisition process—the process of buying customized software. It is not a cookbook, either. The authors believe that management practice cannot be reduced to an unvarying sequence of precise steps. Every project is different. Approaches and practices will have to be tailored specifically for each case. Indeed, the ability to recognize this point is critical to effective management practice.

REFERENCES

[GAO, 1979]: Comptroller General of the United States, *Contracting for Computer Software Development—Serious Problems Require Management Attention to Avoid Wasting Additional Millions,* U.S. Government Accounting Office, FGMSD-80-4, Washington, DC, November 9.

[Schlender, 1989]: Brenton R. Schlender, "How to Break the Software Logjam," *Fortune,* Vol. 120, New York, September 25, pp. 100–112.

CHAPTER 2

The Software Acquisition Environment

This chapter introduces the systems and software development life cycles. It examines the system life cycle, the software life cycle, and their relationships. It then focuses on the management processes in the software life cycle model and concludes with a discussion of some of the standards used in software development.

Most software systems are developed in a total systems environment. Even a simple software program such as a text editor must run on computer equipment and interface with a user, in this case a human being (some programs run in direct communication with other programs without human intervention). Thus the developers of software systems or systems that contain software-intensive subsystems must understand the systems engineering process as well.

This book does not address the development of nonsoftware parts of systems. However, it does recognize interfaces within the system as a necessary part of systems development and a prerequisite to sound software development. Interfaces with the user community, hardware, and other systems are important in systems development.

Software development and its management are based on a life cycle process model that identifies the major activities involved in developing software. It divides the work accoridng to activities related to developing, sustaining, and maintaining a system. It defines the products of these work steps and the reviews held to affirm their adequacy. It provides the basis for communication among managerial, technical, and user personnel, thus contributing to meaningful management of the software development process. It provides a framework for decision making and assimilating lessons learned. Understanding this process is requisite for understanding and applying the techniques of software acquisition management.

The process model is developed incrementally, beginning with the basic life cycle activities, then adding the management and engineering processes to develop

15

a solid software management environment. One caution—the descriptions that follow are not intended to provide profuse detail of the system and software life cycle processes or integral management activities. It is intended to give managers a top-level view that will help them understand the processes. For additional detail, consult the bibliography.

2.1   THE SYSTEM LIFE CYCLE

Basically, a large system acquisition undergoes four phases: concept exploration, demonstration and validation, full-scale development, and production and deployment (Figure 2-1).

2.1.1   Concept Exploration Phase   *Alternatives to mission need*

During the first phase, concept exploration, the original requirements for the system are set forth, and the system is conceived. At this point in the systems life cycle, the statement of requirements is embryonic. It may be a simple statement of need to provide a new capability such as an automated teller system for a bank

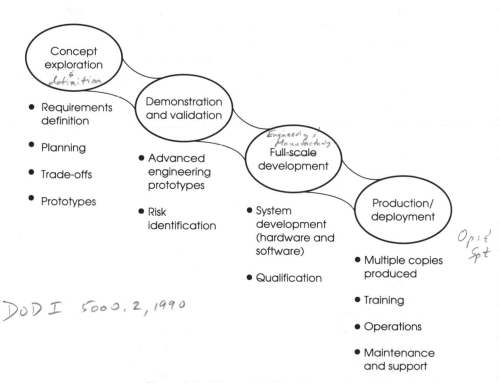

Figure 2-1   The system life cycle

or post office or a defense information system to support command and control of military assets. The requirements may stem from a desire to take advantage of new technology (for example, knowledge-based systems) or to fulfill an operational need (for example, providing timely information on financial holdings or the status of military forces). The broad statement of need is translated into a plan for the development of the system. A preliminary concept of the system's operation is formulated and the operational environment is identified. An early design concept or system architecture may be developed. Initial resource estimates are made and preliminary development schedules projected. Basic trade-offs between technology, cost, and performance are studied to determine the best mix. Early staffing estimates are made for managing the development and operating the system.

During this phase, software and hardware development is minimal. Sometimes prototypes are built to demonstrate concept feasibility or to test a new technology. At this point, system requirements are not clearly allocated to either hardware or software components. However, recognition of software's role in the system should permeate planning. Software planning has to be an integral part of the system's early planning process in order to minimize the risks of cost overruns, schedule slippages and performance deficiencies. The optimal mix of hardware and software, the risks associated with software development, and the magnitude (extent) of the software must be determined. When management and development strategies are devised and the costs of the system acquisition estimated, the role of software is of critical importance.

2.1.2   Demonstration and Validation Phase   *Prototyping of alternative*

The objective of the next phase of the system life cycle, demonstration and validation, is to refine the planning of the conceptual phase and to reduce the overall risks of development. System requirements, resource estimates, schedules, and staffing requirements are further refined. During this period advanced models (prototypes) of the system or selected portions of the system may be built to provide early demonstration of system capability. This leads to better understanding of system requirements and identification/reduction of the technical risks associated with the system's development. A top-level systems architecture is developed that identifies the required hardware and software components. Analyses are conducted to further reduce the risks of development. A systems specification is developed as a prelude to full-scale development. The system requirements are allocated to various hardware and software components. Planning for software development intensifies as the initial management concepts are refined and the risks are further assessed.

In systems where software plays a critical role, it is important to identify software development risk areas. If a new technology is required in order to meet operational requirements, minimizing the risks of utilizing that technology should be part of the advanced development process. For example, an expert system (see Section 12.1) may be required to support a decision support subsystem. The expert system may be prototyped to identify specific software and user interface requirements and to reduce the likelihood of complications when the system is implemented. Other risk minimization approaches like simulations may also be used. While risks are being identified and reduced, system requirements continue to be refined.

During this phase, software development is usually conducted on a somewhat informal basis. One reason is that a full, formal development process is costly. Another is that the software prototype is usually a throw-away product, unsuitable for systems employment. If the software will not be used in the actual operational system, the cost of formal development is not justified. Sound software engineering and management practicies must not be ignored. Software development practices have to be tailored to be consistent with the purpose of the individual component being developed.

It is important for software developers to understand this point so that they can conduct advanced prototyping without trying to preserve software investment by using prototypes "as is" in the operational system. To use an analogy, hardware is often prototyped to investigate feasibility, identify risks, and so on. The hardware prototype usually has a *bread board* configuration. That is, it may be rack mounted for operation in a laboratory setting. Such prototypes are rarely suitable for use in an operational environment. Instead, a new development is initiated to build a production article—one that will function in an operational environment. In a similar manner, early software prototypes are not built to withstand operational use. They may not meet all system requirements, may not attain expected quality (for example, reliability standards), and may not be sufficiently documented. Shortcuts may have been taken in producing implemented code. Such code will be unsuitable for the production article.

This idea is a difficult one for most managers to accept. Separate developement of a production article may be viewed as prohibitively expenseive, resulting in the prototype (or engineering) version becoming the actual article. Consequently, delivered software does not perform in accordance with specified requirements and will need to be re-engineered in the production and deployment phase. Later, we will discuss advanced acquisition concepts, such as evolutionary development, that help avoid this situation. (Section 11.1). Of course, if the software is intended for operational use, the full practice of software development management should be employed. (The software development methodology is described in Section 2.2.)

2.1.3 Full-Scale Development *(EMD) Translation into stable design*

The purpose of the full-scale development phase is to complete the system design, demonstrate that performance requirements can be satisfied, and that the designed system can be produced. In full-scale development both hardware and software components are developed under rigorous engineering and management discipline. The primary output of this phase is production specifications. The engineering process is used to develop the *first article* system or production prototype. During the next phase, production and deployment, multiple units are produced and placed into operation. With software, producing multiple units is quite simple, involving the replication of object code and documentation. The software product specifications describe the *as-built* article. The hardware product specifications describe the specifications for building production units.

During this phase the software requirements are subjected to further analysis and a detailed software design is produced. This design identifes all the components of the software subsystem to its lowest units of decomposition, allocating requirements to each component. The software is coded according to its design, tested, and integrated into a complete software system or set of subsystems. The software has to be integrated with the hardware and tested in the complete system. Building the software is not enough—it has to work within the total system.

2.1.4 Production and Deployment

Stable production base
Operational capability

The last phase of the system life cycle is the production and deployment (sometimes called operations and maintenance) phase. The objective of this phase is to produce and deliver an effective and supportable system. During this phase the system is *produced* for delivery to a user/customer. As described earlier, multiple units of hardware and software are manufactured and placed into operation. The quality assurance function inspects selected hardware items to ensure that they fulfil the requirements of the contract and are of uniform quality. As software uniformity is implied by the nature of the replication process, the quality assurance check is focused on satistfactory delivery and implementation of the software. Systems training, facility preparation, and installation are carried out. The beginning of system operation initiates the maintenance activity.

Hardware maintenance involves fixing broken equipment and performing preventive maintenance. Software maintenance, however, differs because software errors have a different effect on the system. John Munson of UNISYS eloquently stated the difference between hardware error correction and software error correction: "When you correct a hardware error, you return the system to its original state of operation; when you fix a software error, the system is changed to a new state." In addition to error correction, the function of sustaining engineering is performed. This includes user training, system analysis, and facility maintenance.

Software errors come in many varieties: code that does not perform correctly, design errors that hinder fitness for use, and documentation errors that hinder operation. The software may meet specifications but not perform as the user expected. Documentation previously produced may not accurately reflect system implementation. All of these errors may seem like normal system maintenance problems. However, most of them can be traced to the development process. Given the current state of software development practice, it is impossible to test 100 percent of the software system. As a result, errors will and do occur.

Additional circumstances must also be accommodated. Hardware problems (for example, faults in design) are normally easier to address in the software than in the hardware. In addition, software maintenance takes on an evolutionary character. There is the "creeping" feature phenomenon whereby convenient new features are continually incorporated into the design. Modifications may be required to make the software and hardware operate correctly, and new requirements may emerge as the system is used. New technologies may enhance capabilities. The system gradually evolves to meet user expectations and to satisfy new requirements.

Because of its flexibility, software will always evolve in a more dynamic manner than hardware. Managers must recognize this and ensure that the maintenance process accommodates this reality. When it is critical for the software system to operate correctly on delivery such as in space systems where it is difficult to correct errors, advanced techniques to reduce risk and increase software quality must be employed.

We have sketched a four-phase process, but not all software systems undergo all of the phases, at least not in their entirety. The system life cycle is evident in very large system developments, particularly in those of the U. S. government. In other environments and in small system acquisitions, the system life cycle is truncated to accommodate the practical requirements of the acquisition. This usually involves three phases of acquisition. The first phase combines the first two system life cycle phases (concept exploration and demonstration and validation) followed by full scale development and production and deployment. In addition, a complete or full software development process can occur in any life cycle phase. For example, during demonstration and validation there may be a requirement to develop a real-time operating system to support hardware development in full-scale development. Or, in production and deployment, a new version of the software may be required as a result of new user requirements. These situations are guided by the development practices discussed in Section 2.2.

2.1.5 *Operations & Support*   *Ensure fielded system capabilities*

2.2   THE SOFTWARE LIFE CYCLE

The basic model for software development is the waterfall life cycle process model. While advanced models of this process have been formulated to accommodate engineering interactions in complex software developments (for example, incremental build and spiral development), the waterfall model provides a simple and basic explanation of the activities associated with software development. The software life cycle is the basis for the engineering process and is just as important for management of the development process. The software life cycle, like the system life cycle, provides a basis for communicating management and engineering processes across a standard or described set of activities. The software waterfall life cycle model is presented in Figure 2-2. The model progresses through a series of activities from software requirements analysis through software systems testing.

2.2.1   Software Requirements Analysis

The purpose of this phase is to analyze requirements and allocate them to the top-level components of the software system. During this first phase, a functional view and performance model of the software is developed. Thus the software architecture

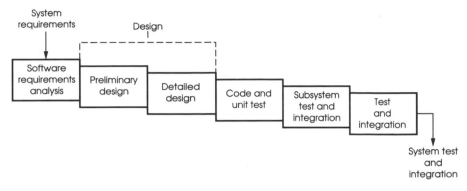

Figure 2-2   Software waterfall life cycle model

is defined. As the process continues, requirements are further allocated across functions and interfaces are defined. Trade-offs are conducted and the system is decomposed into software subsystems. Operational concepts and design constraints are taken into account as the statement of requirements evolves. At the end of this first phase, software requirements are detailed enough for software design to begin. They are often approved by the buyer and, if stable, establish a firm basis for the next phase. The primary output of the software requirements analysis phase is a software requirements specification.

2.2.2 Design Phase

The purpose of the design phase is to map the requirements to the software architecture. This architecture defines the hierarchy of the software design. Each component of the architecture is defined through the allocation process. The design phase normally consists of preliminary design and detailed design.

During preliminary design the software architecture is solidified and its components identified. Requirements are allocated to a number of components, such as objects or functional components. Derived requirements are then defined and allocated. These requirements may stem from the need to reuse existing components or from other factors, such as security, that constrain the design approach. While not originally stated in the requirements specification, derived requirements impact performance and must be accounted for as functions or objects and mapped from requirements to the architecture.

In detailed design, the process continues as each architectural component is designed so that algorithms, controls, and data structures are apparent (see Figure 2-3). The lowest level of the system decomposition represents a simple building block (or unit) that can be traced to requirements, can be coded by a single programmer in a short time, and will perform a well-bounded function. Once detailed design is completed, the software has been laid out in enough detail to allow coding to begin.

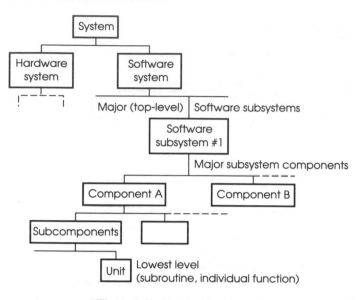

Figure 2-3 Detailed design

The reason for two design phases is quite simple—the architecture and requirements allocations should be in place before the components are detailed. Dividing the process into two or more phases also provides management with the formal means to review the design as it evolves. Thus remedial actions can be taken before the design becomes too detailed. The two-step approach also allows management to subject the high-level design to external review (by systems and hardware engineers, for example). This ensures compatibility with other software and hardware. It is also possible to begin coding units that are ready to proceed before detailed design of the entire system is completed. This parallel development process is consistent with actual practice. The primary output of this phase is a completed design specification.

2.2.3 Code and Unit Testing

In this phase the individual software units, at the lowest level of decomposition, are coded and tested. Coding is usually accomplished in accordance with buyer and/or seller programming standards or conventions. These may stipulate the structure of the code, including, for example, the disallowance of certain coding statements such as "GO TO". Unit testing is conducted by using various methods and techniques (for example, coverage analysis). Testing at the unit level provides the first indication of the actual progress of the software. (It is feasible to conduct earlier testing with prototypes and simulations.) At this point in development, testing is informal, conducted by the programmer, and perhaps reviewed by the internal development team. After coding and testing, software integration can begin.

2.2.4   Subsystem Test and Integration

The purpose of this phase is to integrate the units into increasingly higher levels of the software system until all major software components (subsystems) are tested and ready for complete software system test and integration. More people get involved as the system becomes more functional. Emphasis is on demonstrating that functional and performance requirements are achieved. The testing is informal, conducted by the development team and in some instances a test organization with developers assigned to it with perhaps some degree of monitoring by the buyer. All subsystem activity is completed in preparation for higher-level software testing and integration.

2.2.5   Test and Integration

The last step in the software waterfall life cycle, prior to system level integration and test, is the formal test of each major software deliverable. At this point, all the individual components of each software deliverable have been integrated into a complete subsystem such as an operating system, a display-processing subsystem, or a database system. Each of these subsystems is then subjected to formal qualification testing to ensure that it fulfils all the requirements of the contract. It should be noted that meeting the requirements in the specifications is a necessary but not a sufficient condition. The contract may have other requirements, such as training, that need to be demonstrated.

This formal testing applies to a requirement that is covered by a formal agreement, or contract. The test is monitored by the buyer and established in test documentation. The purpose of this testing is to qualify the software prior to system-level test and integration, the last steps before system level acceptance by the customer. In most systems, especially where there is parallel hardware development, system level testing is required. The customer is buying a capability, not hardware or software. Even if there is no hardware developed, software is often developed on a host computer that is different from the target computer used in the actual system. The goal is to have a complete software subsystem tested prior to system level test. This is not always practical and often software integration and system-level testing are conducted together as it becomes difficult, and somewhat unrealistic, to qualify products in separate tests of hardware and software.

2.3   MANAGEMENT PROCESSES IN THE SOFTWARE LIFE CYCLE

The software waterfall life cycle provides a management model for controlling the software development. The engineering process utilizes a number of techniques and tools to help automate and direct the development. During software requirements analysis, operational analysis techniques can be used to evaluate requirements and facilitate the allocation process. Methods like software requirements evaluation methodology (SREM) and tools like TeamWork™ (Cadre) have been used to aid in requirements analysis. During the design activity, methods such as structured design and tools such as Software-Through-Pictures™ (IDE) are often employed. A number of automated tools support the various methods available in the commercial market as part of CASE toolsets. During coding and testing, methods like structured programming and tools such as compilers, debuggers, and test generators are employed. During test and integration, techniques such as static and dynamic analysis and tools such as path analyzers and coverage or completeness analyzers are used. Every effort is made to automate tedious manual processes and to use methods and techniques to integrate the information necessary to verify that the product of each life cycle phase is satisfactory.

These engineering methods and tools, along with management procedures and techniques, form the software engineering environment. We now examine the management processes that provide control of the development process.

2.3.1 Documentation

Documentation, whether in handwritten or machine-readable form, provides the means to describe the product and the engineering which led to its development. Documentation is neither produced after the fact nor for bureaucratic reasons. It is produced to capture the engineering process so that others can understand and benefit from it. Documentation should be an outgrowth of activities, not an end in itself. For example, the definition provided by requirements analysis should result in a documented statement of requirements.

Documentation falls into three general categories: product documentation, process documentation, and support documentation. Table 2-1 provides an example of the types of documentation used in software development, although it is not all-inclusive. For example, a project management plan is not shown: yet it is normally used on large acquisition projects to interrelate the work tasks that need to be

TABLE 2-1   Software Documentation

Category	Document
Product	Software requirements specifications
	Software design specifications
	Software product specifications
Process	Test plans
	Configuration management plan
	Quality assurance plan
	Software development plan
Support	Software user's manual
	Computer systems operator's manual
	Software maintenance manual
	Firmware support manual

completed with schedules and budgets. The project management plan is described in Sections 6.1 and 7.2.

Product specifications describe the requirements and design on which development is based. They should include system-level as well as software-level, requirements and design specifications. Process documentation describes plans and procedures used to guide the development processes. Examples include software test plans and procedures, configuration management plans, quality assurance plans, and software development plans. Support documentation communicates operational and usage instructions to the operators of the system. This category of documentation includes operator's manuals, users manuals, and operator's scenarios.

A key plan is the top-level plan, that is, is the software development or project management plan. This is most likely introduced before there is a specification. In such cases it is a plan for a plan. Its purpose is to provide a road map for getting the product on time and within budget. It describes the work tasks and their budgets and schedules; the management methods the seller will use to control the development; the seller's concepts for configuration management, testing, and quality assurance; the organization that will be employed for the development; and the individual tools, techniques, and management procedures that will be employed.

Documentation is preprared throughout the development life cycle to capture the results of each engineering activity so that they can be reviewed by the buyer/seller and progress assessed. (Figure 2-4). Planning documentation occurs early in the project. Product documentation occurs in concert with the development phase. While user or support documentation is usually prepared for system delivery, an early version of the user's manual can serve to bound user expectations. This is especially beneficial for systems with a lot of human interaction. Documentation is essential for managing the development process.

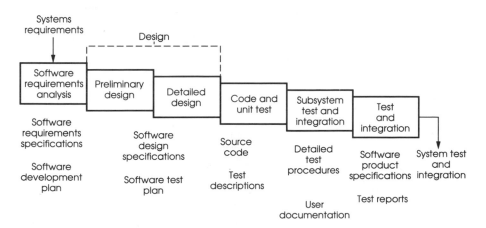

Figure 2-4 Documentation in the software life cycle

2.3.2 Management and Engineering Reviews

Management and engineering reviews directly support the process and provide both buyer and seller management personnel with insight into development progress. Figure 2-5 depicts the formal management reviews held during the waterfall life cycle development process. Notice that each review is a milestone (or quality gate) for some phase of the development, for example, detailed design. Since the completion of an activity is marked by the delivery of engineering products of that activity, documentation of those products is a prerequisite for the review. Thus, at the software specification review, the software requirements and interface requirements specifications or their analogous documents resulting from engineering activity are the subjects of review. The subjects of the preliminary design review are the preliminary design document, which captures the architectural design, and the software test plan, which captures the test and integration approach. Other types of management reviews may be held during the life cycle. For example, the seller may hold weekly schedule assessment reviews to determine progress and pinpoint problems. The buyer may hold monthly project reviews at the seller's facilities to understand and scrutinize technical progress and check financial status. In addition, peer level engineering reviews such as walk-throughs or inspections provide an internal check so that defects can be corrected before they have time to propagate. For example, design and code walk-throughs are often held to focus the team's attention on communications, content, and structure.

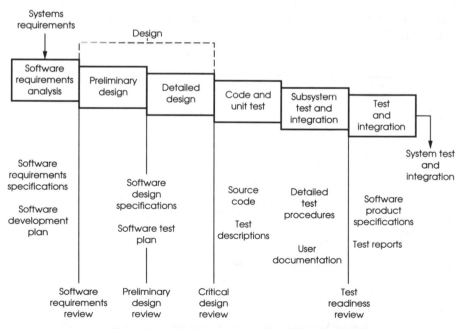

Figure 2-5   Reviews in the software life cycle

Finally, reviews are conducted by the many outside organizations of the buyer and seller. The buyer may audit and review the seller's financial reporting system to ensure that costs can be traced to program accounts. The seller's quality organization may conduct independent evaluations of the products and provide feedback to the developers. Executives may want to review the work while steering groups, councils, and committees may want periodic status reports.

Reviews are protracted activities carried out before, during, and after the actual review meeting. They must be properly planned. An agenda must be set and circulated early to elicit comments and to trigger prereview actions. Personnel whose attendance is required at the review meeting must be identified and contacted to ensure their availability. Review procedures should be in place to describe what is to occur before, during, and after the review. Documentation recording the subject of the review must be provided well before the review meeting to afford a thorough analysis and to provide information for the developer in time for his or her analysis and response. After the review is conducted, postreview actions must be documented, assigned for action, and monitored to ensure timely completion.

The purpose of most reviews is to provide visibility, determine status, measure progress, and assess the integrity of the development process. Each review has specific objectives: to determine the status of the development effort, to review the products of the completed activity (the documentation delivered), and to identify and resolve problems and issues. The culmination of a successful review establishes a milestone or (quality) gate by providing a baseline for continued development.

2.3.3 Configuration Management

Configuration management (CM) is the process that ensures the integrity of the software (and overall) system. Software configuration management is defined as:

> the process of identifying and defining the configuration items in a system, controlling the release and change of these items throughout the system life cycle, recording and reporting the status of configuration items and change requests, and verifying the completeness and correctness of configuration items. [IEEE, 1983]

CM provides identification, control, reporting and auditing of the products of development throughout the entire life cycle of the system. It is a very important activity in software development because it controls changes to baselines and provides a repository for the work-in-progress.

Refer to Figure 2-6 for the following discussion of "George's program," used to illustrate the functions of software configuration management.

1. *Configuration identification.* Assuming that George has been working on the program and it is now ready for the next step in development (in this case, testing), identify the program as version X.1. Identification has to be unique to the system. We cannot have duplicate schemes for identifying and relating programs, documentation, baselines, versions, and releases.

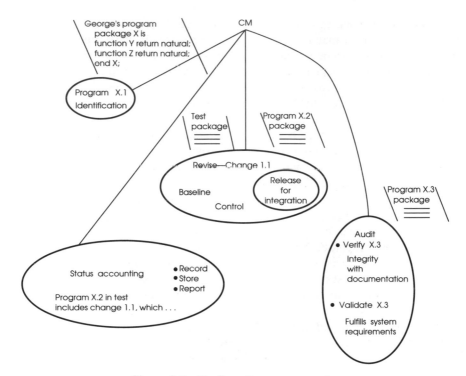

Figure 2-6   Configuration management

2. *Configuration control.*   After identification, the changes to the program and its documentation must be controlled. While George is working on the program, he controls it. When he turns it over to the CM system as version X.1, he no longer controls it. The program is stored in a library, and access to it is limited so that it cannot be changed without appropriate authority. If a change is required, it will be reviewed, approved for implementation; then George will implement it in the software. In this case change 1.1 is implemented and a new version of the program, now called X.2, results. Thus the identity of the program is retained—version X.2 is X.1 with change 1.1 incorporated. Assuming that X.2 is ready to be tested, a test baseline can be established. This simply means identifying that specific version of the program with a specific milestone activity (in this case, testing). Control of the program during testing ensures that it retains its unique identity and cannot be changed. It also ensures that the program is qualified against its requirements. After additional changes, made as a result of testing, the program is released for integration. The released version is identified as X.3.

3. *Configuration audit.*   There are two functions of the configuration audit: verification and validation. Verification ensures that the software configuration is what it is intended to be, and validation ensures that the configuration meets specified requirements. In this example the audit is performed on X.3.

The audit ensures that the program released for integration is correctly identified, includes approved changes, agrees with its documentation, and meets stated requirements.

4. *Configuration status accounting.* This primarily administrative function reports on the three other CM functions. The status of program X can be reported as having three versions with version X.3 released for integration. Configuration status accounting also provides information about the documentation and testing that the program has undergone. Thus it reports the status of the software product at any time.

An important aspect of configuration management is the support it provides to the baselining of system products. A baseline is a "reference point or plateau in the development of a system" [Bersoff, 1980]. Baseline management is an integral function of configuration management and an important life cycle management process for controlling the development process. Each baseline provides the basis for product control and orderly progression to the next step of development. Thus the establishment of baselines is a technique for controlling development through a formal configuration management process.

Baselines marked by the completion of major milestone activities are called *formal* baselines. With formal control, changes to the baselined system must be approved by the authority responsible for the integrity of the system as defined at that baseline. This is usually the buyer because changes in formal baselines affect the scope of the contract. In a software acquisition there are three formal baselines: the functional baseline, the allocated baseline, and the product baseline (Figure 2-7).

1. *Functional baseline.* The primary purpose of the functional baseline is to firmly establish the requirements the system must satisfy. Upon establishment of the functional baseline, the system specifications are placed under control. Changes to formal system baselines usually impact both cost and schedule.
2. *Allocated baseline.* Once the requirements are allocated to individual software subsystems, the allocated baseline is established, marking the completion of the software analysis phase. The allocated baseline captures the mapping between the architecture and software requirements.
3. *Product baseline.* When fully designed, developed, and tested a product baseline is established. This baseline identifies the produced software system and provides a basis for modifying the system by correcting errors and incorporating new requirements.

Informal CM begins the day the project starts. In informal CM, control of the product resides with the seller. The seller team leader makes all decisions as products are internally baselined and put under seller control. These baselines are called development baselines. As the product progresses through development and impacts other products being developed, control over it moves to higher levels of

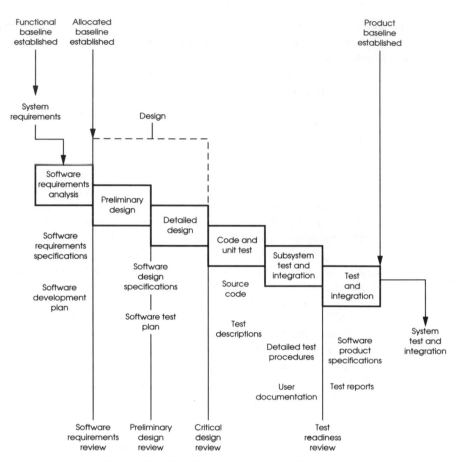

Figure 2-7 Baselines in the software life cycle

authority. Placement of the product under the control of buyer/seller management (formal control), occurs at various gates (for example, software design review) after successful review of the product at that milestone.

Control of the software is aided by several board activities. These provide a forum and mechanism to review, approve, and check the status of proposed changes to the system. Two board activities are normally evident in a life cycle software environment:

1. *Configuration control board (CCB).* This board meets to control changes to formal baselines. The board is assisted by personnel and procedures that provide engineering review of the changes and administration of the CCB process. The configuration management function normally includes this last activity.

2. *Software fault or discrepancy review board (DRB).* This board acts much like the CCB, but it normally reviews changes to the software that do not

affect formal baselines. During development the DRB is under the control and authority of the seller. Changes found to affect a formal baseline are referred to the CCB.

The configuration management function is supported by the software development library, which provides a repository for housing the product under appropriate control. It is administered by personnel who support the various configuration management activities.

2.3.4   Quality Assurance

Implied in buying custom software systems is the hope that the delivered product will satisfy requirements, will be delivered on schedule, and will stay within cost projections. Although this may be a minimum expectation, there is also hope that the product will be a "quality" one. The very nature of quality is largely undefined. It means many things to many people. It could mean that the product should have an expected degree of reliability; that is, it does not contain errors that render the operation so faulty that it is unusable. Or it could mean that the product is fairly maintainable, that is, the product is constructed so that changes, whether correctable errors or designed improvements, may be made with relative ease and at reasonable cost.

The objective of a software quality assurance program in an acquisition environment is

> to assure the quality of (a) deliverable software and its documentation, (b) the processes used to produce deliverable software, and (c) non-deliverable software. [DOD, 1988]

A quality program begins with the definition of quality requirements such as efficiency, effectiveness, and readability. These must be identified at the onset of development and included in the requirements specifications.

A quality program is instituted to specify the quality requirements that the product must satisfy, monitor the development process to ensure that it can address these requirements, and work with the developers to ensure that the provisions of the quality requirements are achieved. A key aspect of a quality program is prevention, the aims of which are to stop problems from originating and propagating. Within the seller organization, the quality program is normally managed through an independent quality assurance function. This helps to ensure objectivity and to provide a focus on quality throughout the development.

2.3.5   Assessment

Integral to any production process is the need to measure and control outputs. The software process, like manufacturing, needs instrumentation that will allow meaningful indicators of progress to be captured and reported as the work flows.

Such feedback may help to identify trends so that remedial actions can be taken before disasters occur.

The management environment should be designed to be self-measuring. The buyer/seller should identify the measurements to be taken and the indicators and metrics to be used as the environment is developed. The indicators should be reported to all to encourage performance that will meet expectations. Indicators support four assessment aspects of acquisition: process, product, productivity, and project.

1. *Process.*   These indicators provide insight into the software development process and how it is working. The indicators should be used to provide feedback to refine the process and contribute to positive control—they should

TABLE 2-2   Indicators by Area of Interest

Indicators	Process	Product	Project	Productivity
		Areas		
Schedule attainment (6.4.2)			X	X
Memory utilization (6.4.6.1)		X		
CPU utilization (6.4.6.1)		X		
Problem reports (6.4.6.2)	X	X		X
Software size (6.4.6.3)		X		
Software size-units (6.4.6.3)		X		
Personnel stability (6.4.6.4)			X	
Development progress (6.4.6.5)	X		X	
Incremental release (6.4.6.6)	X		X	
Test progress (6.4.6.7)	X		X	
Documentation (6.4.6.8)	X			
Cost attainment (9.5.1)			X	X
Earned value (9.5.2)	X		X	

not be after the fact. Some indicators that are useful are rework rate and fault intensity.

2. *Product.* These indicators measure whether or not the product meets minimum levels of quality. For example, if the requirements change frequently, the specifications are unstable, and their quality should be in question.

3. *Project.* These indicators provide progress-oriented measures such as staffing rates, schedule attainment, and deliverable rates. For example, if staffing requirements are not met on schedule, then you are probably going to be playing catch-up throughout the development.

4. *Productivity.* This indicator measures the rate at which work is progressing and focuses primarily on people and what they produce. It is desirable to know how productive your teams are and whether or not your investments in process, methods, and tools are yielding projected benefits. Being productive does not necessarily imply that costs will go down. Also it should be realized that hard work does not always suggest high productivity.

Indicators are discussed throughout this book. They are not unique to any specific area—they can and should be used across areas and combined when appropriate to provide a synergistic effect. Table 2-2 lists the indicators discussed in the book by the topical areas just addressed. Many other indicators may be used, but those listed are fairly easy to apply and are particularly appropriate.

2.4 THE ROLE OF STANDARDS IN THE MANAGEMENT PROCESS

In the management process, standards play a stabilizing role because they allow organizations to communicate in common terms within a decision framework that everyone understands. Without standards each management environment would be unique. There would be no consistency across projects, and each team would have to relearn what others have already learned on past projects. Both buyer and seller would have to train each project team in a unique way of doing business.

Thus standards are an essential ingredient in an orderly software management environment. A number of competing standards and sets of standards are in place within the industry. These are usually associated with specific market segments or contracting environments (for example, DOD, NASA, IEEE, and ISO). In each environment, standards provide for common practice that allow the seller to relate to the buyer. Standards are thus the backbone of the management environment. A number of standards are described, with focus on how they relate to software management practice.

2.4.1 IEEE Standards

The IEEE Computer Society, through the software engineering subcommittee, has been actively developing software engineering standards. The most pertinent one from a life cycle model perspective is the *Standard for Software Life Cycle Pro-*

cesses [IEEE, 1989]. The standard defines life cycle management processes, activities within each process, and the interrelationship of processes and activities. It does not define a specific life cycle model. Instead, it uses a life cycle model process to provide for the development of a project-specific life cycle and guidelines to map the life cycle processes into a full life cycle management model.

The life cycle project model is based on four life cycle processes: project management, predevelopment, development, and postdevelopment. These are called processes instead of phases to facilitate mapping the individual processes and activities into specific life cycle models on a project-specific basis. Figure 2-8 shows the organization of the IEEE standard. While the standard does not provide a time-phased model, it is useful to map the processes into the general model depicted in Figure 2-8.

1. *Project management processes.*   These processes prepare the project for implementation and help to sustain management throughout the life cycle. Included are activities such as defining standards, methodologies, and tools/tool sets; allocating resources; establishing the project environment; and developing risk analyses and contingency plans.

2. *Predevelopment processes.*   These processes are normally performed before the seller activity begins, namely, before contract award. Predevelopment activities include identifying needs, formulating potential solutions, conducting feasibility studies, planning system transition, analyzing and allocating requirements, and developing a system architecture.

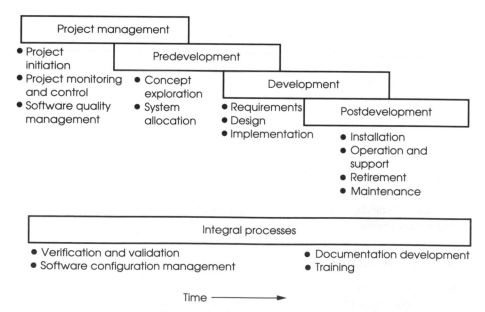

Figure 2-8   Life cycle processes

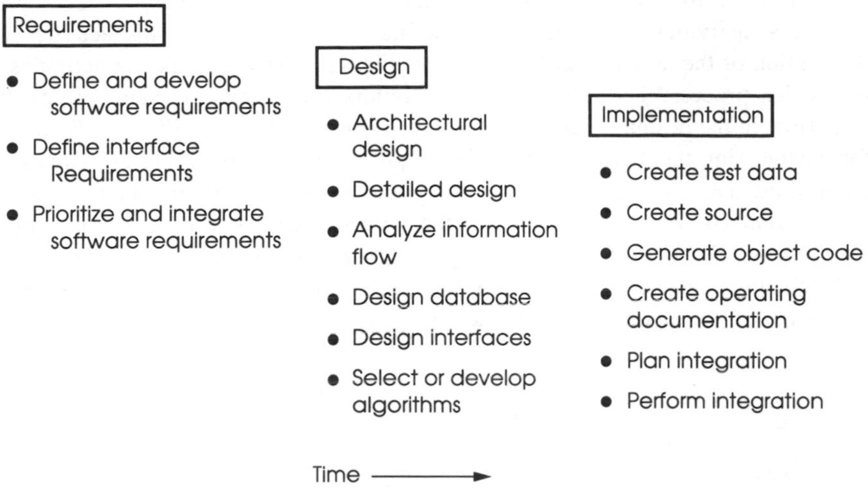

Requirements

- Define and develop software requirements

- Define interface Requirements

- Prioritize and integrate software requirements

Design

- Architectural design

- Detailed design

- Analyze information flow

- Design database

- Design interfaces

- Select or develop algorithms

Implementation

- Create test data

- Create source

- Generate object code

- Create operating documentation

- Plan integration

- Perform integration

Time ⟶

Figure 2-9 Development processes

3. *Development processes.* These processes include defining and developing software requirements, defining software interface requirements, performing detailed design, and implementing the detailed design. Figure 2-9 depicts the processes of development in a time-ordered sequence. These processes most closely resemble the waterfall software development model.

4. *Postdevelopment processes.* These processes include installing, operating, supporting, maintaining, and retiring the software product.

Included in the methodology are the so-called integral processes such as software configuration management. These processes augment software development with management-oriented support activities such as reviews and audits. The integral processes defined in the IEEE standard are: verification and validation, software configuration management, documentation development, and training.

1. *Verification and validation.* This process includes "planning and performing all the reviews and audits (verification) and testing (validation) to be conducted throughout the software life cycle" (IEEE, 1989).

2. *Software configuration management.* This includes the traditional configuration management activities of planning, identification, control, and status accounting.

3. *Documentation development.* This process includes planning developing and producing all project documentation.

4. *Training.* This process provides for planning, developing, testing, and implementing the training program. This activity represents a marked difference from other methodologies by including training in the life cycle model.

Each of the life cycle process areas defines a number of processes composed of several activities. Each activity is defined by the inputs to the activity, the description of the activity, and the outputs. Figure 2-10 shows the six activities of the design process. The figure shows the inputs and outputs of each activity and their flow in the design process. Thus the activities are related, allowing flexibility for customizing the activities for different project situations. Table 2-3 shows the inputs and their sources and the outputs and their destinations for the activity *design database*. Each activity invokes the appropriate integral processes to support the activity. For example, the activity *design database* invokes the verification and validation process activity *evaluate processes and products*, and the software configuration management process activity *perform configuration control*.

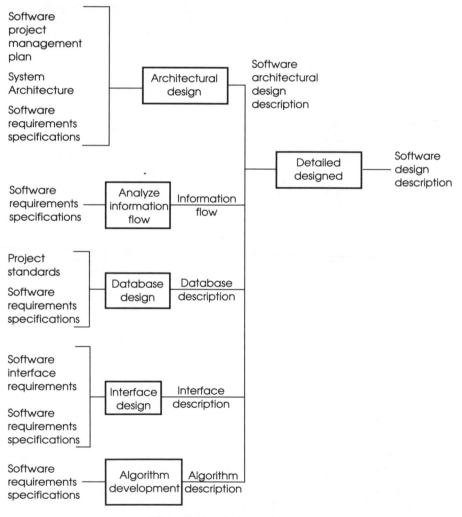

Figure 2-10   Design activities

TABLE 2-3   Design Database

	Source	
Input	Process	Activity
	Project standards	External to standard
Software requirements specifications	Requirements	Prioritize and integrate software requirements
	Destination	
Output	Process	Activity
Database description	Design	Perform detailed design

The IEEE standard does a nice job of relating the life cycle activities to existing IEEE standards. For example, Figure 2-1 of the standard contains a reference [13] to ANSI/IEEE Std 1012-1987, *IEEE Recommended Practice for Software Design Descriptions*. Thus the standard is backed up by a number of IEEE standards that define documentation formats, testing standards, configuration management plans, and other elements. A complete list of the available IEEE software engineering standards is provided in Appendix B.

Tailoring is built into the process of defining a life cycle management methodology. The standard may be tailored for an organization, a particular project, or a specific development effort, such as prototyping. Of course, tailoring requires expenditure of resources to define the life cycle management structure the user wishes to employ, and reasonable expertise in the organization is necessary to accomplish this. The standard also includes front-end project planning and concept exploration activities as well as tail-end postdevelopment activities. On the whole, the IEEE approach is an excellent one that will satisfy the needs of a wide range of users.

2.4.2 Department of Defense (DOD)

Within the U.S. Department of Defense, the predominant software standard is DOD-STD-2167A, *Software Development Standard* [DOD, 1988]. It is a management and engineering standard that provides for phased activities. It establishes baselines used to control development and formal documentation that describes the processes and products of development. Developed between 1979 and 1984, the standard has progressed through one revision, "A." Figure 2-11 depicts the development life cycle of the DOD standard. The standard provides detailed guidance for the management processes, including configuration management, product evaluation, informal and qualification (formal) testing, and documentation. Although

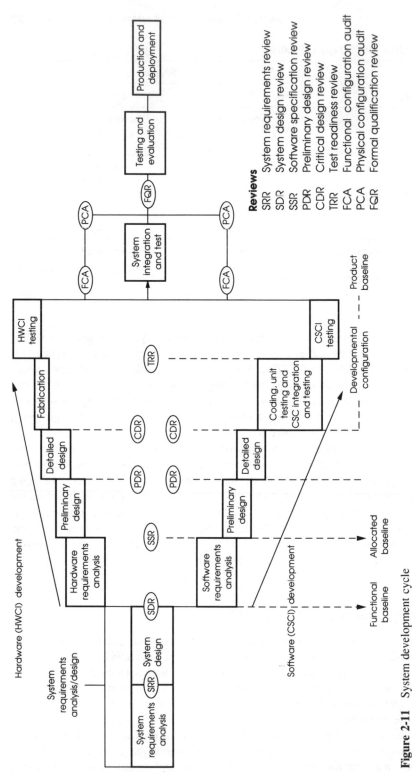

Figure 2-11 System development cycle

Source: [DOD, 1988] *Department of Defense Standard 2167A, Defense System Software Development*, Feb. 29.

2167A purports to cover total systems development, including hardware development and system-level testing, it provides minimal guidance with respect to those aspects of development.

Eighteen standard documents are specified by the DOD standard. Called *data item descriptions* (DIDs), they are arranged in three categories: product documents, management process documents, and operations and support documents. (Table 2-4). The first document, the *system/segment design document*, captures the results of the front-end systems engineering processes. There are, however, no system-level integration or testing documents included in the standard.

Figure 2-12 shows how the documents are ordered in the development process. At each major milestone a formal review is conducted (for example, preliminary design review). As a part of the review the engineering products are assessed and the documents that are generated are evaluated.

The 2167A standard is supported by a number of other closely related standards:

1. *Defense System Software Quality Program (DOD-STD-2168).* The purpose of this standard is to ensure the quality of deliverable software and its documentation, the processes used to produce deliverable software, and nondeliverable software. It sets requirements for the contractor quality assurance program and provides for a standard planning document (*Software Quality Program Plan*), conduct of software quality evaluations, and maintenance of software quality records.

TABLE 2-4   Documentation Hierarchy

Document Class	Documents
Product	System segment design document (SSDD)
	Software requirements specification (SRS)
	Software design document (SDD)
	Interfaces requirements specification (IRS)
	Interface design document (IDD)
	Software product specification (SPS)
Management processes	Software development plan (SDP)
	Software test plan (STP)
	Software test description (STD)
	Software test report (STR)
	Version description document (VDD)
	Engineering change proposal (ECP)
	Specification change notice (SCN)
Operations and support	Computer system operator's manual (CSOM)
	Software user's manual (SUM)
	Software programmer's manual (SPM)
	Firmware support manual (FSM)
	Computer resources integrated support document (CRISD)

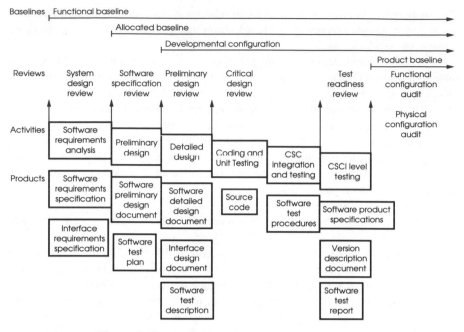

Figure 2-12 Computer software development cycle

2. *Configuration management (MIL-STD-483).* This standard details requirements for the seller configuration management program.

3. *Specification practices (MIL-STD-490A).* This standard describes the specifications used in the development process and procedures for their preparation and control.

4. *Reviews and audits (MIL-STD-1521B).* This standard prescribes practices for the conduct of formal reviews and audits conducted to assess development projects (for example, software requirements review and physical configuration audit).

One alternative management and engineering development standard used within DOD for software development is *DOD-STD-1703*. Like *DOD-STD-2167A*, it defines the process and its activities, reviews, and products. Unlike *DOD-STD-2167A*, it contains development guidance, including for example, Ada design guidelines. In addition, *DOD-STD-1703* employs a more flexible tailoring process that allows the buyer and seller to add, delete, and combine requirements and deliverables (documentation) as appropriate for the project.

2.4.3 NASA Standards

Traditionally the U.S. National Aeronautics and Space Administration (NASA) development centers have operated autonomously, allowing each center and project to use its own versions of development and documentation standards. There have been recent efforts, however, to provide a NASA-wide standard for software management and development. This work has its origin in the NASA Software Management and Assurance Program, commonly called SMAP.

The NASA SMAP software standards (Release 4.3) are defined in a five-volume set. The parent document, *Information System Life-Cycle and Documentation Standard*, provides terminology, life cycle definitions, and guidelines for adaptation to various life cycles. Four *Documentation Standards and Data Item Descriptions (DIDs)* volumes describe the format and contents for each of four fundamental types and guidelines for tailoring the documentation set. These four volumes together establish a complete framework for all relevant software documentation: specifications, plans, assurance, and reports.

1. *Management Plan Documentation Standard and DIDs* volume.   This volume contains the planning information for the project. The outline of a project's planning document is shown in Table 2-5. This planning document, as any document in the set, may consist of one or more physical volumes.

TABLE 2-5   Management Plan Framework

Introduction

Applicable documents

Resources, budgets, schedules and organization

Acquisition plan

Independent verification & validation

Certification

Development plan

      Risk management
      Engineering and integration
      Configuration management
      Assurance
      Training
      Delivery and operational transition

Sustaining engineering and operations

Evolutionary acquisition

Abbreviations and acronyms

Glossary

Notes

Appendices

Source: NASA, *Software Management Assurance Program (SMAP) Information System Life-Cycle Documentation Standards,* Release 4.3, 28 February 1989.

The DIDs provided in this volume contain structure and description for each section of the planning document.

2. *Product Specification Documentation Standard and DIDs* volume. This volume contains all the engineering and technical information. Thus a product specification would consist of the following topical areas:
   - Concept
   - Requirements
   - Design
   - Version description
   - User's guide
   - Maintenance manual

3. *Assurance Specification Documentation Standard and DIDs* volume. This volume contains all technical assurance information for both the acquirer (buyer) and provider (seller). The taxonomy provides for quality assurance, safety and security, testing, verification and validation, and certification.

4. *Management Control and Status Reports Documentation Standard and DIDs* volume. This volume contains all the reports, change papers, and the like that are specified in the management plan.

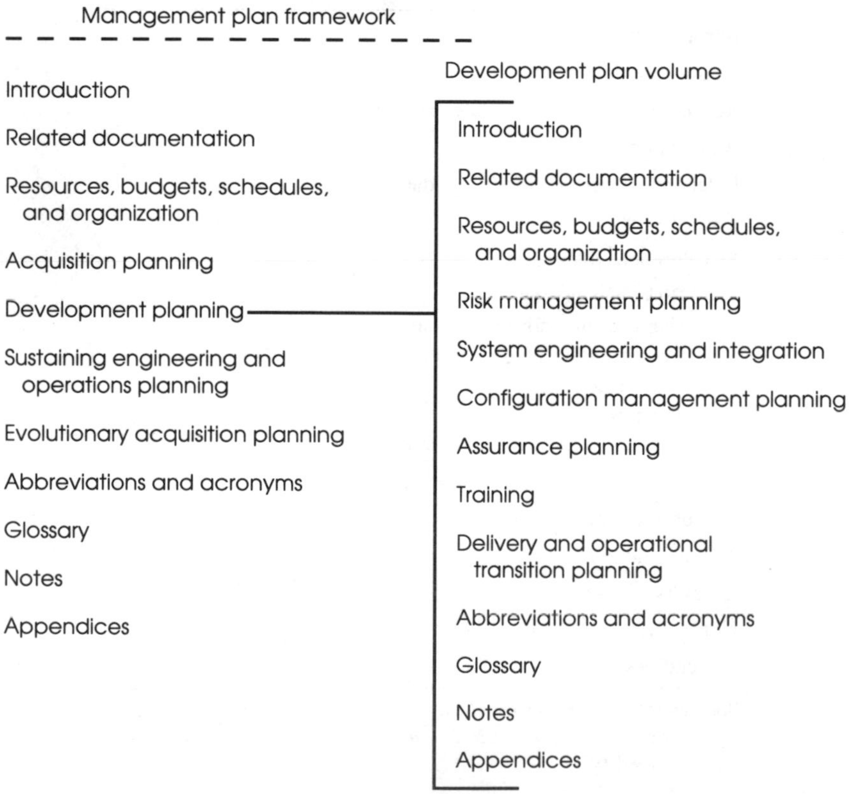

Management plan framework

Introduction

Related documentation

Resources, budgets, schedules, and organization

Acquisition planning

Development planning ——

Sustaining engineering and operations planning

Evolutionary acquisition planning

Abbreviations and acronyms

Glossary

Notes

Appendices

Development plan volume

Introduction

Related documentation

Resources, budgets, schedules, and organization

Risk management planning

System engineering and integration

Configuration management planning

Assurance planning

Training

Delivery and operational transition planning

Abbreviations and acronyms

Glossary

Notes

Appendices

Figure 2-13 Roll-out of development plan

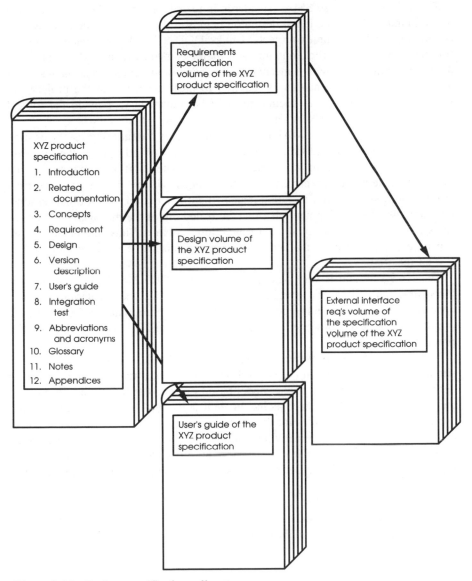

Figure 2-14 Product specification roll-out

Source: [Barr, 1988] Barr, C. P., E. D. Callender, and M. J. Steinbacker. "Life-Cycle Management and Documentation Concepts for the Space Station Program," *Proceedings of (COMPSTAN) Computer Standards Conference 1988*, Washington, DC, March 21–23, 1988. Los Alamitos, CA: IEEE Computer Society. ©1988 IEEE.

The objective of these SMAP standards is to reduce the number of documents to a minimum. Thus, the initial definition begins with a four-document set, which is sufficent for less complex projects. Unlike DOD-STD-2167A, which requires a full set of product specifications for each major component, the SMAP standards define a minimum set with a mechanism for expansion. The project management team tailors the documentation as required to meet the needs of the project; for more complex projects the documents may be expanded to provide the logical coverage required in a *2167A* set.

A unique feature of the SMAP documentation set is the tailoring mechanism by which one of the four individual documents can be "rolled out" of the top-level document. This can occur when the amount of material is voluminous, special treatment is required, preparation of the sections will be detailed to a distinct organization, separate configuration management is required, or for other reasons. For example, the development plan may be rolled out of the management plan, as shown in Figure 2-13, to produce a stand-alone volume. Thus, the document set can be expanded to meet the needs of large projects while reducing boiler-plate textual material.

The NASA system is very flexible; unlike DOD-STD-2167A, it facilitates tailoring through rolling out or rolling in sections in the documentation set. The concept is that the numbers of documents should be appropriate for the size of the project and the levels of system decomposition. Figure 2-14 shows a roll-out of a product specification.

The NASA SMAP software standards system defines a basic life cycle model similar to the model used in the DOD-STD-2167A, but it requires each project to define its own instantiation of the model based on levels of system decomposition and development methods such as incremental delivery. The SMAP standards life cycle definition also provides for the concept of parallel life cycles. That is, there are active system life cycle activities during subsystem development. The model is intended to support as many levels as required, depending on the complexity of the system. For each life cycle, or subsystem decomposition, a complete set of documentation is required.

One major difference between the NASA and DOD standards, in general, is that DOD standards are mandated, whereas NASA standards are available for any projects wishing to use them. Selection and enforcement of the SMAP standards is a project responsibility.

2.5 HOW SOFTWARE FITS WITHIN THE SYSTEM LIFE CYCLE

Software has been viewed as a productionlike process in which one simply "turned the crank" when the software part of the system was needed. In avionics systems, for example, the airframe was developed first, and then the avionics (airborne electronics) was developed and computational hardware selected. Once the hardware was defined, software development began. As software has become a more integral part of the system this situation no longer holds. There remains, however, a pervasive industry perception that software is a manufacturing or "turn-the-crank" process. Instead, it is an engineering process, and one cannot use a cookbook because the recipes for success are often too complex.

In modern systems, software provides 90 percent of the system's features and functionality. That is why software is so important—it allows an unbelievable degree of flexibility. Of course flexibility does not come free. Added costs and headaches occur because software engineering today is largely a manual, personality-dominated team activity that takes skill, patience, and persistence to accomplish correctly.

The software development community has experienced major catastrophes when blindly pushing the software through a cookbook type of development process. Many of these attempts have resulted in projects that never became operational or dramatically exceeded cost and schedule projections.

2.5.1 Incremental Development

Software development is a complex process, typically consisting of a number of parallel developments at the subsystem level. In many projects, as depicted in Figure 2-15, the design process is a series of parallel activities with several individual software subsystems undergoing development at any one time. In other words, the waterfall process is replicated within the project many times depending on the complexity of development. Strategies of this type approach development in a single way: as a series of smaller "mini" development projects. They cope with large, complex projects by breaking them into manageable components.

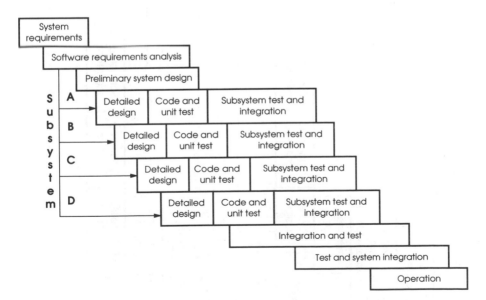

Figure 2-15   Parallel development

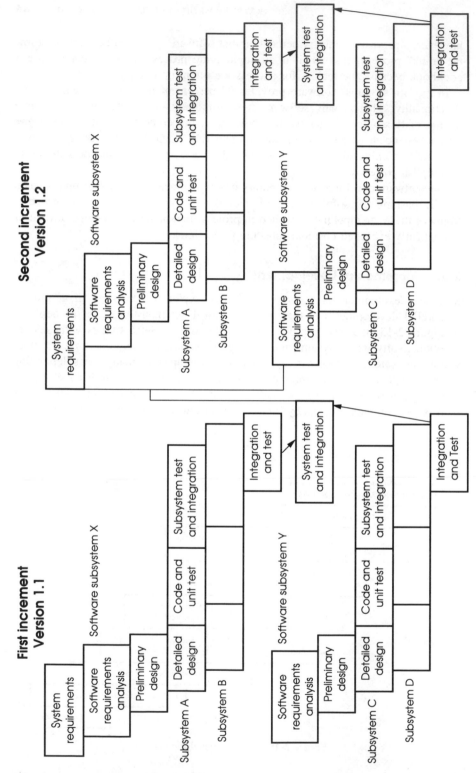

The complexity of the develoment process is managed through various techniques. The parts of the system may be decomposed, or organized into smaller development components as described above. These components may be organized into increments, or builds, that provide a snapshot of the system at any point in the development process. This process affords the developer an opportunity to gauge overall progress before the system is complete. The system may also be delivered in increments as a series of capabilities that are integrated over time (Figure 2-16). Control must be exercised on each, and each must be integrated into a complete system as the acquisition progresses. If management is not astute, a misstep in one direction will cause a failure in another. Because of the interactions between the activities, careful planning and control are required to maintain the integrity of the development.

Incremental development may be used within the system or at the systems level itself. This typically occurs when a breadboard or model of the system is developed prior to production of the overall system. This underscores the practice of prototyping systems before major production decisions are made. In the past,

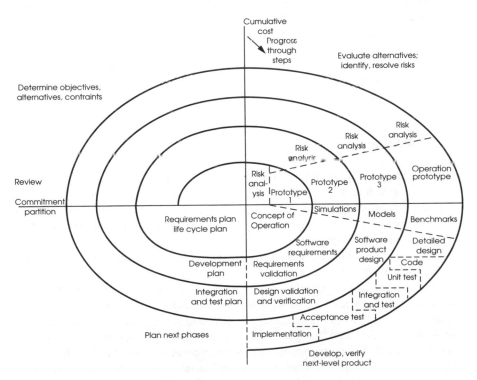

Figure 2-17   Spiral model of the software process

Source: [Boehm, 1988] Boehm, B. W., "A Spiral Model of Software Development and Enhancement," *Computer*, Vol. 21, No. 5, Los Alamitos, CA, May 1988, pp. 61–72. ©1988 IEEE.

decision processes for advanced system prototypes have been dictated largely by hardware issues. In recent systems engineering practice the need for advanced software prototypes has been recognized as well.

2.5.2 The Spiral Model

Several advanced software development models have been proposed to accommodate the parallel and incremental nature of software development. One of these is the spiral model [Boehm, 1988]. The basic object of this model is to reduce risk by using an iterative process that builds upon its own development experience. As indicated in Figure 2-17, at the project's inception a judgment is made about the overall risk of development. If the risk is high, an initial prototype is developed based on the objectives of the project. During this phase in the spiral model, documentation and the formal management processes are minimal in order to contain the cost of development. As the spiral model progresses through its cycles, the degree of documentation and development rigor increases.

When the development reaches *risk analysis* (a point depicted in the right quadrant of the model) a reassessment of risk is made and a decision is required either to continue in the spiral or to "jump" to another spiral path. If the development risk is deemed low, the development could jump to the last phase, the traditional waterfall model of development.

This advanced model is not in widespread use, but it is receiving increased attention. The principal problems with such complex models are the need for personnel training and the requirement to integrate the model process with the developer's engineering practice.

2.6 SUMMARY

Software engineering is similar to other engineering processes. It would be a mistake to look at it as a discipline separate from the systems engineering process. In systems acquisition, software and systems engineering go hand in hand. The systems engineering team must be multidisciplined, including personnel that understand software development as well as hardware development. In many software-intensive systems, systems engineering is performed by a lead systems engineer with a strong software background.

Management and engineering personnel must not make the mistake of viewing software development as a contained process implemented by a number of software "magicians." Although senior management personnel may not have solid software backgrounds, the need for good software engineering must be recognized and accommodated. Just as important, software personnel must not insulate themselves, by hiding behind the "software is different" label. Management must be able to recognize this syndrome, within both the buyer and seller organizations, and take appropriate action to correct it.

The management of this process, when governed by a formal vehicle such as a contract, is called software acquisition management (sometimes simply referred to as software management)—as opposed to managing the software development on a project (called software project management). The waterfall life cycle software development model provides the basic framework for software development and management of the development process.

The next chapters provide detailed treatment of the individual requirements and practices of these management processes The next chapter, Acquisition Management, sets the stage for the procurement or acquisition process.

REFERENCES

[Bersoff, 1980] E. H. Bersoff, V. D. Henderson, and S. G. Siegel, *Software Configuration Management*, Englewood Cliffs, NJ: Prentice Hall.

[Boehm, 1988] B. W. Boehm, "A Spiral Model of Software Development and Enhancement," *Computer*, Vol. 21, No. 5, May, pp. 61–72.

[DOD, 1988] *Department of Defense Standard 2167A*, Defense System Software Development, February 29.

[IEEE, 1989] *IEEE Draft Standard P1074/D4, Standard for Software Life Cycle Processes*, New York: The Institute of Electrical and Electronic Engineers, Inc., August 8.

[IEEE, 1983] *ANSI/IEEE Standard 729-1983, IEEE Standard Glossary of Software Engineering Terminology*, New York: The Institute of Electrical and Electronic Engineers, Inc.

CHAPTER 3

Acquisition Management

The purpose of this chapter is to discuss acquisition management as it relates to software. The chapter discusses acquisition strategy, proposal preparation, contract negotiations, source selection, and other acquisition topics. Many of the topics are generally applicable to systems acquisition as well as software acquisition.

Acquisition management involves the purchase of software via a contract. The buyer specifies what the system requires, when the software will be needed, and how it will be accepted. The seller determines how the software will be developed and the resources required (people, equipment, facilities, technology, and so on). Although both parties are concerned with technical performance, schedules, and cost, each addresses these concerns differently. The buyer tracks development progress to ensure that the seller is performing as expected and that cost and schedule goals are being realized. The seller manages the development and tries to make a reasonable profit. The seller also wishes to please the buyer and so provides information concerning the development's progress to help relieve buyer anxiety.

Acquiring large software systems requires both the buyer and the seller to formulate effective management strategies. The buyer's strategy is aimed at using competitive market forces to get the seller to agree to develop the desired product on an acceptable schedule and at reasonable cost. The seller's strategy is directed toward getting the buyer to share risk and to earn a reasonable profit. Technical, financial, and contractual terms must be negotiated and conditions established under which the joint conduct of the effort will be guided. Both buyer and seller need to understand each other's expectations, and both need to work to establish trust, rapport, and good working relations as the acquisition life cycle unfolds.

The acquisition of a software system follows the life cycle depicted in Figure 3-1. Phases in the procurement of the system include concept exploration, source acquisition, and performance management. Notice that this is a truncated version of the system life cycle described in Section 2.1.

During the concept exploration phase, the buyer develops the requirements for the system; prepares a functional specification; devises a management strategy; and generates a technical, political, and economic case justifying the acquisition. The seller may be one of several working with the buyer during this phase to help determine requirements, evaluate alternatives, and establish concept feasibility.

During the source acquisition phase, the seller responds to the buyer's request for proposal (RFP), and the buyer chooses a contractor to develop the system. Considerable effort is expended by both parties to prepare for and respond to RFPs and negotiate a contract. The contract that evolves serves as the basis upon which the system will be built. If the contract is defective, the buyer may not have enough leverage to get the seller to build what is needed. Contract changes, which cost time and effort, may be needed to rectify such problems.

During the performance management phase, the buyer monitors the seller's progress and compliance with the contract's provisions. The buyer is involved in *performance measurement*. The seller focuses on getting the job done and achieving the interim milestones called for in the contract schedule. The buyer and seller identify problems and work as a team to correct them whenever possible.

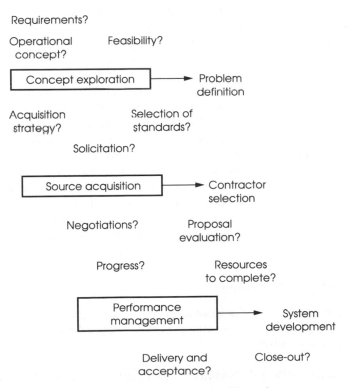

Figure 3-1 Software acquisition life cycle

Finally, the contract is closed out when the seller delivers an acceptable product and the system becomes operational.

Managers in both buyer and seller communities understand how important adequate and timely funding is to project success. Their activities must be keyed to the planning, programming, and budgeting process used by the buyer during the acquisition process to acquire and allocate funds. Managers must navigate the technical traps present in an acquisition process that often must accomodate competing interests. Politics and availability of funds will often determine tradeoffs among technical performance, cost, and schedule goals. Compromises are made to accommodate decisions dictated by funding limits and some desirable technical features may have to be forgone.

Acquisition management is an industrial contracting process. Its structure, organization, and flow are governed by a series of gates imposed by the buyer to ensure selection of the best source and to enforce the terms and conditions of the contract. The remainder of this chapter introduces the reader to the principles of acquisition management.

3.1   ACQUISITION MANAGEMENT STRATEGIES

There are many possible acquisition strategies for software systems. Selection of the appropriate strategy is governed by various technical and fiscal factors. If a development is fairly risk-free, a straightforward approach may be taken. If the software is complex, deeply embedded in a hardware system development, then the acquisition strategy may be more complicated. For example, acquisition of avionics software usually follows airframe development and selection of avionics hardware. The airframe developer might select a subcontractor to develop very sophisticated software used to mechanize complex weapons delivery systems.

In some systems, software development is intensive and hardware development minimal. Selection of an appropriate strategy may be dominated by technical considerations such as integration complexity within the system. For example, a system for the Internal Revenue Service is primarily served by general purpose computers. The strategy might be different for precedented systems where a seller has experience with the product and can readily adapt it for new applications. Subsidiary issues to be considered as a strategy is formulated include schedule, risk of development, and cost.

3.1.1   Strategies Explained

There are three basic types of acquisition or procurement strategies to be considered: competitive, two-phase, and sole source. Each is discussed and related to the major factors that impact selection.

3.1.1.1   *Competitive Acquisition*   In a competitive acquisition, sources, or sellers, compete for the job based on an open solicitation specifying definitive system requirements. The sellers' proposals are evaluated based on predefined

criteria such as ability to meet requirements and minimize risk. Usually such criteria are assigned numerical values to obtain scores by which the proposals are ranked. After ranking, a competitive range is established by eliminating the lowest-ranked proposals, those deemed technically unacceptable. Depending on the acquisition tactic, the offerer with the lowest price may be awarded the contract. If, however, the competitive range is narrow, the buyer may select a winner based on best technical approach even though it may cost a little more. Normally the buyer's strategy, including its detailed evaluation criteria and point system used, is not divulged to the sellers competing for the contract. The relative order of importance, however, is addressed in the RFP (Figure 3-2).

In some cases, after the competitive range is established, the buyer will ask for best and final offers. All of the sellers still within the competitive range will be asked to submit a final cost proposal. Usually the seller shaves fee; however, if competition is severe the seller could be faced with a dilemma. In order to remain competitive, the seller may have to shave cost at the expense of fully meeting the requirements of the statement of work, or "buy in" to the effort through the use of corporate funds. Such practices may compromise the acquisition. The buyer should exercise caution when considering such shaved bids. Although offering a low up-front cost, the seller is probably operating in an extremely cost-competitive environment and may be forced to recover cost through change proposals or

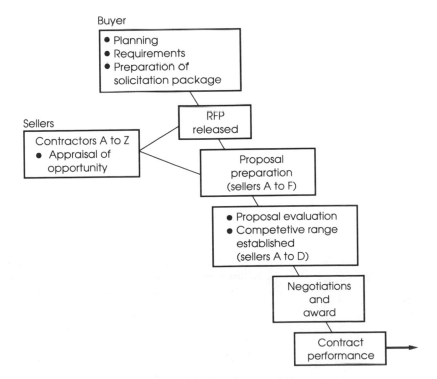

Figure 3-2 Competitive acquisition

by reducing functionality or performance. The buyer usually evaluates the cost realism of the offers and may look on major unexplained decreases in the best and final offers negatively. If the software product is proprietary, the buyer might be dependent on the seller for maintenance and support.

In some cases the buyer is justified in going back to the seller base established by the competitive range. The buyer may want to clarify technical issues in the proposals prior to making an award or discuss various costing and pricing options with the seller. This activity results in the *negotiated contract*. The tactic is perfectly acceptable except as a guise to lower costs.

3.1.1.2 Two-Phase Acquisition
In a two-phase acquisition, the full-scale development of the system follows a competitive concept definition phase. In the first phase, sellers are selected based on a fully competitive procurement process. Several sellers, usually two or three, are selected to further define requirements, system concepts, and possibly a design. During this first phase, the responsibility of the buyer is to ensure that all teams are treated fairly and no seller accrues an unfair advantage through access to privileged information or through preference. After the competitive first phase effort, usually a single source is selected to conduct the full scale development (Figure 3-3).

The buyer has several alternatives at the end of the competitive phase. A contract can be awarded to the seller who has done the best job in the first phase and who

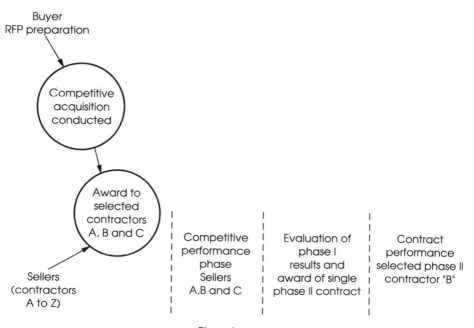

Figure 3-3   Two-phase acquisition

submits the most attractive proposal for the follow-on phase. This is the most common course of action. Another option is to initiate the second phase with an open solicitation using the results of the first phase as a basis for competition. It is also possible, though unusual, to continue the competition into or even through full-scale development. For example, the design of two competitive systems may be the objective of the procurement. One desire may be to establish a second source environment, thereby reducing the risk of dependence on a single supplier for the system or product.

3.1.1.3 Sole-Source Acquisition

A sole-source acquisition is one where the buyer simply negotiates and awards a contract to a single offeror. Typically, this type of acquisition is appropriate when only one seller can do the job and the conduct of a competitive procurement would be a waste of time and resources. A sole-source contract should be awarded only when there is no other alternative. The buyer must take extreme care to ensure that adequate value is obtained for the funds expended under this acquisition strategy.

3.1.2 Selection Factors

The selection of the appropriate acquisition strategy and its effective implementation depends on many factors:

1. *Risk.* Those technical factors with the potential to adversely impact cost, schedule, or performance. If development risk is high, the acquisition strategy should contain provisions offering the developer incentives to contain risk. Source selection may be conducted by having competitors demonstrate how they would reduce risk to an acceptable level should they receive the award.

2. *Complexity.* A relative gauge of the difficulty of the software product development. If the development of the product is complex, sellers with the right resources, talent, and qualifications to do the job must be sought. The availability of such sources is a factor in determining the appropriate acquisition strategy. Limited source availability may be sufficient cause to justify a sole-source strategy.

3. *Uniqueness.* The degree to which competition can be used during source selection. In some cases, only one seller has the capacity to perform the job because of prerequisite experience, patents, or technological expertise. In procurement environments such as that of the U.S. federal government, a sole-source strategy is predicated on the existence of only one capable source. In other more liberal environments, merely establishing that there is a clear choice of a single source is enough to establish that conducting a competitive selection would waste both time and resources.

4. *Cost.* A measure of the dollar resources available to do the job. When budgets are limited, cost may dictate the acquisition strategy. For example, a two-phase procurement may use competition to contain costs below a

predefined level. As another example, a sole-source strategy may be used to lock a supplier into a fixed-price contract attractive to the buyer.

5. *Schedule.* A measure of the amount of time available to get the job done. The more competitive the acquisition process, the longer it takes to establish a contract and begin work. When time is scarce a sole-source procurement may be justified.

6. *Size.* Larger efforts, in terms of the work, dollars, or amount of code involve greater risk. The buyer can reduce risk by keeping the project to a manageable size. Because the two-phase strategy emphasizes more definition at the beginning of an effort, it is an appropriate candidate for large acquisition projects.

7. *Requirements volatility.* A measure of the definition and stability of the requirements for the system. If requirements are fuzzy, a competitive definition phase should be considered before major commitment of resources to full-scale development.

Table 3-1 illustrates how the various factors influence the selection of the buyer's acquisition strategy.

3.1.2.1 *Competitive Acquisition* A competitive acquisition is usually the most desirable strategy. Such an acquisition assumes a fairly definitive set of requirements. Technical risk is bounded, and the project likely can be realized within cost and schedule goals. Guidance on selection factors for a competitive acquisition strategy is as follows:

1. *Risk.* Risk should be bounded. If risk is high, a fair and equitable competition to select a single seller may not be practical. In such a case, a risk-reduction contract or two-phase acquisition strategy should be considered as a precursor to full-scale development.

TABLE 3-1 Acquisition Strategies Matrix

Factor	Sole-source	Competitive	Two-phase
Risk	low	low–medium	high
Complexity	low	medium	high
Uniqueness	yes	no	no
Cost	moderate	high	high
Schedule	tight	flexible	flexible
Size	small	large	large
Requirements volatility	stable	volatile	volatile

2. *Complexity*. Complexity should be amenable to management. If development complexity is high, a two-phase approach should be considered to reduce risk and to improve the accuracy of cost and schedule projections.

3. *Uniqueness*. Unique criteria or factors preclude a competitive effort. To afford competition, any uniqueness associated with the effort must be removed. Otherwise a fair competition is not possible.

4. *Cost*. Developments with higher cost usually demand a competitive strategy. A competitive design phase should be considered and commitment to a single seller deferred until confidence in cost and schedule forecasts can be achieved.

5. *Schedule*. Generally, the schedule for a competitive effort is not overly constrained. If the schedule is tight, a sole-source procurement could be justified.

6. *Size*. Typically, larger efforts entail greater cost, schedule, and technical risks. In such cases, competition should be extended as long into the development as possible. A competitive design effort is one means to contain the risk associated with the sheer volume of work to be performed.

7. *Requirements volatility*. The requirements used as the basis of a competitive acquisition should be fairly well-defined. If they are not, contract completion could be risky. Cost and schedule projections may be unrealistic. A competitive design phase or requirements definition phase should be considered if requirements are not stable enough for use as a basis for selection.

3.1.2.2 *Two-Phase Acquisition* A two-phase procurement generally takes longer and costs more at the outset than a competitive procurement. It is used when the buyer intends to keep competition open for as long as possible, often for six months to a year. After the first phase, the number of offerors is reduced and a single seller is selected from the remaining competitors. The buyer takes advantage of the work performed by all the teams during the design phase and factors the results of those efforts into the subsequent competitive procurement. The buyer must take care during this process to guard against competitive leveling (that is, making it apparent to one offeror what another is doing).

One disadvantage of a competitive design phase is that the buyer requires additional time, personnel, and dollars to manage the effort. In addition, strict procedures must be followed to ensure that the selection of the winning seller is done impartially. All activities must be conducted so that one seller does not gain an unfair advantage over another. For example, proprietary or privileged information of one seller should be protected from disclosure to the other sellers.

Guidance on selection factors for a two-phase acquisition strategy is as follows:

1. *Risk*. Generally, initial risk can be relatively high because the first phase affords multiple risk-abatement tactics. The buyer can take advantage of different seller approaches for developing the system.

2. *Complexity*. The development is normally complex. The approach attempts to reduce complexity to a manageable level so that (1) the risks associated

with it can be controlled and (2) the resources needed to contend with it can be managed.

3. *Uniqueness.*   There should be no unique development factors that would preclude competition. Each seller should be able to propose its own plan for satisfying system requirements.

4. *Cost.*   The more uncertain the cost, the greater need there is to expend resources up front to more priesly define system requirements. A major advantage of this strategy is that it provides a better definition of the effort before major development is undertaken. As a consequence, costs can be more accurately estimated and risk more readily contained.

5. *Schedule.*   The schedule must allow the additional time required for a competitive requirements or design phase. The purpose of taking longer at the beginning of the program is to reduce the overall schedule risk of development. It may be difficult for management to accept this approach because the world looks perfect at the beginning of a project and a single contract schedule always appears shorter.

6. *Size.*   The effort should be fairly significant in size to justify the additional resources expended in conducting the competitive design phase. Larger developments entail greater uncertainty and the need to resort to this acquisition strategy is more pronounced.

7. *Requirements volatility.*   Poorly defined or unstable requirements justify the added expense of a comparative design phase to better establish them. Of course, requirements for the design phase need to be defined in enough detail to permit a fair competition.

3.1.2.3   Sole-Source Acquisition   The sole-source procurement is infrequently used, particularly on large contract efforts. Buyers are encouraged to pursue competitive awards whenever possible because typically they result in reduced cost and improved leverage with sellers. Sole-source awards are most common when it is evident that there is only one qualified seller. It should be readily apparent that it would be impractical for the buyer to conduct a competitive effort. Sole-source awards are often made on continuation efforts or on developments that capitalize on a specific talent, capability, or technology that the source possesses. A sole-source process is used only when the buyer clearly demonstrates that competition would degrade, rather than enhance, the buyer's ability to obtain a satisfactory system that meets cost and schedule goals.

Guidance on selection factors for a sole-source acquisition strategy is as follows:

1. *Risk.*   Use of a single source to perform a well-defined job within cost and schedule goals is acceptable for only low-risk developments. For riskier projects, this acquisition strategy is inappropriate. In some cases, using a competitive acquisition strategy may actually introduce greater risk, indicating that a true competitive environment is not practical.

2. *Complexity.* Generally, complexity is not a major consideration in a sole-source effort. Occasionally a complex development, for which only one source is qualified, may compel the buyer to utilize this strategy.

3. *Uniqueness.* Sole-source awards are appropriate when it is clear that a single offeror has the only viable solution and that to develop alternative sources would be impractical.

4. *Cost.* Cost risk is normally low on a sole-source acquisition. The risk of the seller overrunning cost projections should be a lesser concern than the contractor's ability to meet technical and schedule requirements.

5. *Schedule.* A tight schedule will often justify a sole-source award. A more flexible schedule may enable a competitive procurement that uses market forces to reduce cost.

6. *Size.* Generally, the size of a sole-source acquisition should be fairly small. For large efforts, it is extremely difficult to contain cost with a sole-source strategy. The buyer is unable to utilize market forces to protect against cost concessions and unfavorable terms and conditions in the contract.

7. *Requirements volatility.* It is important to have a well-defined and stable statement of requirements. Otherwise, the scope of the award cannot be precisely defined so that both the buyer's and the seller's risk can be bounded and managed.

3.1.3 Approaches Reviewed

A competitive strategy is most commonly used for software acquisition. The other two approaches, two-phase and sole-source, are generally used in acquisitions that are complex or that have extraordinary requirements. There are a number of variants to these basic approaches. For example, a two-phase procurement is a variant of a competitive procurement. Management, both technical and administrative, should evaluate the acquisition in light of the seven factors discussed to select the one most appropriate for their specific effort.

Assessing the acquisition factors is a first step in building the acquisition environment, but other less predictable factors must also be considered. These factors can greatly influence the selection of the acquisition strategy. They are defined by management policy and the sociological mind-set of the organization. For example, management may not understand the two-phase acquisition strategy and why it might be appropriate for a specific acquisition. They may not understand the apparent increase in the schedule to implement a two-phase strategy. They may be unwilling to accept a new approach or an unknown supplier. To create a more open-minded atmosphere, management must be educated as to the strengths and weaknesses of the alternative acquisition approaches and why they are needed. The options need to be traded off against program risks using factors management can understand (including the seven discussed previously). Once the alternatives have been identified and evaluated, management may be more receptive to accepting a recommended alternative strategy, even one that runs counter to organizational culture. Of course, if the culture is too rigid, it may be impossible to change preexisting mind-sets and convince management to choose the best alternative.

Although a sole-source procurement should ordinarily be avoided, at times it is in the buyer's best interest (as noted previously). In certain customer environments, however, the use of sole-source contracts is strictly taboo. There may be no other option except to proceed with alternatives acceptable to the organization even though they may not be optimal. In any event, it is usually to the buyer's advantage to avoid sole-source contracts.

A buyer facing a sole-source situation may try to reduce dependency on a single seller. One way of accomplishing this is through a two-phase procurement. The first phase, conducted on a sole-source basis, could be directed toward developing a specification for a competitive second phase. This is of course predicated on the assumption that the basis for sole-source can be removed. This may not be the case if, for example, the system is based on proprietary software.

The buyer may conduct a competition for the first contract based on development of an alternative to the restricted capability offered by the sole-source. The buyer should examine carefully the advantages and disadvantages of such an approach. How important is the need for competition or a second source supplier? Is dependence on a single seller unacceptable? Is the system large enough to warrant the additional time and resources required to implement this approach?

3.2   GETTING ON CONTRACT—BUYER ACTIVITIES

Independent of acquisition strategy, the buyer must expend considerable effort in selecting a source and getting the contract in place. The buyer (1) works with the customer to determine that organization's expectations for the system; (2) develops a statement of work detailing the tasks to be performed and how they will be structured; (3) defines the products, reviews, and documentation to be delivered as part of the contract and identifies who needs them and how they are accepted; (4) develops testing, training, and support strategies and factors them into the acquisition plans; (5) generates estimated costs and schedules; and (6) decides the criteria used to evaluate the offers and sets minimal acceptable standards for each.

The product of all these efforts is a *solicitation package*. The package typically contains the following items:*

- Project management plan
- System specification**
- Operational concept document
- Statement of work**

---

*Naturally, the size and complexity of the acquisition will determine which items to include. For smaller projects, the set should be narrowed to those appropriate.

**Items in a suggested minimal package.

- Work breakdown structure
- Documentation list (In U.S. government acquisitions this is known as the contract data requirements list (CDRL).)**
- Schedule**
- Cost estimate**
- Evaluation criteria**
- Draft contract
- Proposal preparation guidelines

1. In the *project management plan* (PMP), the buyer identifies who is responsible for the system acquisition and how they will manage it. The PMP describes the tasks both buyer and seller need to complete in order to deliver a product acceptable to the ultimate user on time and within budget. In essence, the PMP describes the acquisition goals, strategy, and process. It describes what needs to occur during the acquisition in order to preserve the overall integrity of the schedule.

2. The *system specification* describes the functional and performance requirements for the system. It describes what is needed to satisfy customer expectations. It defines all interfaces with other systems and factors that may constrain the system design (such as security or manufacturability concerns). It lists the standards and protocols used by both buyer and seller to guide design, development, test, acceptance, and implementation of the system.

3. The *operational concept document* describes the overall approach used to operate the system once it is deployed. It contains the usage scenarios, operational sequences, and management protocols the customer will employ to use, operate, and sustain the system once it becomes operational. In addition, it describes the support concept for the system.

4. In the *statement of work* (SOW), the buyer defines the tasks required to successfully develop a system that fulfils all the requirements of the system specification. The SOW must describe the work in enough detail to allow offerors to scope the job, cost it, and provide a responsive technical solution to the requirements of the solicitation.

5. The *work breakdown structure* (WBS) helps the buyer keep tabs on cost, schedule, and technical performance and track the development's progress once the contract is under way. The WBS establishes an architecture that permits work to be related to the accounting structure so that results can be compared with plans on a task-by-task basis throughout the acquisition. Figure 3-4 presents an example of a WBS. The seller is usually afforded the opportunity to propose changes to the WBS to more accurately reflect that organization's approach.

6. The *documentation list* itemizes the data items (documentation, databases, and so on) to be prepared and delivered as part of the contract. It details

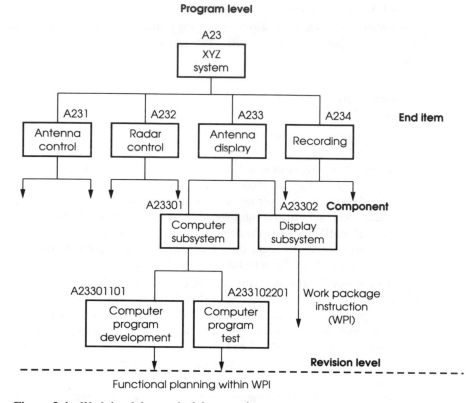

Figure 3-4 Work breakdown schedule example

Source: [Evans, 1983] Evans, M. W., P. Piazza and J. B. Dolkas, *Principles of Productive Software Management*, New York: Wiley. ©1983 Wiley. Reprinted with permission.

for each data item its format, its relationship to the SOW, its delivery schedule, its review procedure, and its distribution. In addition, it may provide reference standards used to guide the production of the data item.

7. The *schedule* summarizes the tasks to be performed, the relationships among them, and the amount of calendar time allocated to complete them. The schedule relates the tasks in the WBS with the data items called out in the documentation list.

8. The *cost estimate* establishes a financial baseline for what the buyer thinks it will cost to develop and operate the system over its expected useful life. This estimate is needed in order for the buyer to establish a budget and get funding authorized and allocated to the project. The buyer uses this cost estimate as the standard for evaluating seller proposals. For government jobs, an independent estimate by a third party is required.

9. The *evaluation criteria* establish the standards against which each proposal will be compared and scored. Proposals are evaluated against these stan-

dards and not against each other. Typical evaluation criteria include the offeror's understanding of the problem, responsiveness to requirements, past performance, and risk assessment. The buyer details the criteria in an evaluation guide, while only top-level criteria are given to the sellers.

10. The *draft contract* contains the contract terms and conditions that will be used to manage the award. Legal, warranty, patent, data rights, termination, accounting, and payment provisions specify how the contract is administered in practice. Contract clauses often have a profound effect on what buyer and seller can and cannot do once the award is made. For example, a clause pertaining to personnel replacement could affect who the seller can place on the project. Extreme care should be taken to ensure that the contract contains clauses that are pertinent and well understood.

11. The *proposal preparation instructions* tell the offerors how to package their proposals. To make the job of proposal evaluation easier, the buyer typically puts limits on the page count and provides a format for the response to the requirements of the request for proposal (RFP). Such limits force each offeror to make its case in as few words as possible.

Once the solicitation package is completed, the buyer submits it to be reviewed by the buyer's and customers' organizations. Review boards are often formed, and criticism is invited from all organizations affected by the procurement. In addition, the buyer may solicit feedback from potential sellers by providing them with draft copies of the request for proposal (RFP) for their review and comment in advance of its release to interested sellers. This has proved a popular way for the buyer to obtain free advice and to notify potential sellers to prepare for a forthcoming procurement. The RFP typically contains everything in the solicitation package but the PMP, evaluation guide, and any other source-selection-sensitive items.

A list of potential sellers must be composed for any competitive acquisition. This can be accomplished in many ways. The buyer may formally advertise for potential sources for the procurement in trade publications or government solicitations like the *Commerce Business Daily*. The buyer may find potential sellers through existing source lists or word of mouth. Many firms maintain lists of qualified sources who can provide particular goods and services. Sources may be classified by type, capability, and geographical area. The buyer might consider making the draft RFP available to potential sellers. The buyer will gain useful feedback and the seller earlier information about the opportunity. Sellers will have more time to prepare for the effort, thus enhancing the competitive environment.

Once a list of sources is established the buyer sends the RFP to the potential sources. A listed seller or any other qualified source may submit a proposal. The buyer ensures a fair competition by preventing any seller from gaining access to information that would give it an advantage over another.

As soon as the bids are closed (the announced date for submission of proposals passes), the buyer embarks on proposal evaluation and source selection. Each proposal submitted is evaluated and scored against the standards in the evaluation guide. Strengths and weaknesses of each offer are tabulated and deficiencies noted. A competitive range may be established which comprises those sources that have successfully met the requirements of the RFP. The buyer may then choose to continue the process with only those sellers that are within the competitive range. Recommendations are then made and the source selection committee may solicit additional information from each of the bidders (or only those in the competitive range). Proposers are usually given the benefit of the doubt during this process, and bidders are allowed to clarify their offers through a question and answer exchange with the buyer. As answers to the buyer's questions are evaluated, offeror proposals are rescored. Finally, a source is selected and negotiations may begin with one or more of the sellers.

Negotiations are the final step in the process. They are held to update offers and seek concessions on either the buyer's or seller's part based upon events that may have occurred during the source-selection process. Technical, cost, legal, and other contract terms and conditions may be negotiated. For example, the requirements may have changed during this time period. The buyer may not want to communicate this information to all offerors because the changes may disturb the baseline against which offers are evaluated.

3.3 GETTING ON CONTRACT—SELLER ACTIVITIES

The seller also has a great deal of work to do to compete successfully for the award of a contract. As the buyer's acquisition management strategy unfolds, the seller is brought into the acquisition cycle and must complete various tasks. The seller starts tracking the procurement early on. This permits sufficient lead time to get ready to compete for the award. The next task is to presell the buyer on seller capabilities and on a sole-source award, if possible. If the probability of winning is acceptable, buyer marketing personnel will try to persuade management to allocate the bid and proposal money, talent, and facilities needed to pursue and win the award. To get such a commitment from management, a competitive analysis is performed to determine the likelihood of winning the award and successfully completing the work. Financing, teaming, team staffing, and subcontracting possibilities and their fit to customer preferences need to be investigated. Once approved by management, the proposal effort is organized and staffed. Proposal teams develop win strategies, proposal themes, and technical backup needed to fulfil the buyer's requirements as stated in the RFP package. Emphasis is usually placed on risk reduction and making an acceptable profit. If a draft RFP is issued, these teams will evaluate it and try to shape it to improve their chances of winning through comments and suggestions to the buyer.

A proposal responsive to the requirements of the RFP is generated and management's commitment to its provisions secured prior to submitting it to the buyer. The seller may be subjected to a preaward survey or a software capabilities audit during these preparatory activities. If so, preparations are made for a customer visit and inspection. The seller will have to respond to the buyer's questions and try hard to satisfy buyer concerns in order to place within the competitive range. If qualified for negotiations, the seller will negotiate technical and cost terms and conditions with the client and submit a best and final offer (BAFO). Long-lead activities, at the seller's expense, may be undertaken to get ready to perform the job should the seller be awarded it. Such activities include keeping key personnel available during the proposal and selection periods to answer the buyer's questions, refining project plans, working technical problems, acquiring long-lead equipment and facilities (often at the seller's expense in anticipation of the contract), and getting people ready to move to the project once the contract has been awarded. Because the buyer may negotiate with several bidders, the selection process may be drawn out over a period of months.

For a sole-source acquisition, the seller will be asked to generate a proposal and may be asked to provide the buyer with a rationale for accepting it. Because sole-source awards are difficult to get, considerable time and effort may be expended to convince the buyer that the seller is the only qualified source for the project. Within the U.S. government, the Federal Acquisition Regulations (FAR) prescribes the rules for conducting a procurement. The FAR identifies a number of specific instances in which the buyer can make a sole-source award.

In certain cases, for federal, state, and possibly local government procurements, minority or disadvantaged set-asides permit the buyer to contract certain types of jobs on a sole-source basis with qualified businesses owned and operated by members of such groups. For the U.S. government, the FAR contains guidelines for such contracts awarded by various government organizations.

For competitive awards, the seller will have to go through the competitive process outlined previously to be selected to perform on the contract. The federal government prefers the competitive process because it can use market forces to pressure qualified sources to keep prices low and quality high. The buyer may even pretend that there is competition (when, in fact, only one bid is received) to maximize leverage during negotiations.

3.4 DEVELOPING A REQUEST FOR PROPOSAL

The request for proposal (RFP) is the document that culminates the buyer's planning and initiates the source-selection phase. It represents the formal means of communicating the requirements of the acquisition to the source that will be awarded the effort. Too often, the RFP is viewed as an administrative rather than a technical document. Although it may be imperfect, it should contain sufficient technical detail for completing the award of the ensuing contract. It is important that the RFP adequately scope technical requirements, the work to be performed, and the administrative terms and conditions of the contract. Inconsistencies, insufficient detail, and inappropriate requirements could make it difficult for the bidder to develop a proposal that is responsive to the buyer's desires.

As already discussed, the buyer must expend a lot of time and effort to develop a comprehensive RFP. The buyer must work with the customer (the ultimate user of the system) to establish requirements, expectations, schedules, and support needs. The customer usually has a concept of a system but not the detailed requirements to build the system. As a consequence, the buyer may need to go through the time-consuming process of developing prototypes or draft specifications to focus and define the user's expectations for the system. Studies may need to be conducted for this purpose, perhaps by an outside organization if staff or resources within the organization are scarce. Independent of the method used, the quality of this specification effort directly impacts the quality of the RFP. To get the desired product, the buyer must remember, "Good contracts come from good specifications," and "The better you scope the acquisition, the more acceptable the offers will be."

In addition, the larger the system, the greater will be the political pressure exerted within the organization. Power battles often erupt as organizations and individuals try to exercise control of the development. Issues such as which user has priority and who is responsible for system maintenance emerge. Management policies need to be established as issues associated with development and support of the system get ironed out. Procedures need to be established for monitoring activities of the seller. Configuration management and quality control approaches need to be devised so that the buyer can manage the masses of documentation that may be delivered during the development. Protocols need to be devised to handle how organizations communicate and deal with one another as the system is developed and then enters operational use. Investment issues need to be considered and monies allocated as long-lead items such as facilities and equipment are identified. Personalities and cliques are involved as decisions are made and changed. To survive, the buyer must understand both the process and the participants.

3.5 LEGAL AND ADMINISTRATIVE ACTIONS AND REACTIONS

Acquisition management deals with legal and administrative issues in addition to technical, programmatic, and political matters. RFPs often contain pages of seemingly meaningless legal and administrative clauses dealing with all sorts of issues:

- Equal opportunity requirements and reporting provisions
- Compliance with labor law legislation
- Patent claims and rights to computer software
- Invoicing and payment terms and conditions
- Use of toxic chemicals in the workplace
- Termination for convenience and/or default
- Rights to inspect accounting records and claims
- Conflict of interest
- Use and replacement of key personnel

Terms and conditions governing these subjects provide buyer and seller with a framework whereby they can administer the contract and enforce its provisions through the courts, if necessary. Though unfamiliar to most technical personnel, such terms and conditions can have a profound impact on the acquisition. For example, placement of a conflict of interest clause in a RFP could discourage several qualified sources from bidding on a job where they are prohibited from defining requirements for equipment and/or software similar to that which they market. They would rather wait and bid for the equipment rather than compete for the definition efforts.

Normally, both buyer and seller consult with an attorney to specify any special terms and conditions needed to maximize their leverage after the contract is awarded. For example, the buyer may want to provide financial incentives for software reuse. The attorney may help identify incentives to be placed into the contract and the way they would be administered. For example, a bonus could be provided for every thousand lines of planned code taken from a reuse library and not developed specifically for the current project.

Likewise, the seller would consult an attorney to determine whether or not the terms and conditions are acceptable, and to devise alternatives when warranted. For example, the buyer may want the rights to any software developed on the contract, even that not delivered. The buyer would specify this as a contractual term and condition. The seller may offer the buyer such rights at a reduced cost if the seller is able to retain commercial rights. This would allow sale of the product to anyone (but the buyer) and thus improve profit margins. As another example, the key personnel clause specified by the buyer may be viewed by the seller as overly restrictive. During negotiations, the seller may therefore seek to have these terms relaxed for compromises in fee and/or schedule.

3.6 THE COMPETITIVE SOURCE SELECTION

As discussed earlier, the buyer utilizes the competitive process whenever possible to take advantage of market forces. The selection of a source and award of a contract follows a process structured to fairly and impartially pick the best source. After the RFP and draft contract containing the legal and administrative clauses are completed, the following eight steps are normally taken to select a source.

1. *Complete solicitation package.* The buyer must assemble the items which make up the solicitation package and get them approved. Often, a review committee is formed called a murder board. This committee forces the buyer to address items that the reviewers consider important, for example, life cycle support and usage issues.

2. *Prepare source list.* The buyer must prepare a list of qualified sources who can perform the job. Sellers are solicited through advertising or by directly asking sources to compete. The buyer may ask potential sources to submit their qualifications for screening prior to placement on the source list. The U.S. government is not allowed to preclude an interested seller from proposing on a procurement without just cause.

3. *Issue solicitation.* The buyer next issues the RFP to those sellers on the source list and ask for responses within some nominal period from 30 to 60 days. During this time, the buyer prepares to receive the proposals from the sellers vying for the job.

4. *Score and rank responses.* The buyer evaluates each of the proposals received in response to the solicitation. A source-selection authority and board are constituted to score each offer using the preestablished evaluation standards and to rank candidates based upon their strengths and weaknesses. A competitive range, including those sellers who have met the requirements of the RFP, may be established to narrow the number of sources to a more manageable level.

5. *Issue questions.* The buyer gives each offeror the benefit of the doubt during the evaluation. However, questions that arise must be answered so that all offers can be scored fairly. Questions are directed to offerors whose proposals require clarification. Because each question represents an opportunity to improve the score, great care is taken in developing a response.

6. *Rescore based on responses.* The buyer evaluates the sellers' responses to the questions and rescores the offerors using again the standards established for this purpose. The technical response may be weighted higher than the cost offer if the buyer so chooses. The relative importance of criteria announced in the RFP most not be changed. The buyer's goal is to select the offer that provides the organization the most value for the money. The final decision on the selection of the winning seller is made by the source-selection authority, the person authorized for this function.

7. *Negotiate.* Contract negotiations with one or more of the offerors commences after the buyer has rescored the proposals. The buyer may elect to negotiate with several offerors in the competitive range to apply pressure for better terms and conditions. The buyer may negotiate only with the selected source; however, that can become difficult if the preferred offeror is inflexible. The buyer may then elect to negotiate with a second qualified offeror.

8. *Award.* The buyer awards the job to the offeror who best satisfies the evaluation standards and provides the best value.

Personnel typically involved in source selection include the following individuals in the buyer organization:

- *Source-selection authority.* The person authorized to make the source-selection decision. Typically, the larger the contract, the higher up in the organization this person is placed.

- *Source-selection advisors.* These individuals advise the source-selection authority. They have been chosen for their expertise in some specialized area. Typically, each customer and each functional specialty associated with the job (for example, cost, software development, systems engineering) is represented in this small but skilled group.

* *Source-selection evaluators.* These specialists are selected to perform the evaluation of seller proposals. Evaluators may or may not come from the organizations involved. They are chosen specifically because of their ability to ferret out answers to questions important in determining whether the offerors have satisfied the buyer's minimum standards.

3.7 WRITING A WINNING PROPOSAL

The proposal should attempt to establish the seller as the best candidate for completing the job defined by the solicitation. By fully understanding buyer activities in the selection process, sellers can improve their chances of winning the award. Bidders may act to improve their competitive position through the eight-step competitive source-selection process presented in Section 3.7:

1. *Complete solicitation package.* The seller tries to influence what goes into the solicitation package. If called on to review a draft RFP, seller comments are often slanted toward approaches that put the seller in a favored position during the selection process. For example, a source with an advantage in some technical area may suggest that advantage be factored into the scoring equation for evaluating risk minimization. On large acquisitions, sellers may invest in research, prototypes, or special studies to gain an advantage on an anticipated RFP. If performance is important, the seller may develop prototype algorithms for a target process to demonstrate to the buyer possession of a sound solution to a particular problem.

2. *Prepare source list.* To compete, the seller must be on the source list. Missionary work well in advance of the procurement may be required to establish seller qualifications. The seller may prepare a qualifications statement presenting capabilities and credentials to the buyer. In any case, some effort must be expended on the part of the seller to be considered one of the players.

3. *Issue RFP.* The seller must next prepare a proposal that responds fully to all provisions of the solicitation. Such efforts take time, talent, and commitment. The proposal must demonstrate why the seller should be chosen to perform the job and how that choice will benefit the buyer.

4. *Score and rank responses.* The seller must make it easy for the evaluators to assess the proposal. Evaluation standards should be addressed fully and faultlessly in proposal themes and content because those standards are the basis for the buyer's selection of the winner.

5. *Issue questions.* The seller must realize that any question posed by the buyer represents a potential discrepancy that could cause the competition to be lost.

Answers should address the intent of the question relative to the evaluation standards and should be pointed and factual.

6. *Rescore based on responses.* The seller must again make it easy for the buyer to rescore the offer. If necessary, the seller may have to explain to the buyer why the answers are responsive and why a higher score should be awarded.

7. *Negotiate.* Once contract negotiations begin, the seller must be flexible. The seller must develop a strategy that anticipates the buyer's moves and keeps the seller in a favored position. Sellers must be willing to play the game of give and take.

8. *Award.* The seller must be prepared to perform should the award be received. This preparation may involve keeping staff on and investing in long-lead acquisitions.

The seller needs to devise strategies that will earn a favored position in the selection process. Often such strategies are developed after a competitive analysis has been performed and the strengths and weaknesses of the competitors have been ascertained. Strategies sometimes take a seller's biggest weakness and make it appear a strength and sometimes take a primary competitor's strengths and make them appear to be weaknesses. For example, the theme "Our people are better, that's why we need fewer" might be interpreted "Our people are more expensive than the competition and this is how we justify offering a similar price."

3.8 NEGOTIATIONS AND APPEASEMENTS

As the source-selection process nears its end, the buyer and seller enter into negotiations. Both parties want to enter into an agreement. The buyer wants to get the best possible value and the seller wants to receive a fair return. Both try to appease the other as they negotiate the following:

1. *Technical terms and conditions.* The buyer and seller negotiate changes to the specifications that formed the technical baseline for the source selection. Such changes could result from a number of reasons. For example, the seller may have a better idea, or the user may desire some change in the requirements.

2. *Financial terms and conditions.* The buyer and seller also negotiate changes to cost and schedule. Again, such changes may result from a number of reasons. For example, the seller may reduce the cost if the buyer reduces the degree of functionality to be provided. As another example, the schedule may be extended because the buyer may not have allocated enough money to handle the full job as defined by the RFP.

3. *Contract terms and conditions.* The buyer and seller may negotiate changes in the way the contract is administered. For example, the seller may reduce the price if the buyer concedes certain commercial marketing rights to the seller.

The final result of competitive negotiations is a best and final offer (BAFO). The sellers provide this to the buyer. The buyer assesses it and issues a contract to the selected seller if it is acceptable to all of the parties concerned (including the customer, developer, user, and reviewers).

3.9 DELIVERING AS PROMISED

Both the buyer and seller can now focus their attention on the job once the contract has been awarded. The buyer's job is to monitor the seller to ensure the provisions of the contract are being met. The seller must perform the work and deliver the product promised in the contract (not the proposal). Both the buyer and seller must work together to handle the problems that typically arise during system development:

- *Administrative overload.* The administrative burden placed on the team to monitor contract terms compliance is so large that the team cannot focus on technical matters.
- *Creeping functionality.* The customer keeps trying to add scope to a job in progress and on an aggressive schedule with sparse resources.
- *Fragmentation.* Members of the team (both buyer and seller personnel) are pulled off the development at random times to work on other jobs (for example, tiger teams, source selections).
- *Goldplating.* Sophisticated rather than simple technical solutions are proposed and adopted.
- *"I'm paid to engineer."* The buyer tells the seller how to do the job, not what the job is.
- *Missing indicators.* The measurement of progress and overall performance is qualitative, not quantitative.
- *Who's in charge.* There are so many bosses that nobody can make a decision in a timely manner.

The roles and responsibilities of the players change once the contract is awarded. The buyer focuses on requirements and on making sure that the seller performs. The seller focuses on the technical work, deciding how to realize the requirements in the most advantageous manner. Both look at the contract to settle disputes. If the contract is deficient, both parties will suffer.

Often, there is distrust between buyer and seller. Many times this is a result of miscommunication and a lack of information on the status of the job. Assessing progress and determining performance present challenges to both the buyer and seller. Both need to keep the other informed of status and problems and both need to work out problems that come up during the development. In addition, a system of measurement needs to be implemented so that the seller can provide the buyer with information about technical progress and the resources required to complete the job.

Numerous techniques discussed in the second half of the book are aimed at reducing distrust and improving communication as the contract unfolds. It is said that to be trusted, one must trust. Such expressions sound trite but are important because of the wisdom they embody.

3.10   CONTRACT MANAGEMENT AND CLOSE-OUT

The buyer and the seller must administer changes to the contract during its execution. Change proposals must be prepared, evaluated, and implemented based upon their usefulness. Equitable adjustments must be made (for example, to rates and schedules) and compensation for the seller must be negotiated. Approved change proposals must be managed and implemented.

There are two basic types of changes that occur during contract execution: contract changes and engineering changes. Contract changes deal with adjustments made to such items as billing rates, compensation structure, and overhead rates. These come about due to new accounting schemes, legal requirements, organizational structures, and so on. Although established within the framework of the contract, these changes must be negotiated and approved before they are employed to render progress payments or compensation of any form. Engineering changes deal with changes made to form, fit, or function. These come about primarily due to new requirements or value engineering changes. Again, the manner in which these changes are administered is covered by the contract. However, they must be assessed, approved, and incorporated into the project schedule in a timely manner.

Once the contract is completed and all required items called out in it have been delivered and accepted, it must be closed out. The following activities are normally necessary to close out a contract:

- Overhead rates need to be finalized and final payments made.
- Excess property needs to be disposed.
- Any claims need to be released and the status of excess funds determined.
- The seller's performance needs to be documented.

3.11   SUMMARY

The acquisition process is complex and needs to be tailored to the circumstances of each specific project. As can be seen, the life cycle illustrated in Figure 3-5 needs to be superimposed on top of that discussed in earlier chapters to illustrate the activities that must be completed to acquire software. The life cycle of Figure 3-5 is the subject of the detailed discussions that follow in the remainder of this book.

Each topic in this chapter warrants additional attention in order that it be appropriately employed. Some of the subjects are broad enough to justify a whole book

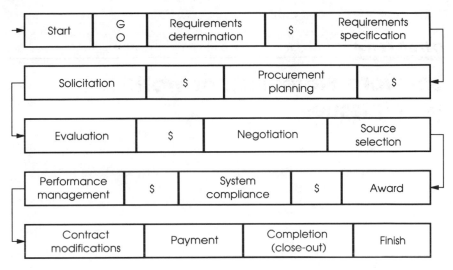

Figure 3-5   Another view of life cycle

or several chapters. For example, complete books have been written about the negotiating process. The remainder of this book focuses on subjects relevant to software acquisition in order to introduce them at the very least, and to provide additional detail so that the reader can apply them to specific software acquisition projects. The next chapter discusses elements of the statement of work and evaluation criteria.

CHAPTER 4

Software Statement of Work (SOW) Issues

Issues important to managing a software acquisition project are addressed in the request for proposal (RFP). This chapter explores selected issue areas and provides a salient set of requirements that should be considered for the RFP as well as criteria to evaluate the seller's response (proposal). The discussion begins with the planning process for preparing a statement of work (SOW).

To provide a proper and effective software management environment, appropriate management requirements must be communicated to the seller. The seller cannot respond to the buyer's desires unless they are explicitly stated in the RFP. If not so stated, the buyer will be dependent on the seller's management program. This is normally an unacceptable situation because the buyer has special requirements. For example, the buyer may want a certain configuration management plan format or may require certain procedures to be used for controlling changes.

There is a fine line between management requirements that afford the buyer control over the project and those that dictate seller management procedures. The buyer must take care to specify only requirements appropriate to buyer needs and avoid imposing internal management procedures that conflict with the established procedures of the seller. This latter practice can drive the seller to adopt new management procedures. For example, the requirement to make risk management visible may force changes to the seller's management systems.

The RFP statement of work (SOW) is the basis for communicating management requirements to the seller. As discussed in Chapter 3, the buyer initiates the procurement by releasing the request for proposal. The statement of work is that part of the RFP describing the tasks that the seller must perform to meet system requirements (for example, building or delivering a system) and how the project should be managed. If technical specifications are the basis for the development effort, they are normally attachments to the RFP or SOW and are referenced in the SOW. Similarly, documentation requirements are normally provided by a documentation list or data list. The data list provides details about what documentation is required, documentation formats, delivery requirements, and review and delivery dates. Documentation is a natural by-product of the development effort. It is referenced in the paragraphs of the SOW describing the technical and management efforts of development.

The primary intent of the following discussion is to promote understanding rather than to explain how to organize or detail a statement of work. There are many organizational formats that a buyer may use for the RFP. Figure 4-1 shows the organization for an RFP used in federal government procurements. Notice that the SOW is section C (description/specs/work statement) of part I, the schedule. The federal government has many guidelines for organizing and developing SOWs. In the commercial sector, the RFP may take other formats and names. Content, rather than format, is important.

Many requirements are contained in the RFP and SOW. They may concern reliability, quality assurance, maintainability, configuration management, logistics, training, supportability, safety, security, metrics, documentation, acceptance, and test and evaluation. Their placement in the RFP will depend on what the buyer needs to procure goods and services. This chapter focuses on issues pertinent to the

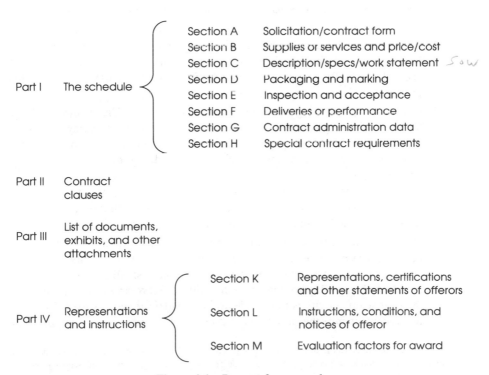

Figure 4-1 Request for proposal

management of the software project, beginning with the SOW planning process. Several systems and software engineering issues are then treated. Although technical in nature, these issues impact the management of the project. Next, traditional management issues such as configuration management and documentation are discussed. The chapter closes with a discussion on organizational issues.

4.1   PLANNING—ITS IMPORTANCE TO THE SOW PROCESS

Irrespective of the particular organization of the RFP and its included SOW, the buyer must have an orderly planning process to collect SOW requirements. This process should afford adequate time and resources for preparation of the SOW. When statement of work preparation begins, the effort is typically parceled out among various functional activities. If it is a complicated SOW, management must bring together the various functional elements involved in preparing the SOW and coordinate the preparation activity. The following is a suggested procedure for managing the SOW development process. Although appropriate for a large project, these guidelines can be modified for use with smaller projects.

1. Identify the functional elements needed in the SOW activity (system/software engineering, configuration management, quality assurance, test, documentation, and so on). In most cases, these activities will also be involved in the ensuing management of the development project.

2. Arrange an initial meeting of the SOW preparation team. Prior to the meeting, send out an announcement detailing the meeting agenda and include a schedule for SOW preparation (Figure 4-2). Include material relevant to the project that should be reviewed prior to the meeting.

3. Use the initial meeting as an organizational activity. The members of the team must be acquainted with the needs of the project, including technical, schedule, and costing requirements. Encourage member participation in the meeting to increase/promote communication among the members of the prospective management team. Task the members to prepare a concept for each area in the SOW. For example, the CM member should be asked to prepare a conceptual approach for the CM program, including requirements for the SOW and evaluation criteria to be used to evaluate seller proposals.

4. Identify a Blue team to help evaluate the SOW.* This might be composed of key members of the development team and senior members of the functional activities represented at the meeting. Keep the team small and choose people based on their ability to contribute broadly to SOW areas. The purpose of the Blue team activity is to provide an independent review of the SOW prior its placement into the procurement process. This activity will improve the

---

* It is common to use colors to describe the various teams in RFP and SOW preparation and proposal evaluation. For example, a Red team is a team that reviews the draft proposal and scores it as if it were the seller.

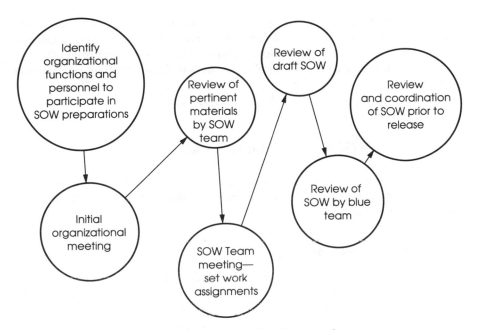

Figure 4-2 Statement of work preparation

product, reduce coordination time, and help establish a cohesive management environment. The members of the Blue team should attend the kickoff meeting.

5. At the second meeting of the SOW preparation team (including the Blue team), review the conceptual approaches prepared by the various functional activities. This meeting should result in firm guidelines for the various participants' approaches and draft inputs of the SOW. Discussion at the meeting can be summarized in written minutes at a later meeting of the Blue team. With further written guidance, the SOW team should begin to prepare its sections of the SOW.

6. The SOW draft inputs are integrated into the SOW according to the established SOW preparation schedule. The SOW is reviewed by the Blue team, which provides feedback and identifies remedial actions. Depending on the schedule and complexity of the project, this process may be repeated a number of times. The result is an SOW ready to be submitted to the appropriate management authority for approval and transmittal to the appropriate procurement organization.

The SOW process is not intended to promote bureaucracy or voluminous paperwork, but each meeting should be documented by minutes. This ensures accountability for assigned actions and establishes guidance in written form. Procedures for conducting meetings should be based on the review procedures discussed elsewhere in this book (Sections 2.3.2, 6.4.1, and 7.6). At certain key meetings, such as kickoff meetings, it has proved useful to invite personnel from activities that are not normally engaged in SOW preparation. Personnel from procurement (contracting), finance, and other areas can provide inputs to the SOW and help expedite coordination throughout the contracting cycle.

4.2 SYSTEM/SOFTWARE ENGINEERING ISSUES

A number of issues bridge the technical and management processes. How technical issues affect management of the project and guidelines for dealing with them are discussed in this section.

4.2.1 Requirements Management

One of the most important, yet often overlooked, systems issues is the definition and management of technical requirements. Most people assume that requirements are defined just prior to, or as a part of SOW preparation, then placed under contract and frozen while the system is designed and built by the seller. This may be an ideal engineering arrangement, but it is impractical for most software projects. Requirements evolve from the inception of the project, during SOW and proposal preparation, throughout development, and over the operational life of the system. Figure 4-3 depicts this evolution. Requirements must be managed continuously because their impact on development is great.

The developer must take the system specification, analyze it, and convert it to an implementable design. During this time, two things can occur: new requirements are conceived by the user community, and derived requirements are defined by the developer.

Derived requirements are fallout from the development design process. The initial engineering design process starts with the high-level requirements statement and develops this into a more detailed set of requirements. For example, the system may require an operator interface. This requirement may be prototyped and evolve the specific nature of the interface—the individual displays that provide user information to the operator. Another example concerns the performance needed in order to satisfy display response times. This could place a requirement on hardware performance, thus creating a derived hardware requirement. Project engineering personnel take the basic set of requirements and extrapolate from them a full set of derived requirements as the design is defined.

New requirements may arise due to changes in operational procedures, in new technology, or in operating policy. If these changes are not accommodated in the system, there is a high probability that the system, when delivered, will be "old" in the sense that it satisfies a need that no longer exists.

In a turnkey arrangement, a firm set of requirements is established and requirements management by the buyer can be minimized. In this type of program, require-

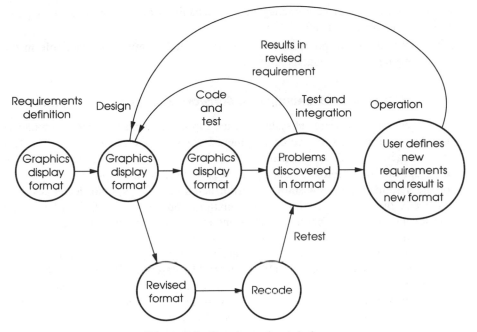

Figure 4-3   Requirements evolution

ments changes are accommodated by the normal processes of development (that is, specification management) and normal development functions (for example, configuration management). In a more dynamic environment in which there are numerous proposal changes, managing requirements is more critical and extraordinary actions may be required.

The requirements process must be managed. The seller must have the capability to develop and implement suitable management mechanisms for reviewing requirements, for making recommendations on how to satisfy them, and for integrating them into the development or deferring them to a later version of the system. The buyer and seller must both play active roles in this process to ensure the ultimate success of the development.

Requirements

1. The seller should have a process for managing requirements. This process must be integrated with, and supported by, the CM function.
2. The seller should describe the requirements management process.

Evaluation Criteria

1. Does the seller understand the importance of managing requirements?
2. Does the seller have hands-on experience with managing requirements on similar projects?

3. Does the seller have management mechanisms and procedures for requirements management?

4. Does the seller procedure provide for an authoritative customer role in the requirements management process?

4.2.2 Selection and Definition of Software Subsystems/Components

The selection of software subsystems or the top-level software system components is a key decision in software development because it often determines the extent of management and documentation needed for the system. In many software development methodologies, management is focused on the top-level components of the system. Figure 4-4 shows a partial taxonomy of a system decomposition. Typically the reviews, testing, documentation, and so on are all focused on the top-level subsystems. Therefore, the extent and degree of management on a project is determined by the number of these subsystems.

This situation is often dictated by management policies such as the *DOD Software Development Standard (DOD-STD-2167A)*, described in Section 2.4.2. This standard defines the management focus at the subsystem level (designated by the term *configuration item* (CI)). All major management activities are identified with this level. In other words, the CI is managed as a complete system. In the NASA SMAP software standards, described in Section 2.4.3, the basic documentation set must be expanded to provide a unique set of specifications for each subsystem. Once the subsystem is defined, management can focus control at this level. Thus, the high-level architecture of the system determines the degree of management rigor applied. The number of subsystems, or CIs, is both an architectural and management issue. This number must allow an appropriate balance between the two so that visibility, control, and affordable management of the project are in balance.

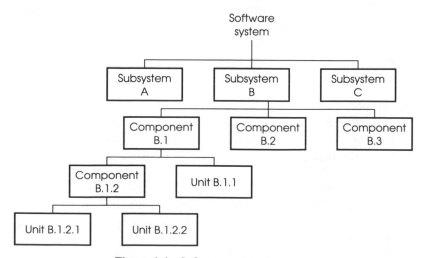

Figure 4-4 Software system taxonomy

The buyer must decide the degree to which the job should be supervised and focus the seller's attention in that direction. In the planning process, it is important to consider management style and manner of application. In the absence of an existing development standard that defines management methods for each major software subsystem, buyer management must define the appropriate focus and the level of necessary scrutiny. If using an existing methodology, management must tailor the methodology to provide an appropriate level of management visibility and control. For example, management may choose to focus at a lower level of detail, that is, at a subcomponent level. Thus the subcomponent is managed with the same rigor as the higher-level components.

The selection of major software components, therefore, is a critical process of development. It provides the first cut of the design and sets the framework for how the system will be managed. The issue becomes how to select the major components and who should make the selection. It is a SOW issue when the buyer chooses to establish the number of top-level components or to provide guidance on the level of management applied to the project.

There is a danger here—selection of top-level components by the buyer predetermines the initial design of the system. The buyer may fix the number of top-level components and thus preempt design decisions that should be made by the developer. This situation should be avoided because it puts the buyer in the design process. This may interfere with the design concept the seller wishes to employ. In general, it is poor practice to establish the design of the system before the seller has an opportunity to evaluate alternate designs.

In order to accommodate such concerns, the following procedure is suggested. The buyer should make an initial judgment of the appropriate number of top-level components and provide that judgment to the seller in the SOW. This gives the seller guidance on the level of management rigor the buyer desires. The seller can refine this initial guidance with rationale in the proposal. During negotiations, buyer and seller can establish the number of top-level components and level of management required. Thus, the buyer can make an initial determination of the top-level components of the system to define the desired degree of management control. The difficulty is in determining the right mix.

To arrive at the number of components, the system is broken down into its major subsystems. These may be complete software functions, subsystems, or components for the purpose of achieving management visibility. For example, in Figure 4-5 the radar system is subdivided into three components: the signal processing subsystem, the data processing subsystem, and the operating subsystem. Each will be managed separately with its own sets of documentation, tests, and reviews before being integrated into the radar system. In this example, management has decided that each element should be identified and managed seprately to achieve visibility and reduce risk. Another example is the operating system shown in Figure 4-6. Here the subsystems are individual functional elements, each of which is managed separately.

Another possible factor for determining the number of components is the size of the system. Although this should not be the primary criterion for determining suborganization, it is practical, especially when applied with other criteria. The

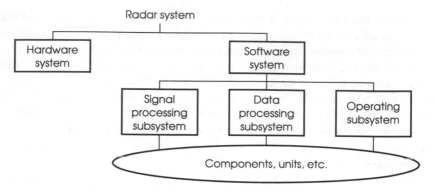

Figure 4-5   Radar system

right number is a matter of judgment. Too many top-level components will require excessive management resources, whereas too few will reduce management visibility and control. The following activities should be considered in assessing or determining the number of top-level subsystems:

1. Look for major functional elements that naturally subdivide the system, for example, a display processing subsystem and a database management system.
2. Examine the complexity of the system and its subsystem functions. Break the complex functions into smaller subsystems, where possible, to provide more visibility and control.
3. Determine if the size of a subsystem is unwieldy. If the subsystem is fairly simple or straightforward, it may be justifiable to manage it as a single subsystem. If, however, the subsystem is large and complex, it is desirable to subdivide it into smaller, more manageable components. In this process the best form is to align the subsystems according to their logical functions.
4. Make certain that a single organization is responsible for each subsystem. Shared responsibility for a subsystem means no responsibility.
5. Don't cross hardware boundaries with a single software component. This will complicate control and qualification of the component.

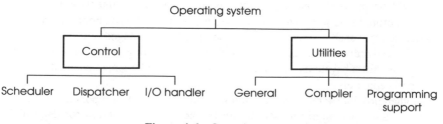

Figure 4-6   Operating system

Requirements
1. Provide a suggested decomposition at the top level of the system.
2. Require the seller to evaluate this decomposition and recommend appropriate changes.

Evaluation Criteria
1. Does the seller demonstrate an understanding of the need to identify a manageable set of subsystems?
2. Does the seller strike a balance between the number of subsystems and the cost of management?
3. Does the seller understand how to achieve an appropriate balance between the number of subsystems and the need to provide management control and visibility over the project?

4.2.3 Tools and Environments

In order to develop a software system, a software production capability is required. In the past, insufficient attention was given this detail, but modern software development demands the availability of modern tools. Early development environments comprised the operating system and support software delivered with the system (libraries, compilers, assemblers, linkers/loaders, and so on). Today such a capability is considered very basic. In modern development environments, tools are much more comprehensive and sophisticated. They include syntactic analyzers, symbolic debuggers, language-oriented text editors, test tools, requirements analyzers, design tools, data flow diagrams, and more. These environments are commonly called software support environments, software development environments, software engineering environments, or integrated programming support environments. In this book, the term software support environment (SSE) is used. The environment includes not only tools and methods, but also management practices and organizational resources (see Figure 4-7). Table 4-1 presents the tools and methods commonly included in these environments.

A software support environment is embellished with a number of tools unique to the system being developed or to that particular environment. In an avionics system development (for an aircraft), a flight simulator may be used to integrate the flight dynamics of the aircraft into the avionics software and to enhance testing. In a banking system, a model may be constructed to simulate the flow of transactions and to assess/predict hardware and software performance characteristics. In maintenance environments, individual tools may be employed to check or test changes made to the system without rerunning the entire qualification test suite employed during development. Thus, while a basic off-the-shelf environment may be employed, it may need to be embellished by special tools, procedures, and in-house methods.

Though impractical to specify the entire environment that will be employed (each seller will have a different approach), it is feasible to specify a set of general characteristics based on the specific needs of the project. The buyer must ascertain

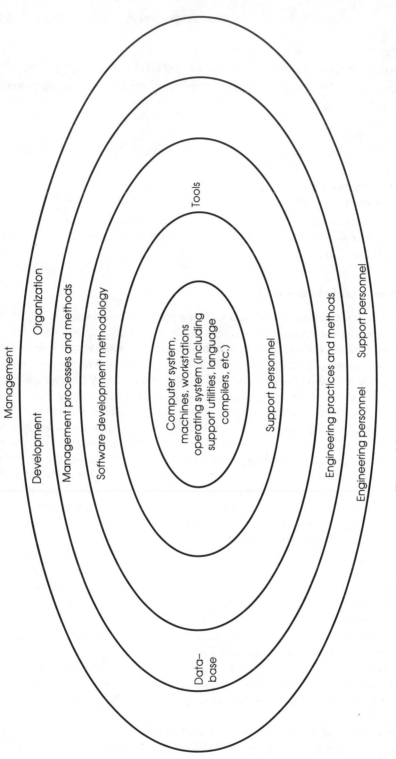

Figure 4-7 Software support environment

TABLE 4-1   Common Tools and Methods of a Software Support Environment

Life cycle phase	Tools*
Software requirements	CASE (computer aided software engineering) Consistency analyzer Simulation support Rapid prototyping Requirements traceability
Architectural design	Architectural analyzer CASE
Detailed design	Complexity analyzer Design language
Code and unit test	Assembler Compiler Complexity analyzer Cross compiler/support system Debugger Editor Linker/loader
Software integration and test	Coverage analyzer Emulator Performance analyzer Regression test manager Simulator/stimulator Test generator Trace facility
Software maintenance	Comparator Conversion tools

Phase-independent	Tools*
Communications support	Electronic mail
Configuration management	Library system
Documentation support	Publishing system
Project management	Planning system Resource estimating models
Quality management	Metrics analyzers
Tool integration	Object management system

* Tools and methods listed are provided as examples only. The list is not intended to be exhaustive. In addition, the authors neither endorse nor offer any of these tools or methods.

that the proposed contractor has a suitable environment, has experience with the environment, and has the capability to tailor it to the specific development.

Requirements

1. The seller should have a software support environment conducive to developing and maintaining software. That environment should include an integrated set of compilers, debuggers, simulation tools, testing tools, design tools, requirements aids, and so on.
2. The tool sets should be mature and stable. The risks associated with seller selection of tools should not contribute to the inherent risks of the development.
3. The seller should have the capability to tailor the environment to the specific needs of the development project.
4. The seller should have experience with the environment. The seller should be able to analyze the development requirements of the project to determine specific needs and additions for the environment and have a rational plan for acquiring tools in consonance with the development schedule.

Evaluation Criteria

1. Does the seller have a modern software support environment that has been employed on previous projects?

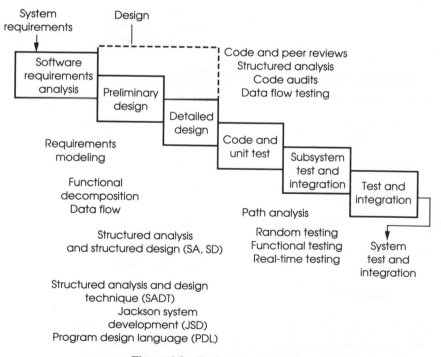

Figure 4-8 Engineering methods

2. Do key personnel proposed for the project possess experience with the environment? Have they employed the environment on previous projects?
3. Has the seller demonstrated the capability to tailor the environment for the project, proposed additions, and planned for their timely acquisition?
4. Is the proposed environment stable? Is it based on off-the-shelf non-proprietary components?

4.2.4 Methods and Methodologies

Integrated in the software support environment are the specific engineering methods that the seller will employ during the development project. Methods are procedures and rules used to order the processes used by engineering and management. Examples of engineering methods are structured analysis techniques used during requirements analysis and structured design analysis techniques used in the design phase (Figure 4-8). Examples of management support methods are procedures for managing the control and evolution of requirements, procedures for conducting reviews and audits, and procedures for managing the testing process (Figure 4-9).

It would be impractical to specify the exact methods to be employed on a project,

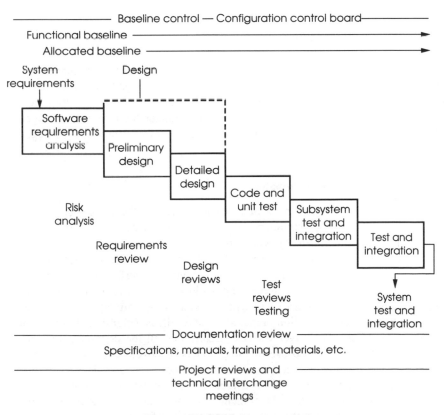

Figure 4-9 Management methods

except in unusual circumstances, but it is proper to evaluate the seller's proposed methods to ensure that they exist. The methods should be adequate and the seller should have experience with their use. They should be applicable to the project. In certain situations it may be desirable to specify a certain method or set of methods. For example, in a global system, involving the networking of multiple resources and development by a number of contractors, it might be appropriate to use a standard language to ensure compatibility and reuse of code. In cases where the customer plans to assume maintenance of the system after development, it might be appropriate to specify a standard configuration management system. These considerations must be addressed in the planning phase and included as requirements in the SOW.

Evaluation Criteria
1. Does the seller have a management and engineering environment with sound methods for supporting the development and management of the project?
2. Do proposed development personnel have experience with the proposed methods?
3. Are the proposed methods mature and have they been applied in prior seller efforts?

4.3 MANAGEMENT ISSUES

Management requirements, like system requirements, must be realistic (that is, attainable and pertinent to program needs). Compliance must be actively monitored by the buyer. Pro forma requirements placed into the RFP for bureaucratic reasons should be avoided. They increase cost and may hinder the effective management of the project. Following is a discussion of the more important management issues.

4.3.1 Software Documentation

Documentation, whether in print or electronic form, is the formal description of the products of the engineering process that are generated during development. Documentation is the means by which the development process is planned, including the description of the processes of development and the specification of the products of development. It supports the management interface between the buyer and the seller. It behooves the buyer to pay close attention to the requirements for documentation by both number and type, as well as the delivery and inspection of documentation. Documentation preparation, after all, is a significant portion of the development effort. The buyer wants to ensure that all the documentation needed to support development and use of the products of development is produced and delivered. The documentation, however, should not exceed project requirements. Documentation costs are not only involved in engineering preparation, but include costs of review and validation. Documentation costs may range from 20 to 40 percent of overall development when the engineering effort is included. If too much documentation is produced, management will be encumbered by excessive review, control, and administrative burden. If too little is produced, maintenance costs could skyrocket. Thus the specification of documentation must be given careful attention.

The buyer specifies the documentation requirements for the project. The seller has the prerogative to do less, but will usually adhere to stated requirements, especially in a competitive environment. It is possible to alter documentation requirements after the contract award. However, this is not practical because the contract price is based on the requirements contained in the RFP. An increase in documentation requirements will necessitate a contract change proposal and increased costs to the buyer.

Software documentation should be tailored to the needs of the development effort. For example, a prototype effort would require much less documentation than a production article or product effort. The best time to tailor documentation is before the contract is awarded. The buyer should specify a candidate documentation set, then solicit recommendations on documentation requirements from the seller. An acceptable set can be negotiated prior to contract award.

If a documentation standard such as *DOD-STD-2167A* is employed, the buyer is sometimes reluctant to reduce documentation requirements after the contract award. The buyer considers the documentation already "paid" for and expects it to be produced and delivered. It is practical to tailor the documentation within the overall requirements of the documentation specification, that is, to change documentation format and detail. Thus, if a certain paragraph in a documentation specification is not required, it can be negated or marked nonapplicable when justification for the change is offered.

Requirements

1. Require the seller to describe the methods that will be used to generate, record, store, and control documentation.

2. Require the seller to describe the management of documentation in the software development plan.

3. The buyer should specify the types of documents required. Whenever possible, documentation standards, such as the IEEE software engineering standards (Appendix B), should be used as a point of departure. It is useful to address documentation requirements in three areas: product documents, process documents, and support documents.

   • Specify the exact types and formats that must be developed for product documents, for example, system requirements specifications, design specifications, and so on. (Depending on the size and complexity of the development project, system-level documentation may not be required. Software-level requirements and design documentation may be sufficient.)

   • Specify all the planning and test documents that are required. As a minimum, a software development plan and test development notebook (including test plans, procedures, and reports under one cover) should be required. In more complex development efforts, there may be a requirement to prepare project-unique configuration management and quality assurance plans in lieu of seller-developed generic plans.

- Specify all user support documents that may be required. Again, the complexity of the effort and its end use will determine the specific documentation required.

4. Specify the degree of detail expected. This will vary depending on the complexity of the development and will not ordinarily be covered in the standards and conventions document.
5. Specify how documentation tailoring will be handled.
6. Specify the use of a standards and conventions document. As an alternative, require that the seller develop a standards and conventions document or detail the internal procedures employed in creating effective and professional documentation in the software development plan.
7. Specify or require the seller to detail a documentation generation, review, and approval cycle.

Evaluation Criteria
1. Does the seller have an overall plan for documentation preparation?
2. Does the seller have a standards and conventions document that includes procedures for preparing documentation?
3. Does the seller understand the use of documentation to support development?
4. Are seller tailoring and scaling recommendations consistent with the requirements of the development?
5. Does the seller demonstrate experience with documentation preparation? Does this experience reflect previous projects where documentation was prepared on time and effectively integrated into the development methodology— used for milestone reviews?

4.3.2 Engineering Data Management

Perhaps the most overlooked and least understood area of the development project is the management of engineering data. Although data are necessary to documentation, they are not synonymous with it. Data are all the individual bits of information that hold together the engineering process, including the outputs of tools and methods such as data flow diagrams, requirements matrixes, and database designs.

Engineering data provide the basis for documentation and communication in the engineering process. Without them the engineering process is seriously deficient. Even though the data may be totally contained within the automated tools utilized throughout the development process, the data act as the bridge connecting individual methods, the phases of the development process, and the documentation products of development.

It is important that engineering data be properly managed. Data must be properly recorded in some media, whether electronic or print, and controlled so that they can be utilized at any given point in the development effort. Without this capability, the development process is uncontrolled. Even data originated by an individual software engineer must be recorded and controlled, usually in software development folders. If a new person has to take over the project, the necessary information to assume engineering responsibility must be available.

Data is important to valuative efforts. Quality assurance and test personnel require access to project engineering data in order to perform their responsibilities. In a software project the product does not materialize until fairly late in the development cycle. Therefore, visibility on progress is assessed through different means. Data provide those means.

Requirements

1. Require the seller to describe the methods that will be used to record, store, and control engineering data.
2. Require the seller to describe the management of engineering data in the software development plan.
3. Require the seller to describe how data generated will be used to support the processes of development from analysis through document preparation.

Evaluation Criteria

1. Does the seller understand the importance of engineering data to the development process?
2. Does the seller have a plan to manage engineering data? Does that plan identify all data to be generated in the project and provide for recording, storing, and controlling the data?
3. Does the seller understand the use of software development folders to house engineering data throughout the project?
4. Does the seller provide for the integration of engineering data with the documentation products of the development effort?

4.3.3 Configuration Management

No one questions the need for configuration management (see Section 2.3.3). Quite often, however, CM is taken for granted. True, standard requirements are placed into the SOW for CM. These usually invoke CM standards or cite requirements in available configuration management standards. A typical SOW statement might be, "The contractor will employ sound configuration management procedures, or the contractor will institute configuration management in accordance with Standard 123.4." Such a statement indicates that the project management team has not seriously planned a configuration management environment and does not understand the CM requirements for the project.

Where available and appropriate, a CM standard should be invoked, but this alone is not sufficent. The buyer needs to ensure that the seller understands CM, its importance to the current project, and the manner in which it will be evaluated in the proposal and throughout the development. Important aspects of CM should be covered in the SOW. The buyer can thus specify desired improvements to the development environment and inform the sellers as to how they will be evaluated.

4.3.3.1 CM Plan   In some cases the buyer will require that a CM plan be developed as a part of the contract. The seller will normally have a standard plan that can be customized for the project. If the seller develops a plan for each new project, it could imply that an effective CM organization does not exist or is pro forma. If the development standards for the project do not require a CM plan, the SOW should require a CM plan for the project. It should be available for review by the buyer, either during the proposal process or after the contract award. If the buyer does not want to evaluate a CM plan during the proposal process, CM requirements important to the project should be addressed in the RFP. This will ensure that the seller understands the emphasis and focus that the buyer intends for CM.

4.3.3.2 Organization   The statement of work should require the seller to explain the internal organization for CM. A CM function should be in place and include experienced personnel and detailed procedures. Normally, CM will be separate from the project organization, providing support from a matrix technical support organization. A CM person, however, should be assigned to the project. When CM is totally contained within the project organization, it is possible for the project manager to de-emphasize "control" of development products or require fewer than the necessary tools or procedures for effective CM.

4.3.3.3 Tools   It is totally impractical within a modern software development project to provide effective CM without some form of library. A number of organizations build their own in-house products and some computer manufacturers provide capabilities that will support a CM system (for example, the Digital Equipment Corporation VAX 780 computer system code management system [CMS]). There are also commercial tools on the market that provide this capability.

An automated tool is not used simply for maintaining files. It should support release management; problem report management; control of hardware, software and data; builds; status accounting, audit trails, and the relationships among all the products. The more automated the tool the more useful it is in CM.

4.3.3.4 Personnel   The CM function should be staffed with experienced personnel. The project should have an identified CM support person or function directly supporting the development project. If this CM person is a junior staff member, more experienced personnel should be available to assist. This arrangement should prove satisfactory, particularly in small and less-complex development efforts.

Although a smaller contractor may not have all the bells and whistles described, its size does not excuse the contractor from exercising sound CM practice. For example, an independent CM function may not exist in the seller organization.

Project personnel should, however, understand CM practice, and possess the appropriate tools and procedures to support it. The time to build CM into the development is before the project begins, not during the development process. Poor CM can create serious problems and a seller that does not understand CM should be avoided.

Requirements

1. Require the seller to have a CM plan or develop one for the project. If the CM plan will not be delivered with the proposal, require the seller to address CM capabilities in the proposal.
2. Require the seller to assign experienced personnel to perform CM on the project.
3. Require the seller to utilize a modern library. (There may be some question about what modern means; however, this will allow the buyer to subjectively evaluate the seller's response.)
4. Require the seller's CM procedures to support control of the products of development throughout the life cycle of the development, and not only the formal baselines invoked by the buyer.

Evaluation Criteria

1. Does the seller have an in-place function for CM? Does the CM function have the capability to ensure sound CM practice?
2. Does the seller have a companywide CM plan and CM procedures? Are the plans and procedures used across the board? Has the plan been used on previous projects? Is the plan supported by written and proven procedures for identifying, controlling, auditing, and reporting on the development project?
3. Does the seller have experienced CM personnel? If assigned personnel are not experienced, do they have access to experienced personnel? A rule of thumb is that at least one member of the CM function assigned to the project have a minimum of 10 years experience in CM including actual practice on at least two projects.
4. Does the seller intend to use an automated tool for CM? Do CM personnel have experience with the tool? Has the tool been used by the seller's organization, or is it being proposed for the contract at hand?
5. Do the seller's internal procedures for CM include provisions for generating status accounting reports and for managing changes, including baseline management, support of control board activities, and life cycle support (development through operation of the system)?

4.3.4 Quality Assurance

Quality assurance is an activity "to provide adequate confidence that the item or product conforms to established technical requirements" [IEEE, 1983]. The software quality assurance program (Section 10.2) is instituted by the seller and carried out by the seller's quality assurance function.

QA has been one of the most misunderstood and ill-practiced disciplines in software engineering. Often the QA team is treated with disdain by the engineering team and looked on as an unwelcome inspector. With growing emphasis on developing sound software systems, more attention is being placed on QA especially in the area of prevention. The worst situation, aside from having no QA program, is paying for one without enjoying the benefits it can bring to the development. It is important for management to understand that QA should not supplant or directly support engineering and will not be effective without the support of both buyer and seller management.

4.3.4.1 Organization   The seller should have an in-place and effective QA function. The QA function supporting the project should report independent of the project manager. The function should maintain personnel that understand QA practice. The buyer should take pains to ensure that the seller provide qualified QA personnel that function as teachers as well as inspectors. It is the quality assurance function's responsibility to ensure that the development process is sound and that the software products meet technical requirements.

4.3.4.2 Procedures   The seller QA organization should have established procedures for prevention, assurance, and verification. These should have been implemented and proven on previous projects. If the seller or the QA organization is new, it is acceptable to borrow existing procedures. After all, everyone has to start somewhere. The important point is to ensure that the QA function has a real purpose and is recognized as an integral part of the development project.

4.3.4.3 Personnel   If QA personnel are inexperienced, it is difficult, if not impossible, to have effective QA. QA is not like engineering—a newly hired engineer can be expected to produce upon graduation from school. Only experience can make QA personnel effective. Preferably, QA personnel will have experience with software development. Thus they will understand the job and know what it takes to accomplish it.

Requirements
1. Require the seller to have an independent organizational effort to perform QA for the development project.
2. Require the seller to have existing procedures for the conduct of QA.
3. Require the seller to prepare a software quality assurance plan.

Evaluation Criteria
1. Does the seller management actively support the QA function? Does the QA function report independent of the project management team and is it integrated into the oversight management process?
2. Does the QA manager assigned to the project enjoy independent reporting within the seller organization?

3. Does the seller have internal procedures that address the conduct of reviews, audits, and inspections?
4. Does the seller have personnel qualified to perform QA? Has an experienced QA manager been assigned to the project? A rule of thumb for gauging experience is 5 to 10 years of QA work on a minimum of two previous projects.
5. Does the seller have an existing QA plan? Has this plan been utilized on prior projects? Is the QA plan a model for the seller QA function across the organization? Does the plan describe the seller's procedures for recording the results of quality assurance functions?

4.3.5   Assessment

The seller should possess procedures for assessing the progress of development. Procedures may involve milestone schedules, network charts, management indicators, internal reviews, oversight management, and clean rooms (see Section 4.3.5.6). The specific methods should be described in the management and technical proposals.

4.3.5.1   Oversight Management   The seller should have the organizational capability for and interest in conducting management oversight of the development project. Procedures based on the size, complexity, and importance of the project should be established to assess status and determine progress.

Requirements
1. The seller should describe how the organization provides oversight management of the development project. This description should include the levels of reporting and the degree of authority and responsibility at each level.
2. The seller should describe how it provides the buyer visibility into and control over the project.

Evaluation Criteria
1. Does the project manager have the responsibility and commensurate authority to report on the development project?
2. Does the organization display an interest in the project? Will high-level managers be interested and involved?

4.3.5.2   Test and Evaluation   A common misconception about testing is that it follows software coding. Testing is a life cycle activity that begins in the early phases of the project. Test requirements must be stated in the software requirements and design specifications to ensure that requirements and the implemented design can be validated. It is important that the buyer and the seller understand that testing permeates the life cycle and that the buyer convey this vision to the seller in the SOW (Figure 4-10).

Testing should not be confused with quality assurance or other activities that may include testing by a third party. Testing is a normal part of the development

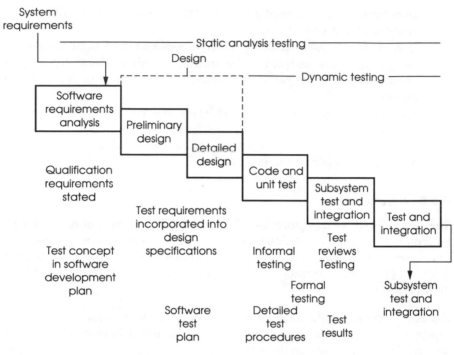

Figure 4-10   Testing in the life cycle

process. It should begin with informal testing, proceed through formal qualification testing (which validates or qualifies the products of development), and culminate in system-level testing (to demonstrate that the system is ready for delivery and operational testing). The function that conducts testing, the testing techniques employed, and the independence of the test team are all important issues to be addressed by the buyer.

The test team employed by the seller should be experienced. It should have the authority and responsibility to conduct impartial testing of the products of development in a structured test environment. Development testing can be conducted informally by individuals directly or closely associated with the software development project, but formal testing should be conducted by an independent and experienced test team. Development testing, which is informal, must be documented, usually in the software development folders, and placed in the software development library. Formal testing is planned, documented, conducted using formal procedures, and witnessed by the buyer. The seller should display a thorough understanding of the testing process, its integration into the development, and its relationship with QA and other functions that supplement it.

Requirements   Perhaps the most important requirement is the implementation of a sound software standard that addresses testing. In the absence of such, or as further guidance, the following points should be addressed in the SOW:

1. Require the seller to describe the testing process that will be employed in the project.
2. Require the seller to relate the testing process to the overall development process by addressing test requirements in the requirements and design specifications, addressing testing processes and methods in the software development plan, preparing adequate software test documentation, and explaining the relationship between the testing process and the other processes of the development (such as QA).
3. Require the seller to describe the internal testing function and how it will be employed in development testing.
4. Require the seller to explain the relationship of the testing function to testing conducted by the development team.
5. Require the seller to explain the function for formal testing and its independence from the development team and project manager.
6. Require the seller to specify the testing environment that will be employed.
7. Require the seller to identify testing personnel and experience levels.

Evaluation Criteria
1. Does the seller have an identifiable test function? Does the test environment contain the necessary tools and procedures? Do test personnel have experience with these tools and procedures? Have these individuals been employed on previous projects?
2. Does the location of the testing function in the seller organization ensure independence of testing?
3. Does the seller demonstrate an understanding of the importance of test documentation and the integration of test requirements into the project requirements and design specifications?

4.3.5.3 *Reviews and Audits* During the development project, a number of reviews and audits of the products and processes of development will be conducted. Some of these will be informal and internal to the seller. Others are formal reviews conducted by the buyer, with the participation of the customer and the seller. Although existing standards for software development methodologies require that these reviews take place, they often do not specify procedures for the reviews or the review process. The burden is on the seller to prepare procedures for the conduct of reviews. Requirements on the seller ensure that reviews and audits take place and appropriate review procedures are followed.

Requirements
1. The seller must perform internal reviews of the products and processes of the development project. These should include formal and informal reviews and inspections of the products and audits of functional processes such as QA and CM.

2. The seller must describe procedures for conducting reviews in the software development plan.

Evaluation Criteria
1. Does the seller have an existing methodology for software development? Does that methodology include detailed procedures for conducting both formal and informal reviews, audits, and inspections?
2. Do seller personnel have experience in the conduct of reviews, audits, and inspections?

4.3.5.4 *Management Indicators*   Management indicators and metrics are used to follow the progress of the development project. (Management indicators are described in Sections 2.3.5 and 6.4.6. Metrics are described in Section 10.4.) Indicator selection is an important management activity. The buyer may impose a broad set of indicators, especially when a suitable standard exists that makes it relatively easy to cite them in the RFP. This often occurs when both buyer and seller lack the expertise to select indicators that are appropriate for the project. There is little rationale for applying indicators that either have little bearing on the development or will not be used. Implementing such indicators can be a serious mistake because the cost of applying them is accrued to the contract.

One strategy is to evaluate the available management indicators, determine those applicable to the project, and require that set in the SOW. An alternative strategy is to have the seller propose a set and then negotiate a usable set for the effort. Either strategy is acceptable. Both will require that the buyer project management team have expertise in management indicators.

Requirements
1. Require the seller to select a set of appropriate management indicators for use on the project, or alternatively, impose a selected set of indicators on the seller.
2. Require the seller to evaluate the selected set and recommend changes.

Evaluation Criteria
1. Does the seller understand the indicators selected and have experience in their application?
2. Is the selected set appropriate for the effort?
3. Does the seller display the expertise required to use the management indicators, specifically those selected for the project?
4. Has the seller demonstrated the ability to collect data to support the indicators and to effectively apply the results to the management assessment process?

4.3.5.5 *Schedules*   It is quite common for the buyer to request, and the seller to provide, a schedule for the development of the system. Often the schedule provided in the proposal is sketchy, containing somewhat superficial milestones such as design reviews and testing. Although this may be satisfactory to top-level

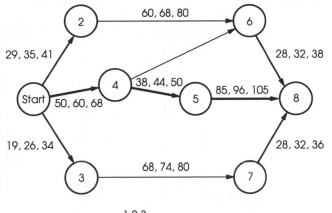

Figure 4-11   PERT network scheduling technique

Source: *System Engineering Management Guide*, Defense Systems Management College, Fort Belvoir, Virginia, pp. 3–5.

management, such a schedule is inadequate for following a complex development project. The degree of visibility achieved is insufficient and the time between milestones too great. The seller's project schedule should contain lower-level milestones (such as for major components, critical subcomponents, and sometimes individual units of the system) to achieve adequate visibility. A rule of thumb is that there should be enough milestones to achieve reporting at one- to two-week intervals.

Various methods are available to support milestone reporting. Indeed, some management indicators are based on milestones (for example, unit-testing completeness). PERT (project evaluation and review technique) provides detailed schedules and relations of events in the development (Figure 4-11). PERT may be applied in the project by seller project management, and sometimes by the buyer. It is not normally useful for high-level management because of its attention to detail. It is important that events be observed and reported at a level suffciently low to provide adequate warning when the project is amiss before severe slippage occurs. The Gantt chart shown in Figure 4-12 provides an example of a detailed schedule that is more suitable for this purpose.

Requirements
1. Require the seller to provide a detailed schedule using a suitable scheduling technique such as milestone or Gantt charts to provide timely visibility into development progress.
2. Require the seller to show how this schedule is integrated into the scheduling methods used on the project.

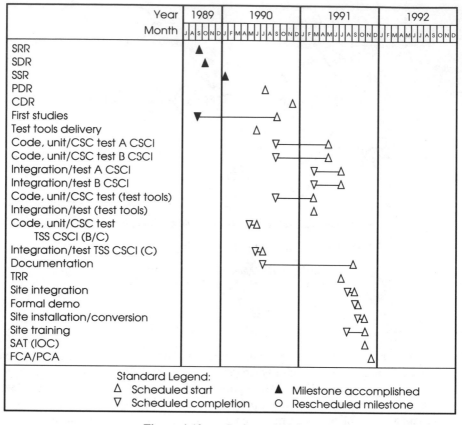

Figure 4-12   Project schedule

Evaluation Criteria
1. Does the seller understand the need for presenting detailed schedule information and is that information tied to detailed project tasks?
2. Does seller oversight management employ these types of schedules as a normal part of management responsibility?
3. Are schedule needs and types described in the software development plan?

4.3.5.6 Clean Room Activity A *clean room* provides a central location to track events in a project. Information on the project can be displayed, usually on the walls of the room, and updated by seller project personnel. When used effectively, it represents a command and control facility for the project and a central focus for project personnel. Buyer personnel can visit at any time to assess the progress of the effort. More than just a management tool, the clean room enhances the entire program environment.

Evaluation Criteria
1. Does the seller employ a clean room for the management of projects?
2. Has the clean room been used on previous projects?
3. Is the clean room used by all project personnel in an effective and honest manner?

4.4 SELLER ORGANIZATION

The nature of the seller organization can reveal the seller's ability to form a project organization that will support software development. Although impractical to dictate how the seller should organize a project, the buyer can influence project organization and its relationship to functional activities within the seller organization. The quality assurance function, for example, should be an effective part of the development project and not a pro forma activity.

The prevalent types of seller organization are matrix, project, or a hybrid of both. Each type carries different implications for the customer. Rather than dealing with the specifics of seller organization, the buyer should adhere to basic principles to ensure a proper development organization, including relations with supporting sellers.

In a matrix organization the project manager normally does not have direct control over all project personnel. Without key engineering personnel reporting to the project manager, engineering decisions will be made by the engineering organization, forcing the project manager to apply "influence" in order to control the direction of the project. In Figure 4-13, both the project manager and the engineering personnel assigned to the project report to the same authority. Thus the engineering supervisor and engineering project manager could have as much influence over engineering decisions as the project manager. The buyer normally deals with the project manager and may believe that the project manager has control when in fact other managers in the seller's organization dilute that authority.

In a project-oriented organization, all resources are assigned to the project manager (Figure 4-14). The buyer can usually be confident that this individual has authority over the development. If, however, the project manager requires additional support from outside the project, there may be a problem. Support organizations may not exist, or the resources assigned to them may be deficient. In addition, assigning QA and test personnel directly under the project manager compromises the independence of action for these disciplines. The size and complexity of the project and the size of the seller organization influence these arrangements.

Requirements
1. Require the seller to describe the project organization and its relationship to all supporting functional activities, for example, configuration management.
2. Require the seller to explain the degree of authority and responsibility of the project manager.

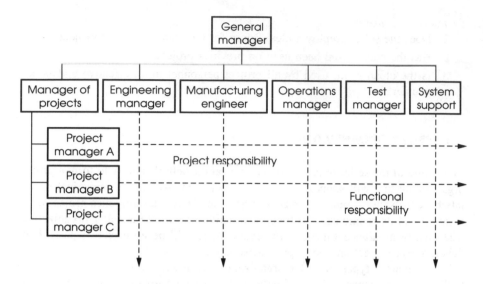

Figure 4-13   Matrix organization

Source: [Evans, 1983] M. W. Evans, P. Piazza and J. B. Dolkas, *Principles of Productive Software Management*, New York: Wiley, p. 241. ©Wiley 1983. Reprinted with permission.

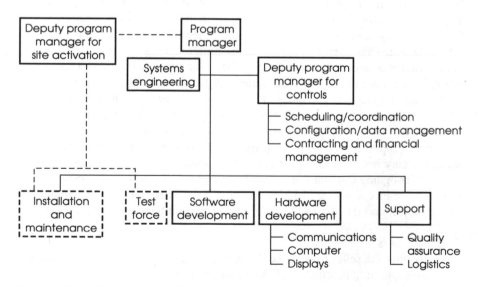

Figure 4-14   Project organization

Source: [Evans, 1983] M. W. Evans, P. Piazza and J. B. Dolkas, *Principles of Productive Software Management*, New York: Wiley, p. 245. ©Wiley 1983. Reprinted with permission.

3. Require the seller to explain internal reporting on the project.
4. Require the seller to explain how supporting functions (QA, CM, and so on) will support the project. Have the seller explain how the testing and QA functions will remain independent, yet be integrated into the overall organization so that their efforts will receive oversight review at an appropriate level. (An appropriate level is best described as one low enough to ensure that appropriate time and resources can be devoted to the activity and one high enough so that corporate-level attention is achieved.)

Evaluation Criteria
1. Does the project manager have direct control over personnel needed to implement the project?
2. Does the project manager have reporting responsibility to a high enough level to ensure control of the project? Is this reporting level commensurate with the importance of the project? Does the reporting level suggest that the project will receive adequate review by senior-level managers within the seller organization?

4.5 SUMMARY

The use of requirements and evaluation criteria will vary from project to project. On small projects, a subset of the requirements may be used. For large projects, the set will probably have to be expanded. Key management areas must be evaluated for inclusion in the SOW and a sound management process used to decide which are important to the current project. Each SOW is a unique document, and SOW requirements should be customized for each project. The chapter provides the basis for understanding these key software management issues and provides basic guidance for appropriate management action.

The next chapter, on contract law, discusses the various types of contracts used, how they are administered, and some of the clauses used in federal government procurements.

REFERENCES

[IEEE, 1983]: *ANSI/IEEE Std 729-1983, IEEE Standard Glossary of Software Engineering Terminology*, New York: The Institute of Electrical and Electronic Engineers, Inc.

CHAPTER 5

Contracts and Contract Law

For the purposes of this book, a contract is defined as a set of promises, the breach of which is provided a remedy by law. Managing a software acquisition necessarily deals with contracts. Buyers and sellers must be well-schooled in the intricacies of the legal and administrative aspects of procurement. A contract can consist of a single promise by one individual to another, or many individuals and promises may be involved. Technically, there is a difference between a contract and an agreement. An agreement is a broader term; it encompasses promises the law will enforce as well as those the law will not enforce.

From a legal point of view, there must be two parties, each with the legal capacity to act, for a contract to exist. The parties to the contract, by offer and acceptance, manifest assent or agreement to the terms of the contract. There must be *consideration* or something of value exchanged in order for the contract to be binding. There must exist provision for redress of any grievances; the terms and conditions governing the administration of the contract must be enforceable by law. For example, an uncertain condition exists when no schedule is specified for the delivery of the item being purchased. The seller could legitimately state that delivery will occur when conditions are favorable to seller profit. Therefore, a breach of contract does not exist.

With some important exceptions, general contract principles apply equally to private and government contracts. The U. S. government can enter into a contract because it is granted the power to do so by the Constitution. Interestingly enough, the making and administration of government contracts is an executive function under the Constitution, and the ultimate authority to enter into a contract is vested in the president. Normally this authority is delegated to various levels within the government. Congress has the power to make laws that impose limits on the executive branch's ability to contract. For example, the government is prohibited from entering into sole-source contracts except under special circumstances such as a national emergency. Such prohibitions are employed to ensure a fully competitive process, in which no organization or person is afforded preferential treatment. Companies employ similar checks and balances to ensure that there is no favoritism and that they are in compliance with the law.

In government procurements, contractual authority is normally delegated to two key individuals: a contracting officer (CO) and the contracting officer's representative (COR). Most companies have similar arrangements.

* *Contracting officer* (CO)—any person, either by virtue of position or appointment in accordance with procedures prescribed by law, given the authority to enter into, administer, and make changes to or modify the contract on behalf of the contracting party.
* *Contracting officer's representative* (COR) (sometimes called the contracting officer's technical representative (COTR))—any person formally designated in writing to act as the CO's duly authorized representative to provide technical direction, approval, and/or surveillance of the technical requirements of a contract.

The technical direction given to the contractor fills details, clarifies or interprets technical requirements, implements lines of inquiry, or otherwise serves to accomplish the technical objectives and requirements of the applicable contract. In order for the technical direction, approval, and surveillance to be valid:

1. They must be consistent with the scope of work set forth in the contract and its applicable requirements.
2. They must not constitute a new assignment of work or a change to the terms and conditions of the contract.
3. They must not constitute a change that will result in any contract consideration or contract delivery schedule.

The terms change order and contract modification are used as follows:

* *Change order*—a written order signed by the CO directing the contractor to make changes that the changes clause of the contract authorizes the CO to order without the consent of the contractor.
* *Contract modification*—any written alteration in the specification, delivery point, rate of delivery, contract period, price, quantity, or other contract provision, whether accomplished by a unilateral action in accordance with a contract provision, or by mutual action of the parties to the contract. It includes bilateral actions such as supplemental agreements, unilateral actions such as change orders, administrative changes, notices of termination, and notices of the exercise of a contract option.

In order for this system to work, the CO and COR must be in constant communication throughout the acquisition life cycle. Each relies on the other's expertise. In addition, both need to understand how to lever the contract vehicle itself to achieve their respective goals.

The CO's objectives are primarily administrative: to enter into a contract that realizes the sponsor's cost, schedule and technical goals, and that equitably rewards risk. The CO strives to minimize the administrative burden as the contract moves along the acquisition cycle.

The COR's goals are primarily technical: to administer the provisions of the contract so that its technical goals are achieved and risk is managed. Technically oriented, the COR may look upon the many contractual and administrative matters as necessary but uninteresting activity best described by the jargon "bean counting." However, an enlightened COR will understand and try to influence the contract structure to ensure that it contains the needed provisions for achieving technical objectives.

The remainder of this chapter is a primer on contracts and contract law. Both buyer and seller require such knowledge to effectively interact and communicate with the CO. For additional reading, the reader is referred to the government documents at the end of this chapter.

5.1 CONTRACTING FUNDAMENTALS

Contracts are normally classified by offeror intention at the time the offer is made. They may be bilateral or unilateral, express or implied, oral or written. Written contracts that expressly state what both parties have unilaterally promised and agreed to are the easiest to administer. The following important principles of contract law are fundamental to understanding contracts:

1. *Contract terms and conditions*—the parties to a contract, either those expressed or implied, must qualify their promises to perform based upon the occurrence, or nonoccurrence, of a term or a condition such as the delivery of an article. The mere passage of time is not a valid condition under this principle.

2. *Divisibility*—the parties to a contract may divide their respective performances into installments or separate units. For example, the buyer can be held liable under the law for not paying the seller within the negotiated time frame for partial services rendered under this principle.

3. *Substantial performance*—if the seller performs only partially, but the performance is substantial, the buyer can seek legal remedies only for partial damages, not the full contract price. This doctrine applies only when the seller has not been guilty of bad faith and promises have not been willfully breached. This principle is extremely important during termination proceedings.

4. *Discharge of contracts*—the obligations incurred by buyer and seller when they entered into agreement no longer exist to bind performance. Contracts can be discharged by having both parties perform as promised or by agreement to rescind the contract or make a new one.

5.1.1 Types of Contracts

Contracts are normally discussed in terms of compensation arrangements and format used in different procurement situations. Although there are many variations, the two basic compensation schemes used in contracts are fixed-price and cost-reimbursement. Under a fixed-price contract, the buyer pays the seller a fixed sum for the goods or services agreed upon. Because the price is fixed, the seller assumes the risk. Profit is a direct function of the seller's ability to deliver an acceptable product for less than the price paid. Under a cost-type contract, risk is shared because the buyer agrees to reimburse the seller's allowable costs plus profit. Different profit incentives are used under this scheme to motivate the seller to keep a lid on costs and to fulfil the provisions of the contract (the goals set for costs, schedules, and technical performance).

5.1.1.1 *Fixed-price Contracts*   There are four basic types of fixed-price contracts: firm fixed-price, fixed-priced with economic price adjustment, fixed-price incentive, and fixed-price redetermination. Each of these are briefly explained:

1. *Firm fixed-price* (FFP). This contract is basically an agreement to pay a specified price upon delivery and acceptance of the goods or services. An FFP contract is often used to order large quantities of goods from a standard price list. Unless performance is affected by other clauses (for example, economic price adjustment), the seller must perform for this price or be liable for breach of contract. The risk associated with this form of contract is therefore assumed by the seller.

2. *Fixed-price with economic price adjustment* (FPEPA). A fixed-price contract may include a special clause allowing for price adjustments when needed to protect either or both parties from significant economic fluctuations in labor or material costs. Adjustments may be either up or down based on the occurrence of events explicitly defined in the contract. For example, the seller might negotiate adjustments for variations in air-fares on a multi-year contract because they are difficult to predict. This form of shared risk between buyer and seller is specified in the adjustment clauses.

3. *Fixed-price incentive* (FPI). In this type of contract, the fee is varied and used to motivate the seller to increase efficiency or reduce cost. The incentive relates profits directly to performance goals. Negotiations set a target cost, a target fee, a ceiling price, and an adjustment formula. The formula is usually expressed as a ratio such as 75/25. This provides for a proportionate division of cost overrun or underrun between buyer and seller. For example, if the final cost is less than the target cost, the formula allows the buyer

and seller to share the underrun on a 75/25 percent basis (Figure 5-1). Costs in excess of the ceiling are not allowed. This cost-sharing arrangement might be used to share the risk associated with a research and development effort where the schedule was the pacing item. Because costs could go up if the schedule is accelerated, risk should be shared.

4. *Fixed-price redetermination* (FPR). A fixed-price redetermination contract provides a means of shifting certain indeterminable risks from the seller to the buyer after an initial price is negotiated. This form of contract could be used when specifications are not firm enough to allow reasonable estimates of cost. The contract price is adjusted up or down at specific times during the acquisition based upon factors negotiated prior to signing. For example, the task may be to develop a quick reaction capability, but the requirements are not well-defined. As the requirements are defined (in parallel with the development), the seller might renegotiate the price and share the cost risk related to requirements growth.

Table 5-1 summarizes the applicability, essential elements, approvals, cost risk, and strengths and weaknesses of these four types of contracts. Needless to say, a fixed-price contract is to the buyer's advantage because it places the cost risk on the seller. Profit depends on the seller's ability to produce the required items and to control cost.

This form of contract is attractive to the buyer because it also minimizes the administrative burden and, in many cases, eliminates the need for buyer involvement in technical direction. The seller may also favor this form of contract because of an increased potential for profit.

Sellers are warned, however, never to take a fixed-price contract unless requirements are well-defined and the profit potential is worth the risk involved in the

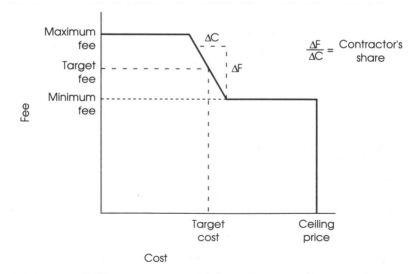

Figure 5-1   Incentive fee-sharing (FPI contract)

TABLE 5-1   Fixed-price Contracts

FFP	FPEPA	FPI	FPR
		Applicability	
Firm design/ requirements available Adequate competition exists Reasonable price/cost comparisons exist	Market/labor conditions are unstable for extended time period	Possibility of cost reduction exists Performance improvements possible Firm target price/ profit can be negotiated	Realistic price cannot be estimated at start Realistic price for later time periods cannot be estimated
		Essential elements	
Buyer/seller must agree to fixed price at inception Fair and reasonable price can be estimated at inception	Established price Ceiling on upward adjustment Downward adjustment reasonable	Target cost Target profit Price ceiling Profit adjustment formula OK accounting system	Ceiling price or initial price fixed Agreement to renegotiate/ redetermine price OK accounting system
		Cost risk	
All of the cost risk assumed by seller	Reduced cost risk in the adjustment areas	Variable fee employed to control cost	Reduced cost risk in the renegotiated areas
		Approvals	
Contracting officer	If adjustment more than 10%, higher-level approval may be needed	Contracting officer	Contracting officer
		Strengths/weaknesses	
Minimum management burden Minimum administrative burden	Increased administrative burden	Increased administrative burden Increased management burden	Even more administrative and management burden

effort. If needed, a seller may negotiate payments for partial deliveries and put a cost of money provision into the contract to penalize the buyer for not paying bills on time.

It should be noted that for government procurements, fixed-price contracts with progress payment clauses are as burdensome to administer as cost-reimbursement contracts. In addition, the government often takes a long time to pay. Therefore, financial capacity to perform may become an issue along with a line of credit availability.

5.1.1.2 Cost-Reimbursable Contracts There are also four basic types of cost-reimbursement contracts: cost and cost-sharing, cost plus incentive fee, cost plus award fee, and cost plus fixed fee. Each of these is briefly explained:

1. *Cost and cost-sharing* (CS). Under a cost or cost-sharing contract, the seller receives no fee. In a cost contract, the seller's allowable costs are reimbursed. In a cost-sharing contract, the buyer and the seller agree on the ratio by which they will share costs. Both contracts are used primarily in research and development efforts. The cost contract is used with nonprofit organizations. The cost-sharing contract is used when the seller will receive substantial present and future commercial benefit from the arrangement. For example, the research and development associated with advanced aircraft may require a cost-sharing arrangement. The buyer, usually a government agency, receives cost reductions while the contractor receives subsidies for work that has commercial value.

2. *Cost plus incentive fee* (CPIF). Like its fixed-price counterpart, this form of contract uses fee to motivate the seller to control costs. Negotiations set a target cost, a target fee, a ceiling price, and an adjustment formula. Minimum and maximum fees are established and related to performance goals. The minimum fee is sometimes set to zero or a negative number. In all cases the seller's allowable costs are reimbursed. The risk associated with research and development efforts is normally shared with fee used as the primary incentive for the seller to keep the lid on costs, meet schedules, and effectively manage the effort (Figure 5-2).

3. *Cost plus award fee* (CPAF). The CPAF contract extends the concept of financial incentives into more subjective areas. The buyer establishes a number of performance criteria that are difficult to measure quantitatively (such as quality, ease of use, and so on). The buyer and seller then structure incentives based upon subjective evaluation of performance using these factors. The fee structure is then established so that there is a base fee and an award amount. The base fee is usually fixed and does not vary as a function of performance. The award fee is used to motivate the seller to excel in the negotiated areas using the criteria for performance established through negotiation. The base profit is normally set low (around three percent of target cost). The maximum profit allowed is set higher than that allowed in CPIF contracts (around 20 percent). The seller is reimbursed allowable costs according to the rules

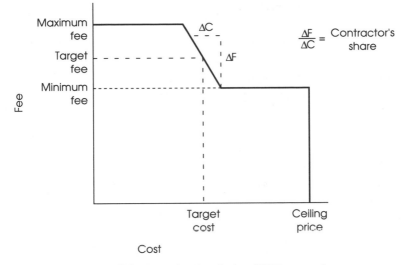

Figure 5-2 Incentive fee sharing (CPIF contract)

established for that purpose and under the limits set. The amount of award is determined through periodic evaluation by an award fee board whose function it is to assess the seller's performance relative to the established criteria. Such evaluation places a severe administrative burden on the buyer. As a consequence, CPAF contracts are limited in use.

4. *Cost plus fixed fee* (CPFF). This type of contract reimburses the seller's allowable costs and pays a fixed fee or profit. The fee does not vary and is not used as an incentive to control costs or manage effectively. The CPFF contract is normally used for research and development efforts where the parties involved cannot reasonably predict the costs and the risk associated with the effort must be shared. Often a ceiling on cost is established as the only motivation to control expenditures.

Table 5-2 summarizes the applicability, essential elements, cost risk, approval requirements, and strengths and weaknesses of these four types of contracts. Cost-reimbursement contracts are more to the seller's advantage because they always reimburse his allowable costs. Therefore, the only risk is in the fee, except where fixed (for example, CPFF contracts). Profit, although variable, depends on the seller's ability to manage cost, schedule, and technical performance effectively.

This form of contract is less attractive to the buyer. The administrative burden is higher because allowable costs and fees need to be assessed or determined. The work of managing is greater because progress must be assessed and technical direction given. The amount of paperwork generated is dramatically increased as funds status and performance are reported, reviewed, and evaluated by the buyer and other organizations with a stake in the effort.

TABLE 5-2   Cost-reimbursable Contracts

CS	CPIF	CPAF	CPFF
Applicability			
Uncertainties in performance and estimates	Uncertainties in performance and estimates	Uncertainties in performance and estimates	Uncertainties in performance and estimates
Research and development jointly sponsored	Performance improvements possible	Performance improvements possible	Research and development where the job cannot be defined and the level of effort is not known initially
Research and development done with a nonprofit organization	Cost/schedule improvements possible	Measurements of improvements subjective	
	Variable fee can provide incentives	Variable fee can provide incentives	
Essential elements			
Predetermined cost for both buyer/seller	Target cost	Estimated cost	Estimated cost
	Target fee	Base fee	Fixed fee
No fee	Min/maximum fee	Maximum fee	OK accounting system
OK accounting system	Fee adjust formula	Award fee criteria	
	OK accounting system	OK accounting system	
Cost risk			
Self-motivated to control cost and performance	Variable fee employed to control cost and performance	Variable fee employed to control cost and performance	Seller responsibility for managing cost
Approvals			
Head of contracting	Contracting officer	Contracting officer	Contracting officer
Strengths/weaknesses			
Hard to get parties to agree	Management burden high	Most difficult to administer	No incentives provided to control cost
	Administrative burden high	Difficult to derive award fee and to manage	Administrative burden high

It should be noted that for government contracts, cost-reimbursement contracts are even more burdensome to administer. Different agencies get involved and often the right hand does not know what the left hand is doing. Everyone seems to want to audit the contractor and there are so many regulations it is almost impossible to do everything right the first time through. In addition, the government places many accounting requirements on the contractor, increasing operating and overhead costs. After one has the experience, one understands why it costs the government $300 for a toilet seat.

5.1.1.3 Other Contractual Devices

There are four other contractual devices that require explanation: time and materials (T-M) contracts, letter contracts, indefinite-delivery contracts, and basic ordering agreements. Each of these is briefly explained:

1. Time and materials contract (T-M). A time and materials contract provides for payment for services and supplies based upon some negotiated rate for each direct labor hour and purchased item. The rate negotiated provides allowance for overhead expenses and profit. A time and materials contract is suitable when the extent, duration, and cost of the work cannot be estimated accurately at the start of the job. Typically, the efforts contracted in this manner include engineering services, repair, maintenance, and overhaul work.

2. Letter contract (LC). A letter contract is a preliminary contractual instrument that allows the seller to start an effort as it is being negotiated. It is used only when a definitive contract cannot be negotiated in time to satisfy the buyer's requirements. It is a temporary device used until a more definitive contract can be negotiated to replace it.

3. Indefinite-delivery contract (IDC). When the exact delivery date is unknown, an indefinite delivery contract may be used. Such a contract provides for the delivery of a known quantity of supplies or services within a given contract period for a negotiated price. Various optional forms of this contract type are used to permit requirements to be satisfied with variable deliveries of goods and services during the contract period.

4. Basic ordering agreement (BOA). A BOA is not a contract. It represents a provisional agreement whereby the buyer and seller agree on the services or supplies to be ordered in the future and the prices to be paid or how prices will be determined. In addition, terms and conditions for inclusion in future contracts are negotiated. A BOA is used to minimize paperwork when a buyer anticipates a large number of orders with the same seller.

Table 5-3 summarizes the applicability, essential elements, cost risk, approval requirements, and strengths and weaknesses of these four types of contractual devices. Each is used under specific circumstances when other forms of contracts are not suitable.

TABLE 5-3 Other Contractual Devices

T-M	LC	IDC	BOA
		Applicability	
Initially not possible to estimate the extent or duration of the job Applicable to design or engineering services and maintenance and repair	Requirements are such that commitment is needed for work to start immediately Cost/schedule estimates can be derived in the future	Schedule for delivery may be unknown Quantity may be unknown Requirements may need to be defined during start-up	Multiple jobs contemplated, which can be combined for ease of overall administration under a single agreement Economies of scale exist
		Essential elements	
Direct labor rate fixed Burden and fee negotiated Ceiling price established OK accounting system	Maximum liability spelled out As many contract provisions defined as possible OK accounting system	Provisions for specifying time, amount, and requirements identified Minimum and maximum order quantities OK accounting system	Estimated cost Estimated fee OK accounting system
		Cost risk	
Task orders used as minicontracts to control cost	Cost could grow during negotiations	Variable fee employed to control cost and performance	None — not a contract
		Approvals	
Contracting officer	Head of contracting	Contracting officer	Head of contracting
		Strengths/weaknesses	
Constant surveillance needed Management burden high	Need to get under contract as soon as possible	Easy to administer if fixed-price Management burden high	Do not have to compete jobs Still have to make contract

TABLE 5-4   Type Contract Guidance

Type of effort	Type of contract
Basic research	Cost, CPFF
Applied research	Cost, CPFF
Exploratory research	Cost, CPFF
Advanced development	Cost, CPFF, CPAF
Engineering development	Cost, CPFF, CPAF, CPIF
Full-scale development	Cost, CPFF, CPAF, CPIF, FPI
First production	FPI
Follow-on production	FPI, FFP
Supply	FFP

5.1.2   Selecting the Proper Contract Type

The generally accepted progression of the acquisition spectrum and the contracts recommended for use are shown in Table 5-4.

Many factors govern which type of contract is appropriate. The contracting officer has the prime responsibility for making this determination. The CO must ensure compliance with the law, meet company policies, be fair, adequately compensate risk, and, in general, try to protect the interests of the buyer. The following selection factors are considered in deciding which type of contract is best:

- The degree of competition present.
- The availability of comparative data for use in evaluating the seller's offer.
- The volatility and difficulty of the requirements.
- The urgency of the requirements.
- The degree of risk involved in meeting the requirements.
- The difficulty in measuring performance during the contract.
- The extent and nature of subcontracting contemplated.
- The size of the contract.
- The seller's experience.

Once the contract type is decided, its contents must be finalized. Much more goes into a contract than just a statement of work, schedule, and list of deliverables. Legal provisions are necessary to make the terms and conditions expressed in the contract enforceable under the law.

5.2   CONTRACT CLAUSES AND THEIR MEANING

As discussed in Chapter 3, acquisition management deals with legal and administrative matters, as well as technical, programmatic, and political matters. Contracts are legal agreements designed to make the conditions governing what constitutes acceptable performance of the two parties enforceable by the courts. As a legal device, a contract must enforce the law as it is currently interpreted by the courts. Many people reading a contract for the first time are bewildered by the seemingly endless stream of difficult language and trivial citations. Yet, there is a reason for every one of these clauses. Most implement policies set up to protect the firm from violating laws for which there are civil or criminal penalties. They also deal with the buyer's rights to patents, data, and copyrights. Clauses can be negotiated to protect either the buyer or seller. Perhaps the easiest way to explain them is to comment on those clauses commonly included in most contracts, both commercial and government.

5.2.1 Labor Clauses

Organizations have the right to form unions under the law. The National Labor Relations Act (Wagner Act of 1935) protects labor's right to engage in organizational activity without fear of retribution. In addition to encouraging employees to form unions and bargain collectively, the Act prohibits the use of certain unfair labor practices by employers. It also established the National Labor Relations Board to administer the provisions of the Act. The NLRB investigates violations and refers them to the federal courts for enforcement of the Act's provisions.

Most contracts contain clauses that protect these rights and outline how disputes between labor and management are mediated. Under the Labor Management Relations Act (Taft-Hartley Act of 1947), the Federal Mediation and Conciliation Service was established to minimize interruptions of the free flow of commerce growing out of labor disputes. This act amended the Wagner Act and made significant changes (prohibiting secondary boycotts, requiring cooling off periods, and so on) in the practices unions could employ during labor disputes.

In addition to these acts, contractual clauses enforce work-hour and safety standards established by the states and the federal government. Work-hour standards dictate the manner in which overtime is computed for both management and technical personnel. Safety legislation prescribes rules for the protection of workers in potentially dangerous work environments.

If the seller is dealing with the federal government, other labor clauses must be contained in contracts and subcontracts. For example, the Convict Labor Act of 1887 makes it a criminal offense to employ prison labor on government contracts. The Copeland Anti-Kickback Act of 1934 makes it a criminal offense to interfere with the orderly operation of the government in the field of public works. It states:

> Whoever by force, intimidation or threat of procuring dismissal from employment, or otherwise induces a person employed on a public housing or public works to give a portion of the compensation to which he is entitled shall be fined not more than $5,000 or imprisoned not more than 5 years or both.

5.2.2 Socioeconomic Clauses

The federal government also requires that the seller implement executive orders in its contracts. Clauses are included that prohibit age and sex discrimination in employment (Executive Order No. 11141). Probably the best known executive order (No. 11375) deals with equal employment opportunity (EEO). Firms contracting with the government must provide equal opportunity to their employees regardless of race, color, religion, sex, or national origin. The system established for ensuring compliance with these regulations provides means for filing complaints, determining compliance, and exercising sanctions and penalties.

5.2.3 Patent Right, Copyright, and Trade Secret Clauses

In certain situations, patents, copyrights, and trade secrets afford protection to their holder. The law restricts how information relative to these items may be handled. Both the buyer's and seller's legal rights with regard to patents, copyrights, and trade secrets must be established by clauses inserted in the contract.

If the seller develops a patentable process or product using the buyer's funds, the buyer should have the right to patent it. Unfortunately, this may not be the case if the rights to such patents are not clearly and carefully spelled out in the contract. For example, the seller could patent the item and charge the buyer a royalty if not prohibited by the contract from doing so. Similarly, the seller could copyright or protect material developed using a trade secret. To protect against such occurrences, the buyer expends considerable time and effort generating the relevant contract clauses.

A buyer will usually ask the seller to identify any patents, copyrights, or trade secrets to be used in the performance of the contract prior to the start of the effort. The buyer may be willing to buy rights or pay a royalty for these items if deemed cost-effective to do so. The seller will want to make sure that all protected information is marked as such before it is given to the buyer. The seller should also make sure that the contract spells out how patents, copyrights, or trade secrets materials will be protected by the buyer as they are used during the performance of the contract.

5.2.4 Rights in Technical Data and Computer Software Clauses

A special clause is sometimes included in contracts that states the buyer will own unlimited rights to the technical data and computer software developed on the contract. This means that the buyer can use, duplicate, or disclose this technical data and computer software in whole or in part, in any manner and for any purpose whatsoever, and can grant permission for others to do the same. Technical data in this context refers to any recorded information, regardless of form or character, of a scientific or technical nature. It does not include cost, pricing, and management data, or other information incidental to contract administration. Computer software refers to the set of instructions that cause a digital computer to operate and all associated documentation. (See Section 11.6 for additional material on data rights.)

This clause requires the seller to identify any restricted rights on technical data and computer software that will be used in the generation, production, or operation of items to which the seller has unlimited rights. For example, if a proprietary software tool is needed to generate the operational software, it must be identified so that a price and appropriate rights for the software can be negotiated prior to contract.

Occasionally, this clause is coupled with a deferred delivery clause that allows the buyer to purchase the rights to the technical data and computer software and take delivery for a fixed price at some later time during the acquisition process. Such clauses, though rare, can substantially improve the buyer's leverage, enabling purchase of items at a later time when additional funds may become available (during the operational phase).

5.2.5 Other Clauses

Numerous other clauses are sometimes inserted in the contract. The more popular of these include:

1. *Conflict of interest clause.* This clause prohibits the winning offeror from bidding on related future efforts because a conflict of interest apparently exists between this and the future effort. For example, the buyer may want to discourage hardware vendors from specifying requirements for equipment that they would bid on competitively during the follow-on effort.

2. *Key personnel replacement clause.* This clause requires the seller to obtain the buyer's permission before replacing any of the key personnel that were proposed for the effort. Persons proposed must perform on the contract or the contract will be held null and void. Replacement is possible only with the buyer's approval. The suggested replacement should be at least as capable as the person being replaced. Interviews may be held at the buyer's option.

3. *Use of facilities and/or equipment clause.* This clause specifies the terms and conditions that govern the seller's use of the buyer's facilities and/or equipment during the contract period. For example, the clause would specify remedies for any problems caused by faulty operation of equipment or software. It might require the seller to hold the buyer blameless regardless of the source or cause of the error.

4. *Cost accounting standards clauses.* These clauses spell out how cost data will be collected and reported. They identify the standards to be used in separating allowable from nonallowable costs and set in place a structure to provide for an audit trail. Certain clauses may force the seller to implement a job costing system and to move from a cash to an accrual method of accounting.

5. *Warranty clauses.* These clauses spell out the required warranties and how they will be administered when implemented. They may tie the warranties to the payment clauses as a means to motivate the seller to perform as promised. They may discuss acceptance criteria and how defects will be fixed. A large and often confusing body of statutes, regulations, and judicial decisions must be considered when designing a contract that will afford both buyer and seller adequate protection.

5.3 UNDERSTANDING THE FEDERAL ACQUISITION REGULATIONS (FAR)

The Federal Acquisition Regulations (FAR) were established to codify and publish in one place a uniform set of acquisition policies and procedures for use by all executive agencies within the U.S. government. Its volumes are periodically updated to reflect current statutes, executive orders, and judicial findings.

FAR is organized into eight subchapters and fifty-three parts. (For FAR organization and topics see Appendix C.) It is the bible for contracting officers because it contains the current interpretation of the law on literally every acquisition management topic. It is overwhelming in size and difficult to comprehend due to the complexity of the regulations and the need to have them established in detail. Both buyer and seller must study its provisions carefully to keep current with interpretation.

FAR represents a considerable improvement over the state of affairs that existed prior to its publication in 1984. Until that time, the various government agencies maintained different and often conflicting interpretations of the same laws. As a result, contractors working for the government often had to interpret differently the same contract clauses for the various agencies. This made the task of contract management confusing and hectic for all parties concerned.

FAR has remedied this situation, as well as simplified the task of specifying clauses for contracts. A contracting officer has only to designate the applicable clauses and include them in the contract by reference. Many government organizations publish standard contracts with lists of applicable FAR clauses already checked off. In addition, these same organizations retain a FAR lawyer who can cite the regulations chapter and verse if required, especially during contract negotiations. Of course, modified clauses and negotiated exceptions still need to be spelled out and amplified in the contract.

One important difference between government and commercial contracts affecting interpretations offered relative to FAR involves the concept of apparent authority or estoppel. The government, unlike commercial firms, is not bound by the unauthorized acts of its agents. A party entering into an arrangement with a representative of the federal government is responsible for determining whether or not that representative is acting within the bounds of prescribed authority. This determination is often difficult to make. An agent may presume to have an authority held by the agency, but not by that individual. As a consequence, the interpretation of FAR contained in the contract might be unilaterally changed because the agent acted without proper authority, and the interpretation may be held nonbinding.

5.4 CONTRACT ADMINISTRATION AND TERMINATION

As already discussed, the contracting officer (CO) has the authority to enter into, administer, and make changes to or modify the contract on the buyer's behalf. Once the contract is negotiated and let, the CO's duties and those of the COR normally include:

- Performance measurement—monitoring status and making sure that substantive progress is being made on deliverables.
- System compliance—ensuring that all systems and procedures established by the seller (accounting, configuration management, and so on) comply with contract requirements.
- Contract modifications—negotiating changes to the contract and monitoring performance to ensure that they are properly implemented.
- Property administration—ensuring that property the buyer makes available to the seller for use on the contract is properly cared for and returned as promised.
- Review and consent to subcontract—reviewing subcontracting proposals and providing consent if and when the proposed vendor is found qualified to do the job.
- Inspection, correction, and acceptance—ensuring that all terms and conditions of the contract, including those for warranties, inspection, correction, and acceptance are satisfied.
- Contract termination/close-out—terminating the contract for convenience or default or closing it out upon satisfaction of all of its requirements.

5.4.1 Performance Measurement

The seller has the primary responsibility for the timely and satisfactory performance of contract requirements. The buyer closely monitors the seller's progress to ensure that the requirements are being satisfied and to identify related technical, managerial, and administrative problems. The buyer also helps the seller interpret requirements and provides the technical direction needed to implement requirements provisions.

The buyer must relate technical performance to schedule and cost status in order to determine whether the best value is obtained for the funds expended. When performance problems exist, the buyer will be called upon to provide expertise, assistance, and technical direction. Change requests may need to be evaluated and change orders may require approvals. The buyer may also be called upon to administer progress payments, award or incentive fees, waivers, warranties, and a host of other contractual provisions. Key buyer activities include:

- Maintaining visibility into, communications with, and control over the seller's work.

- Handling disagreements with the seller in a professional manner, calling in specialists, when warranted, to mediate problems.
- Analyzing cost, schedule, and technical performance quantitatively and determining if variances are within acceptable bounds.
- Monitoring costs, both direct and indirect, and taking action when they seem to be getting out of hand.
- Learning about the seller's systems and procedures and using them to supply necessary management information.

Determinations of status and progress are themselves topics worthy of considerable discussion (see Chapters 6 and 7).

5.4.2 Contract Modifications

Contracts change with time as organizations better understand their own needs and requirements. Changes to address newly defined needs or requirements may be made for a variety of technical or administrative reasons. For example, new laws may be passed that impose stricter accounting requirements on the contract. These new requirements will have to be negotiated and incorporated into the contract in order to maintain its legality and enforceability.

Contracts must be maintained as living documents with changes to them processed and implemented in a timely manner. Buyer and seller employ a structured process to deal with contract changes. When the need for a change is recognized by either party, a change proposal is prepared and submitted for review by a change control board established for that purpose. Buyer and seller representatives work together to evaluate change proposals. If a proposal is found acceptable, an equitable adjustment in price and/or delivery schedule may be negotiated.

Some contracts allow changes to be made unilaterally by the buyer without due consideration (that is, without the exchange of benefits taking place). For example, no new consideration is necessary when a contract is repriced under its redetermination provision. As another example, the estimated cost may be increased without due consideration on a cost-reimbursement contract.

The buyer is extremely careful to ensure that changes are within the scope of the original agreement. If they are not, a new and separate contract must be negotiated. The following modifications are examples of changes that are outside the scope of the contract:

- Any change in the essential character of the goods or services originally ordered.
- Any requirement for work, effort, or services beyond those required by the original contract.

Changes are conceived, screened, evaluated, accepted/rejected, processed, and implemented as the acquisition process unfolds. Change processing is important because it represents a means by which contracts can be altered to reflect the current needs and requirements of buyer and seller organizations.

5.4.3 Contract Terminations/Close-out

Contracts are terminated on completion by delivery of goods and services. Contracts can be terminated before completion in two ways:

1. Termination for convenience—termination may occur at any time during the contract, even when the seller is performing satisfactorily.
2. Termination for default—termination occurs when the seller fails to perform satisfactorily.

When a contract is terminated for convenience, the buyer is obliged to compensate the seller for work completed to date, as well as for the costs of termination. In addition, the seller is entitled to a reasonable profit. Because both the direct and indirect costs associated with the termination proceedings become allowable costs, it is sometimes cheaper to let a contract lapse rather than to terminate it. As an example, Boeing's profit soared when the supersonic transport (SST) project was terminated in the 1970s.

When a fixed-price contract is terminated for default, written notice must be provided and the seller should be given a reasonable time to remedy the situation. The notice is sometimes called a *show cause* notice because it states that the contract will be terminated unless the seller shows cause, within a specified time period, why it should remain in force. In some situations, the seller may be liable for the costs involved in purchasing replacement goods or services. When a cost-reimbursement contract is terminated for default, the seller receives all allowable costs incurred up to termination and is not liable for repurchase costs should the buyer elect to purchase replacement goods or services.

Independent of the manner in which termination occurs, the contract must be closed out. Close-out is mostly a cleanup activity where overhead rates are finalized, incentive and award fees are determined, excess property is disposed of, patent disclosures are made, claims are released, equipment is returned, excess funds are deobligated, and performance is documented.

On cost-reimbursement contracts, audits are conducted to finalize overhead rates and to substantiate charges incurred during the contract. Because these activities are time-consuming, contracts are often not closed out until some time after delivery. This means that final payment for goods and services may come years in the future.

We have completed an introduction of software acquisition management, covering the basic acquisition strategies, statement of work issues, and contract law. In the next three chapters we discuss software management issues; first from the viewpoint of the buyer in Chapter 6, and then from the viewpoint of the seller in

Chapter 7. We then discuss issues common to both in Chapter 8, which examines the team approach.

ADDITIONAL READING

Department of the Air Force, *Government Contract Law*, 6th ed., March 1979.

Department of the Army, *Procurement Law*, Pamphlet No. 27-153, January 1976.

Department of Defense, *Federal Acquisition Regulations*, February 1987.

Department of the Navy, *Defense Contracts Management for Technical Personnel*, 1983.

CHAPTER 6

Software Management—
The Buyer's Model

Buyer and seller acquistion responsibilities are different in scope and perspective, but not in kind; they are based on identical management functions. The buyer acts as the project advocate to the customer organization and defends the budget. The seller is faced with directing the development effort, so that an acceptable product is delivered on time and within budget. The degrees of detail and of rigor employed are different. The buyer, for the most part, wants a top-level perspective and does not wish to be included in every aspect of managing the development effort. The buyer normally avoids getting involved in detail except to resolve a specific problem, monitor a high-risk area, or to spot check seller management procedures. The seller, on the other hand, is intimately involved with development detail by the very nature of its task: to make the difficult engineering decisions and provide the buyer visibility into the effort.

These dual perspectives must be complementary because the basic objective of both buyer and seller is to develop an acceptable system. In this chapter and the next, buyer and seller environments, respectively, are discussed. Project planning, requirements assessment, project management roles and responsibilities, project assessment, risk management, and the role of third-party suppliers are covered.

6.1 PROJECT PLANNING (PROJECT MANAGEMENT PLAN)

Project management includes a host of activities. These are usually described in the project management plan. The plan describes the project organizational structure and key personnel responsibilities. It covers standards and methodologies, documentation, development tools, budget, schedules, staffing, assessment, and customer approval and certification.

The project management plan is developed during the initial phase of the project. It is normally a part of the solicitation package detailed in Section 3.3. It should be prepared before the statement of work because it documents the results of the planning phase and structures the way in which the buyer will manage the project. As such, it provides the basis for the seller management program, commonly documented in the project management plan and/or the software development plan. The project management plan will vary depending on the particular needs of the project and the management style of the buyer. A well-considered plan might do the following:

1. Detail project organizational structure, included functions, responsibilities, and required resources (dollars, talent, people, time, and so on).

2. List personnel resources by amount, expertise, job category (for example, test personnel), and number; detail the equipment required to develop and test the system; and detail the facilities required to house the organization and the integration and test facilities.

3. Identify and assess areas of development risk. The plan may describe the criteria for risk assessment and management procedures used for identifying, quantifying, and controlling risk.

4. Outline the approach for the quality assurance program. The objectives of the quality program and specific quality requirements should be identified in terms of prevention, assurance, and verification.

5. Identify the specific requirements of the CM program (the control mechanisms that will be employed, baseline management procedures, control board activities, and the role and authority of buyer and seller).

6. Define the training concept (for example, contractor versus buyer training). The plan may identify different types of training, required resources for training, schedules for preparing training materials, conduct of training, and the distribution of training resources and information. The training program should address the development of training materials, the testing or validation of the training program, and the implementation of the training program.

7. Identify the documents required, the standards used to prepare them, review procedures, and acceptance criteria.

8. Detail initial responsibilities for support of the system. Will the development be supported by the contractor, the user, or the buyer? What support facilities, including hardware, will be required? Will a support facility have to be built?

9. Detail the security requirements, including physical as well as data security (privacy).

10. Identify the expected management environment. Will there be a need to manage a complex contractor environment with more than a single contractor? Or will the concept of a single "prime" contractor be employed?

11. Detail the types and outline the procedures for the conduct of reviews.

12. Detail the schedule and identify the types of reports to be used. How often will milestone reporting occur? What detail will be required in project schedules?

13. Identify the testing concept. Will an independent testing organization be employed? Will operational testing be conducted? Identify the roles of the user, the buyer, and the seller in testing.

14. Determine what metrics and management indicators should be used. Select an appropriate set for the project (see Section 6.4.6).

15. Detail the type of financial reporting. How often will financial reporting occur and with what degree of timeliness?

16. Identify the problem-reporting mechanisms to be employed. Will a standard reporting form be used? Identify problem-report processing and review procedures.

17. Determine whether the buyer management team requires support resources. The plan should detail the requirements and objectives for support. If an IV&V role is envisioned, the plan should define the role and extent of the IV&V effort (see Section 6.6).

18. Detail the standards that will be applied to the effort. Will a development standard be employed? Will a buyer standards and conventions document be required and will the buyer require the developer to provide one?

19. Define the role of commercially available off-the-shelf hardware and software. Who will provide it—buyer or seller? How will it be managed?

20. Address considerations regarding the acquisition of software data rights. Is the software proprietary to the seller? Does the buyer require unlimited rights to the software?

6.2 SPECIAL TOPICS IN BUYER PROJECT MANAGEMENT

There are many important considerations for the buyer during the planning phase. Certain topics deserve special mention. Though often neglected or misunderstood, they are critical to acquisition of an acceptable system.

6.2.1 Establishing Requirements

Project requirements are of two types: the statement of need from the customer or user of the system, and requirements necessary to manage the project. Irrespective of management requirements, adequate attention to the statement of need, or performance requirements, is an essential prerequisite for an acceptable project.

The requirements statement is the foundation for a software acquisition. Collecting requirements would appear a fairly straightforward enterprise. It demands, however, a disciplined approach. The lack of a good requirements statement has been the scourge of many software development efforts. Once the project is under way, the developer may employ methods and tools to analyze requirements and prepare an acceptable specification. A tool such as TeamWork™ enables the developer to identify inconsistencies, eliminate duplication, and understand the hierarchy of requirements in order to architect the software and develop work estimates. In a sense, however, such actions are like closing the barn door after the horse has escaped. Requirements should be definitized before the contract effort is awarded. Thus, a solid functional and performance baseline for the system can be established prior to the design activity. In general, the statement of requirements should meet the following criteria:

1. The requirements should be complete. The statement of need should not lack any requirements necessary for developing a usable system.
2. The requirements should be consistent. Inconsistencies create redundant needs or conflicts in implementation.
3. The requirements should be clear. They must be understandable so that their implementation can be achieved.
4. Each requirement must be achievable. There must be a reasonable expectation, albeit with some degree of risk, that the requirement can be implemented within some bound of cost and schedule.
5. The requirements should be verifiable. Each requirement should be amenable to testing to the satisfaction of the user such that it can, at the very least, be demonstrated.
6. The requirements should bound the functional performance expected by the user. The requirements should be traceable to their source and they should be quantitative.

The fact that an individual user expresses some need does not necessarily imply that the requirement is practical or acceptable to a broad number of users. Management's job is to sort through these requirements in order to develop an integral set that will provide for a sound development. The buyer can use the following check list to provide a top-level assessment for the validity and integrity of the requirements statement:

1. How were the requirements synthesized? Was there a rational plan for their collection? Did the plan detail the conduct of the synthesis process? Are requirements coming from qualified personnel? How should the requirement be evaluated? Were criteria such as degree of necessity formulated to classify the requirements?
2. How was the requirements synthesis process managed? Was there a method? Were the requirements catalogued according to established criteria? Were the requirements controlled and managed through a control activity?
3. How were the requirements reviewed? Was there a method to systematically assess requirements against established criteria? Were initial trade-offs conducted to assess the cost of implementation versus accrued benefit? Was a peer-level review of requirements performed?

These procedures may appear to the reader rigorous. The authors are not so naive as to believe that they occur routinely; they do not. These procedures will allow management to establish the validity of requirements before development is initiated. If the requirements are not adequate, a more extensive requirements definition effort may be warranted.

6.2.2 Estimating Resources

Estimating required resources prior to the selection of a seller is difficult unless the effort is being developed under special circumstances. For example, if the software system is a redevelopment of an existing system where the developer has experience in the application (that is, understands the customer environment and system requirements), then a fairly accurate estimate of development resources is possible. In this situation, the developer of the existing system is best equipped to make the estimate. Usually, the buyer wants to develop the estimate, but may not have the expertise to do so. If the buyer is familiar with the existing system and has actively participated in its development, a fair estimate that will suffice for budgeting purposes (that is, within 10 percent of actual costs) is possible. If the system is a new development, estimation of resources is more difficult and imprecise.

Accurate cost estimates based on requirements statements are extremely difficult to obtain. Given current software practice, a well-bounded estimate of software development resources is only feasible when the design is completed. This, of course, is impractical in most procurement situations. By utilizing the cost-estimation methodologies discussed in Chapter 9, the buyer can acquire a better handle on the required resources. However, management should not be deluded into thinking that the estimate is inviolable. Control and assessment of the resources expended during development is mandatory to ensure that the project meets cost and schedule expectations. If the risk of an inaccurate estimate is not acceptable, the buyer should consider using a risk-reduction phase where requirements can be defined and a system design possibly developed prior to committing major resources to the acquisition.

6.2.3 Risk Management Strategies

Risk is in the eye of the beholder. To the user, risk is associated with whether a usable system that meets performance requirements can be achieved. To the buyer, risk is associated with whether performance requirements are met within cost and schedule bounds. To the seller, risk is measured in terms of ability to meet contractual requirements while achieving profit expectations. The seller is usually concerned with the technical risk of development. To the maintainer or ultimate support organization, risk is associated with whether the system will be maintainable. Risk is any impediment that might jeopardize the attainment of specific objectives of the project.

Risk assessment is an ongoing process throughout the development. During the planning phase, risk assessment focuses on issues of project feasibility. Risk is directly related to the development cost and schedule. If cost is a critical issue, the risks impacting resources should be explored and alternatives that can eliminate or reduce these risks to an acceptable level identified. If schedule is a critical issue, risks impacting schedule have to be identified and eliminated or reduced before the project begins.

In some projects, risk is commensurate with the objectives of the effort. A project may undertake to develop or explore the possibility of achieving a new capability (such as in artificial intelligence applications). As another example, the development may be a prototype effort to define or eliminate a high-risk area critical to a subsequent development effort. The prototype effort is undertaken to reduce this technical risk before major resources are committed to the development of the actual system.

Naturally, one would like to identify and eliminate all appreciable risks before the development contract is in place. Although a laudable objective, it is impractical because one cannot predict all possible occurrences in the acquisition. One can attempt to identify and manage risk before development, but other risk areas will emerge as the development proceeds. The purpose of the planning phase is to identify such risks, determine a suitable set of actions based on trade-off studies, and develop an overall strategy for risk abatement and providing for risk management throughout the development.

The buyer, in the preliminary planning phase, and the supplier, in the early phases of development, should prepare a risk management plan. This plan can be incorporated into other management plans such as the buyer's project management plan or the seller's software development plan. It could be a stand-alone plan. This management choice depends on the character of the acquisition, especially the size and complexity of the effort. The plan should deal with identifying, quantifying, ranking, and controlling risk (Figure 6-1). The basic management process for managing risk is as follows:

1. *Assessment.* Table 6-1 is a guide to possible risk areas on projects. The buyer may rely on this guide as well as personal experience (lessons learned from other projects) to develop a list of possible risk areas. Risk areas can be categorized according to likelihood of occurrence and problem severity. For example, the availability of a mature compiler for the selected high-order language (HOL) to be used on the project may be identified as a possible risk area. A compiler of lesser maturity could represent a critical risk.

2. *Analysis.* Each risk should be analyzed to determine the alternative actions, if any, that should be taken to minimize it. If the risk of an immature compiler is unacceptable, an alternative language or compiler might be identified. If no alternative exists, or if the risk is acceptable, then the risk area should be closely monitored throughout the development effort.

3. *Evaluation.* Appropriate management mechanisms should be in place to provide ongoing assessment of the identified risk areas. These mechanisms should be integrated with the life cycle management of the development

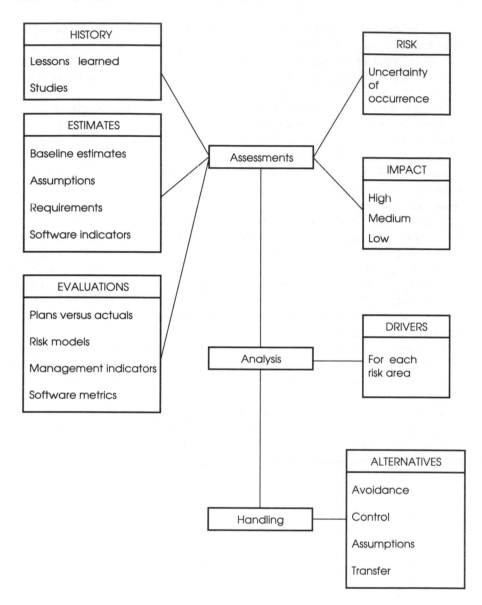

INPUTS   OUTPUTS

Figure 6-1   Software risk management

Source: Department of Defense, *Draft Total Quality Management Guide,* DOD 5000.51-G, August 23, 1989.

TABLE 6-1 Areas of Project Risk

	Performance (Technical)	Cost	Schedule
Requirements			
Completeness	P	S	S
Stability	S	P	S
Complexity	P	S	S
Technology			
Language	P	S	S
Tools	P	S	S
Prototypes	P	S	S
Reuse	P	S	S
Personnel			
Availability	S	P	S
Stability	P	S	S
Experience	P	S	S
Hardware			
Availability	S	S	P
Buyer-furnished	S	S	P

P = Primary
S = Secondary

(for example, formal reviews). In the example of the immature compiler, a management indicator that tracks projected compiled code versus actual compiled code, such as the indicator described in Section 6.4.6.3, could be utilized. Another metric is how efficiently compiled object code utilizes computer memory. Of course, this would have to be compared with some standard.

4. *Management.* It has been useful on a number of projects to conduct risk-management meetings periodically throughout the development effort. In smaller projects, this function can be incorporated into periodic project review meetings. Risks should also be addressed at formal reviews such as preliminary design and critical design.

The management of risk is wielded as a doubled-edged sword. First, risk areas are identified before the project begins. The buyer should attempt to reduce risk to a level consistent with the resources and expertise available for the effort. Second, risk management should be incorporated into the management of the project and documented in appropriate management plans so it is part of the management process.

6.3   PROJECT MANAGEMENT OFFICE ROLES AND RESPONSIBILITIES

The project management office can include from one person to as many as a hundred people. The size of the office normally depends on the size and complexity of the acquisition and the resources that the buyer brings to the project. In small organizations, project offices tend to be small. In large organizations, the offices are usually large. Regardless of size, the office functions for each project are fairly standard. The project office is responsible for the effective management of the project and must exercise appropriate control based on available resources.

The buyer must have the means with which to manage the execution of the management requirements placed in the contract. Lacking such means, the buyer is in a risky situation. A lack of adequate resources implies ineffective control of the project. Of course, experienced personnel can more than make up for a deficiency in their number. Vast numbers of people employed in bureaucratic organizations often turn out to be ineffective. If the effort has been properly structured and management controls effectively employed (including appropriate assessment mechanisms), the project can be managed with a surprisingly small number of people. If sufficient resources are not available, the use of an engineering support contractor (see Section 6.5) to supplement buyer resources should be considered.

It would be totally inappropriate to provide a model for a project office. Clearly, the office setup will be determined by the management style of the organization, its culture, and the size and complexity of the project. Certain functions, however, should be considered for any project organization:

- Project management
- Engineering
- Configuration management
- Test
- Training
- Quality assurance
- Contract administration
- Program control
- Data management
- Interface management
- Logistics support

In small projects, several functions might be combined (for example, configuration management and quality assurance) to make more effective use of resources, or the buyer may rely on seller configuration management if principal responsibility for this function resides with the seller. Through the configuration management plan and appropriate management controls (such as the quality assurance function), review of the CM process is achieved. CM is required for every software project. The buyer must check on its implementation to ensure that it is effective.

It is not suggested that functional responsibilities such as CM be ignored. In a resource-constrained environment, the buyer has to make choices as to where emphasis is placed. By careful planning and judicious application of management mechanisms, such as quality assurance, and assessment techniques, such as management indicators, it is possible to monitor these functional areas with minimal resources. Monitoring, however, is different from controlling. In large and complex efforts demanding the close interaction of buyer and seller, appropriate and sufficient resources must be available.

6.4 PERFORMANCE MANAGEMENT AND ASSESSMENT TECHNIQUES

Perhaps the most important activity for managers to utilize and properly understand is assessment. The proper use of assessment techniques provides visibility into the development effort. One of the most serious mistakes management can make is to rely on superficial reports or broad interpretation of data. For example, cost data may be entirely on track, yet the project could be in serious trouble. Financial status reports may be several months behind actual progress and thus not reflect current project financial status. In another common occurrence, resource expenditure and financial data are tracking normally but the project is actually experiencing technical difficulties. These difficulties will not show up, at least initially, in financial or resource expenditure reports because technical performance may not be related to them.

Every project manager understands the need for early visibility. However, internal mechanisms of the project environment usually act to obscure problems. The development team may believe a problem is of a transitory nature and can be solved before there is any real impact on the project. Human nature leads people to keep problems to themselves, particularly if personally responsible for them. In addition, the seller, hoping to keep the development on course, is reluctant to divulge problems. If management action is not taken to achieve meaningful visibility, the buyer will not obtain accurate and timely information on project status. Software projects get into trouble a little at a time. Therefore, constant surveillance and timely actions are needed to keep the project on target.

Visibility is not attained through reliance on a single management mechanism. The management team must rely on a number of carefully selected techniques to provide a coordinated assessment program. This section considers these techniques, their utilization, and their implications for assessing project status.

6.4.1 Reviews

Reviews are normally of two general types, formal and informal. Formal reviews, such as design reviews, are those mandated by the selected development methodology or contract requirements. Informal reviews are those conducted by the development team in the course of everyday management of the effort, such as walkthroughs.

An effective formal review is much more than just a meeting. The review must be structured around well-defined procedures and objectives and coupled with realistic project milestones. It should be based on a specific product or set of products. Procedures for conducting reviews are described in Sections 2.3.2 and 7.6. The development methodology should define the specific milestones that will result in formal reviews. For example, the preliminary design review is conducted at the time requirements have been allocated to the top-level components of the software architecture.

Informal reviews are normally not monitored by the buyer. These reviews (for example, walk-throughs) are usually conducted during the design and coding phases of the project. Although not under the control of the buyer, the integrity of the review process is checked through the quality assurance function. Thus a degree of visibility is attained. To the extent that quality assurance is an independent function, overall project visibility is increased.

The buyer should schedule formal project review meetings at periodic intervals. The timing of these meetings should be based on the complexity and overall schedule of the acquisition. If the project is of a fairly short duration (from one to two years), biweekly meetings might be scheduled. If the project is to be a long-term effort, monthly or bimonthly reviews may be in order. At these reviews, results of informal reviews can be studied through summary reports published by the development team (for example, test, QA, CM).

6.4.2 Schedules

There are various methods for depicting the project schedule. A typical top-level method is based on milestone occurrences. An example of a top-level schedule is shown in Figure 6-2. The figure uses a Gantt chart as the schedule representation.

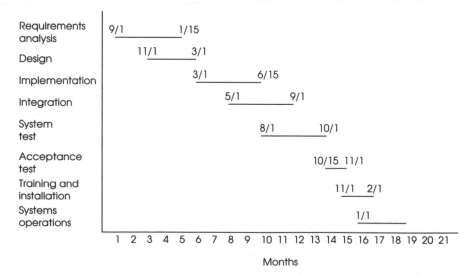

Figure 6-2 Gantt schedule

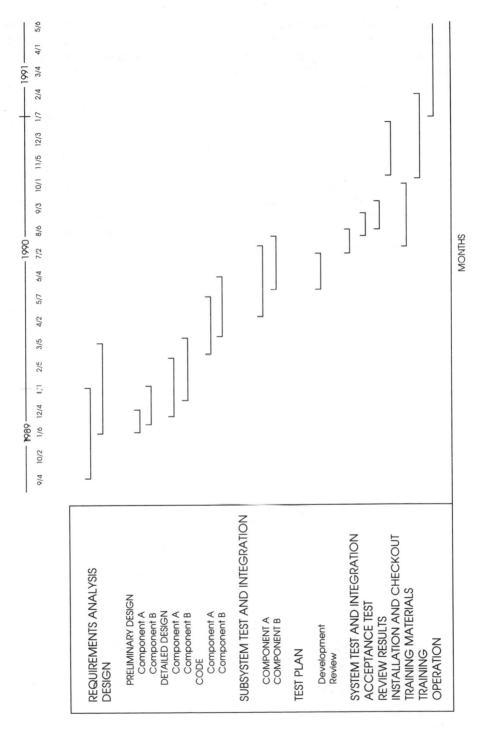

A Gantt schedule technique shows a schedule of events with start and stop times plotted along the time axis of the project. This type of schedule, while useful, does not provide meaningful visibility for the project management team. In order for a schedule to be an effective assessment tool, the events described should be definitive project occurrences spaced at fairly close intervals in the development. For example, scheduling milestones no more than two weeks apart provides a realistic framework for most projects. Figure 6-3 presents an example of a more detailed schedule.

Another popular scheduling method is PERT/CPM, or project evaluation reporting technique/critical path method [Burrill, 1980]. This technique, shown in Figure 6-4, shows the precedence relationships between all project tasks. Each activity or event is described by its maximum (pessimistic) time, its minimum (optimistic) time, its expected time, and its relationship to predecessor and successor tasks. Once the PERT is developed, the critical path, which shows the longest path through the network, can be established. Management can then take action to shorten that path if possible or to monitor path events to ensure that the schedule is being met. PERT/CPM is an excellent technique to track the project schedule. However, the additional resources required to use it may not be warranted except for large and complex projects. The contracting agency must specify its use and ensure that it is reported on at appropriate times during the development.

Because the work breakdown structure describes events at the task level, the data to support detailed schedules are available to the seller. The key is to ensure that the scheduling techniques used are commensurate with the scope and complexity of the project and that they are detailed and reported on at a meaningful periodic rate.

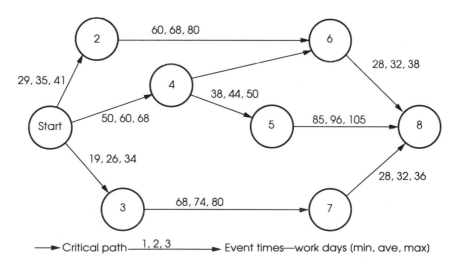

Figure 6-4   PERT/CPM method

Source: Defense Systems Management College, *System Engineering Guide*, Fort Belvoir, VA., 1983.

The granularity of the schedule will differ depending on the level within the project. Typically, the schedule is driven by events at the work breakdown structure task level; however, this may be inappropriate at higher levels within the project. The buyer should ensure that it is not inundated by events at too low a level of reporting, or too-frequent milestones (for example, occurring every week). The buyer needs to have, however, reasonable visibility into the project without having to wait months for a report. The seller, on the other hand, may require a more detailed schedule to exercise effective control over the development. These circumstances are dictated by the complexity of the project.

6.4.3 Problem Reporting

The project management plan should provide for problem reporting. Problems occur at different levels within a project. They can be high-level problems affecting cost, schedule, or performance. They can be of a lower level or more detailed nature, such as errors in documentation or code. The buyer may choose to use an established problem-reporting system. Certainly, the buyer should resolve how problem reporting will be managed. Two systems are required: one for problem reporting and one for corrective action. Management procedure should provide for:

1. Review of the problem. Who will review the problem and the actions taken to address it?
2. Reporting. How will the problem be reported? Who will be able to report problems? What types of problems should be reported?
3. Status. How will the problem be prioritized? How will the status of problems be reported?
4. Management. How will the problem be managed? How will problems be controlled?
5. Correction. How will the problem be corrected? How will the corrective action be controlled?

A problem can be resolved by explanation (requiring no further action), correction, or preparation of a change proposal in the event the problem causes a change in an established contract baseline and the change has a cost or schedule impact.

The problem report should include the following:

1. Problem sources (for example, design documentation and affected module).
2. Products presumed to be in error, including documentation.
3. Description of the problem including the environment and specific conditions.
4. Recommended corrective actions or set of alternatives.

By monitoring problem reports, the buyer can obtain useful insight into development processes. Problem reports should track milestone activities. Thus, during specifications preparation, problem reporting and resolution deal with the appropriate specification. During coding and testing, problems considered deal with errors reported in testing at this level. By evaluating problems and their closure rate, insight is gained into progress.

6.4.4 Test

The testing program is an excellent means to achieve visibility into software progress. If it has a disadvantage, it is that formal testing, witnessed by the buyer, is not conducted until late in the development. Of course, the preparation for testing is important. The progress of test planning must be assessed and a determination made as to whether the test program will meet project objectives and provide meaningful insight into development progress.

In order for the testing program to provide such insight, it must be properly planned, documented, and conducted. The test program is based on test requirements that mirror technical requirements. There must be clear correspondence between test requirements and project requirements. Test documentation should be reviewed at appropriate milestones and monitored by the quality assurance function to ensure that the documentation is adequate and in accordance with project standards and testing is accomplished as planned. Thus, the quality assurance function provides a check on the test program. Independent testing, if utilized, can provide an independent check of the adequacy of the test program. In addition, it can provide testing above and beyond the project testing program.

The test program provides useful insight into the project. The project manager must ensure that the test program is viable and will deliver useful results. To establish a worthwhile test program, the following steps should be taken:

1. Ensure that the qualification requirements are incorporated into early specifications (system requirements and software requirements specifications).
2. Ensure that the early planning documents (the project management and software development plans) cover the testing program.
3. Ensure that the development contractor has and will employ a test environment that maintains the necessary tools to support the testing program.
4. Ensure that long lead actions are identified and the seller has a plan for implementing these actions.
5. Ensure that a viable test organization with responsibility and authority for conducting the program is in place. Ensure that the test program can operate without undue influence from the development team or project manager.
6. Ensure that there are appropriate checks on the testing process (through the quality assurance function and independent engineering support, if utilized).

6.4.5 Independent Testing

Independent testing may be utilized in developments that are complex or carry critical mission operations or developments in which the manager desires an extra degree of confidence. The reasons for independent testing differ from those for the project testing program, and the conduct of the testing is therefore different. A natural motivation of the developer is trying to prove that the product works. The independent test team tries to define the limits of the product: that is, it attempts to determine where and when it will fail. Thus, the independent test team focuses on the fringes, or anomalous test cases, of the product. (This function is sometimes confused with independent verification and validation—IV&V. IV&V includes independent testing but is not synonymous with it. IV&V is described in Section 6.6.) Independent testing should be conducted on projects that warrant the expenditure of the additional resources required for this function.

6.4.6 Management Indicators

An extremely useful methodology that has recently evolved utilizes high-level management indicators or metrics (such as fault density, personnel stability, and test completeness) to provide insight into development progress. (Variously called management indicators, metrics, or quality indicators, the general term management indicators is preferred in this book.) Management indicators, if used in a coordinated manner, provide a very useful assessment technique. They help achieve insight into the various aspects of development, and they help pinpoint problem causes.

The use of indicators requires that data be collected to support their quantifications. Of course, the data required for most of these indicators must be collected in the normal course of the project. For example, the collection of problem reports is a typical function in current development practice.

Indicator selection must be consistent with both project objectives and resources. It makes little sense to require the full set of indicators described in this book for projects that are fairly straightforward, of short duration, and not overly complex. The extra resources required to support data collection and analysis are simply not warranted. On the other hand, if the project is complex and will require considerable resources to develop, the use of the full set may be justified.

There exists a large number of these management indicators. Those included here were selected because of their relevance and ease of application. Indicators that require complex data collection methods or the collection of huge amounts of data are omitted. Although these may be valuable, experience shows that they are not used if the cost of their implementation is high.

6.4.6.1 *Memory Utilization* This indicator tracks, or measures, the utilization of computer memory (or secondary memory such as disk memory) across the project (Figure 6-5). The figure shows memory utilization relative to project schedule, including two milestones; critical design review, where intensive coding begins (the system is completely designed), and test readiness review, the beginning of formal testing. Typically, an estimate of memory utilization across the project is made at the beginning of the project. In order to allow for growth and estimate inaccuracies, memory utilization is projected at twice the expected required memory. As code is implemented, memory utilization usually increases

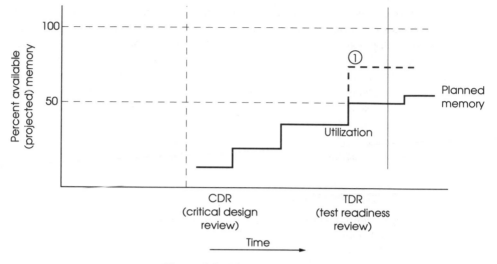

Figure 6-5   Memory utilization

beyond its expected level. (There is an old adage that the amount of code will expand to fill the memory available—not unlike a move into a larger house with more storage space.)

Comparing projected and actual memory utilization gives some indication of development progress. If memory utilization tracks within the planned memory allotted, as shown in the figure, the project is proceeding quite normally. If, however, memory utilization starts to increase rapidly, early estimates of memory or source lines of code may have been unrealistic. If there are sharp jumps (shown by 1 in Figure 6-5), there may be a serious development problem. Code is being generated rapidly in an attempt to alleviate the problem—the brute force method. If memory utilization is tracking below projected levels, the project may be running behind schedule. One can formulate a number of possible explanations for differences between actual and projected memory utilization. By correlating this indicator with others, the project manager can better identify problems and appropriate responses.

The memory utilization indicator is particularly important for systems with limited memory capacity. Typically, these are systems in which memory capacity must be contained due to physical limitations. Examples include a system for a space vehicle and a large real-time system such as a military radar system. In most commercial applications, due to the availability of fairly inexpensive memory systems, this indicator is less critical. Even so, it is useful as a measure of system size and progress. A variant of this indicator, with input/output (I/O) channel access and CPU utilization added, is often used to provide additional information (Figure 6-6).

I/O channel utilization is tracked in terms of the frequency with which it is accessed per unit time or transaction. CPU utilization can be tracked as a percentage of total CPU or cycle time. Each provides information similar to that obtained

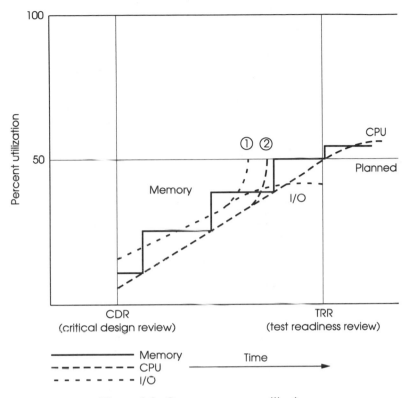

Figure 6-6 Computer resource utilization

through the memory utilization indicator. A combination of the three indicators can provide additional information. For example, if all three are acting in concert with projections, the project is probably on schedule. If all are rising too slowly, the project is probably behind schedule, or if all three rise suddenly, the project may be in serious trouble. If one of the three does not track the projection (for example, the frequency of I/O accessing rapidly increases—see 1 in Figure 6-6) while the other two track according to their predicted courses, the design of the system may be flawed. The system could be I/O bound—hard to get data in and out of it. If CPU time rises while the other two remain fairly predictable (see 2 in Figure 6-6), the system might be CPU bound. In other words, the program design is overly complex, requiring an inordinate amount of processing.

6.4.6.2 *Problem Reports* This indicator, shown in Figure 6-7, is probably the oldest in software engineering practice. It tracks both open problems and the closure of problems against time. Two indications must be considered: the open-problem trend curve and the number of problems relative to total source lines of code.

Problems are anomalies detected during the development process (that is, during requirements analysis, design, code implementation, testing, documentation

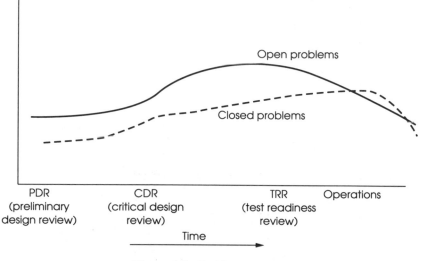

Figure 6-7   Problem reports

preparation, and so on). A problem is different from a failure. A failure is a defect discovered during operation of the code — during testing or operational use. Failure measurement is utilized to assess product reliability. To clarify, the following terms are defined.

- *Problem.*   An anomaly discovered during the development of the system. A problem could involve a statement about requirements, a design inadequacy, or an actual fault in the software.
- *Failure.*   Any event in the software operation that departs from the intended operation [Musa, 1989].
- *Fault.*   A defect in the computer software that causes a failure [Musa, 1989].
- *Failure intensity.*   The number of failures occurring in a given time period [Musa, 1989].
- *Software reliability.*   An assessment of software performance based on the fault density (in terms of faults per thousand lines of code) measured during operation. The fault density measured during the testing program, for example, might be 1.1 faults per thousand lines of code. Statistical modeling may be used to predict fault densities and therefore software reliability. Such predictions can be used to set expectations with which actual measures can be compared.

Measuring the number of faults discovered during testing produces a metric commonly termed fault, failure, or defect density. This measure is used to assess the reliability of the product. Software reliability is a more exact discipline than problem reporting.

Problem reporting is a necessary management function for maintaining control over the development process. The problem-reporting indicator supports this management function. Traditionally, problem-tracking would begin at the start of testing. However, in modern practice, problems are tracked from early in the development (when initial progress reviews are conducted). Problems normally rise gradually as component integration begins and the testing program becomes more active. The shape of the open-problem curve should be a normal bell shape as shown in Figure 6-7. The closure rate should correspond but lag behind the problem curve. This reflects the amount of time necessary to resolve or correct problems. If the project is going smoothly, the number of problems will taper off as testing draws to a close.

Problems have to be managed according to the seriousness of their impact. Some problems have little impact on the development and can be given low priority. These problems may not be fixed until later in the project. For example, a problem that concerns the implementation of a graphic format, but that does not affect the operation, may be left open or referred to a later release of the system. Other problems may need to be corrected on a more timely basis. These may require special attention. If the manager finds that a key problem is not being corrected, a major problem may exist in the effort. The indicator can be modified to track critical problems and their closure.

The problem-reporting trend normally rises as testing begins. As testing nears completion and the product is evaluated for operation, the trend should be downward. If it is not, the product is not ready for operation and additional engineering and testing are warranted. Similarly, if the closure rate drops, there is a problem with correcting or resolving problems. This could be due to resource deficiencies or technical obstacles.

The problem-reporting indicator helps the manager gauge product readiness. The ability to make this assessment is acquired through experience with similar types of developments. An appreciably lower number of problems than expected does not necessarily imply that the product is of high quality. The testing program may have been inadequate. If the peak of the bell curve is appreciably flat, testing has not been thorough.

6.4.6.3 *Software Size*
Tracking software size (based on total lines of code) is a simple way of checking development progress (Figure 6-8). If the number of lines rises above the projected level early in the coding phase, the system may have been underestimated. If the number of lines tracks below the projection, slippage may occur, especially if seller personnel resources have rapidly increased. If the number of lines rises late in the development, that is, close to the beginning of system testing, there could be difficulties in implementing the design. The number of lines rising dramatically during system-level testing (see 1 in Figure 6-8) portends serious development problems. Every new line of code represents new work that requires resource expenditure over and above that originally projected.

In modern software development practice, tracking lines of code alone is not sufficient. There is a famous story in software development practice of a project that was assessed as 90 percent complete. This was based on 90 percent of the code

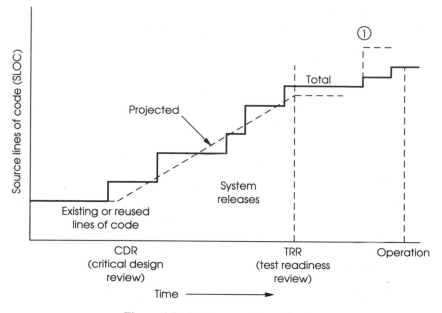

Figure 6-8 Total source lines of code

having been completed. Several months later, and after considerable additional resource expenditure, the prognosis was the same while code completion was still at 90 percent. Obviously, the degree of code completion alone is a poor indicator of actual progress.

Another method for gauging progress is to track the total number of software units as shown in Figure 6-9. The technique is to track total units against the projected number of units. If the number of actual units rises rapidly as the project progresses, the design may have been deficient. Such a rise is of particular concern if it occurs after critical design review, when the number of units should have been fixed. This indicator is useful when combined with the lines of code indicator. For example, if the total number of units is rising, but the number of lines remains fairly flat, the design might be deficient. An increasing number of lines with a stable number of units might suggest that the cost projection was inaccurate. Most cost estimation models are based on total lines of code. Therefore, if the estimate of the number of lines is too low, then the cost too will be underestimated.

An additional dimension of the software-size indicator involves requested changes to the system (engineering change proposals, or ECPs). A seller requesting an inordinate number of changes, or a system requiring so many changes, indicates that project requirements are not stable or that the design is incorrect. The requirements specification may be incomplete or the design may be unable to accommodate all of the requirements. What constitutes an inordinate number of changes will differ for each project. An upper limit of 5 to 10 percent of overall development cost can be used as a rule of thumb. That is, if the resources necessary to implement the requested changes approach 10 percent of projected development

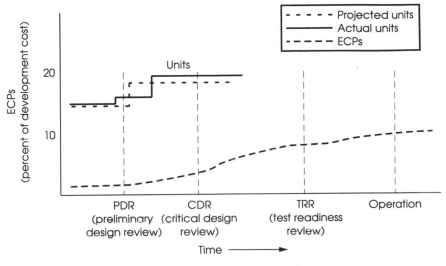

Figure 6-9 Software size—units

resources, and the project is not near completion, there is probably a problem with requirements.

6.4.6.4 Personnel Stability This indicator tracks the total number of people assigned to the project by the seller (Figure 6-10). Actual personnel levels might rise above projected levels early in the project. This could suggest that the seller

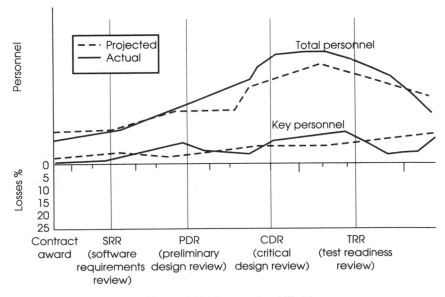

Figure 6-10 Personnel stability

is not well organized or does not have the right kind of resources available and is substituting quantity for quality. If personnel resources increase after coding begins, there are usually difficulties in the programming area. One variant of this indicator is to track key personnel rather than, or along with, total personnel. Key personnel changes are usually strong indicators of potential problems. If key personnel numbers rise early in the effort, the seller is usually having great difficulty in requirements analysis or preliminary design. If key personnel resources decrease early in the project, problems in the later phases may develop.

It is useful to track personnel stability by comparison with the normal attrition rate for contractor personnel. This is assessed periodically as shown in Figure 6-10. The number of people departing is measured as a percentage of total personnel on the project. Only unexpected departures are counted—not normal rotation of personnel due to task phasing. A high turnover rate could be disruptive but not reflected in resource expenditure reports. Most contractors try to stay at 2 to 3 percent attrition. If the rate exceeds 5 percent, the buyer should seek an explanation. The impact on the project due to such losses should be examined.

6.4.6.5 Development Progress This indicator supplements the top-level milestone schedules. It tracks key implementation activities—preliminary and detailed design and early integration. At the successful conclusion of these activities, the product should be ready for system-level test and integration. Figure 6-11 tracks the development by gauging the progress of major components or configu-

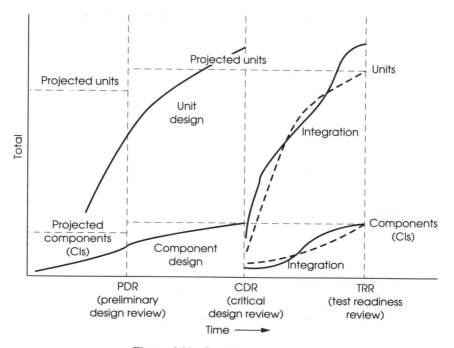

Figure 6-11 Development progress

ration items (CIs) and the total number of units. For example, units are tracked through design and then through coding and integration where they form higher-level components.

If the progress of unit and component design is not keeping up with the projections, it may not be possible to successfully complete the preliminary design review or the critical design review. If units and components are not being successfully integrated according to the projections, formal testing will slip. Thus, schedule slippage can be discovered before major milestones occur.

6.4.6.6 *Incremental Release*   Releases are versions of the software produced at various times throughout the development. Releases are produced for specific purposes, such as to provide a baseline for testing or to provide a check on development progress. Each release is controlled so that the integrity of the product at that point is maintained. Changes to the product are usually held and applied to a subsequent release. Releases are produced throughout the life cycle of the product. Each release is a new version of the software. It includes corrections to earlier versions as well as added capabilities. The incremental-release indicator is a measure of the contents of each release.

Figure 6-12 shows release contents, measured by the number of units contained in each. In the development process, the number of units in successive releases should gradually increase, approaching the total number as the development reaches system-level testing. A release that contains fewer units than an earlier release may suggest a technical problem. For example, in Figure 6-12, release 2A represents a potential problem in the development effort. By reviewing the status of any missing units, the problem area may be identified. It is useful to couple this indicator with the lines of code indicator. If the number of units is rising with each release but the number of lines of code is flat, a problem exists.

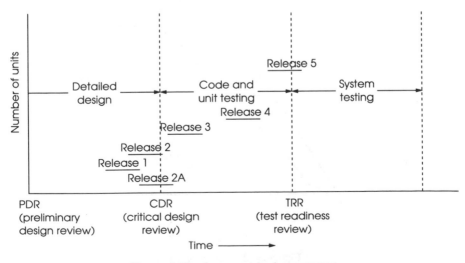

Figure 6-12   Incremental release content

6.4.6.7 Test Progress   This indicator measures testing progress and is based on tests scheduled and successfully conducted. Management must decide when this tracking should begin. Testing begins with informal unit testing as the individual components of the system are coded and checked by the development programmer. During this embryonic period, development is dynamic and tracking testing progress may not be warranted or practical. Tracking test progress becomes feasible when the units are starting to come together, namely, in the early stages of software integration.

The indicator tracks planned or scheduled tests, tests that have been completed, and tests that have been termed successful (Figure 6-13). The figure shows a normal pattern for these curves relative to specific milestone points of the development schedule. If the rate of tests passed relative to tests conducted shows a downward trend, the product may not be coming together as planned. It is useful to compare this indicator with the problem-report indicator. If the number of successful tests conducted is tracking according to the projection while the expected number of problem reports is less than expected, more rigorous testing may be in order. Conversely, if the number of problem reports is excessive even when success is indicated, more testing may be warranted.

6.4.6.8 Documentation   This indicator tracks the progress of documentation against the schedule of documents for the project. The indicator provides a method for tracking documentation that has passed inspection, normally by the quality assurance function. It tracks the three general categories of documentation: product, process, and support (Figure 6-14). If the first category, product documentation, falls behind schedule, it is an indication of early trouble in requirements analysis or

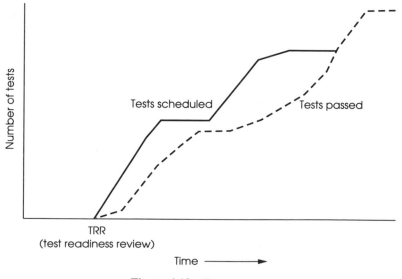

Figure 6-13   Test progress

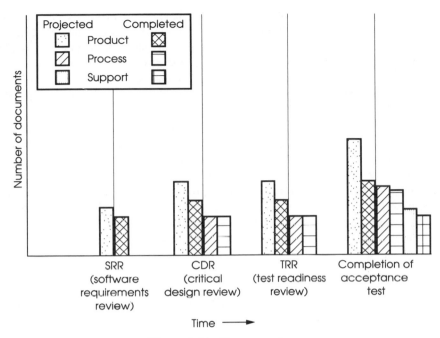

Figure 6-14   Documentation

TABLE 6-2   Management Indicator Impacts

Indicator	Quality	Schedule	Cost	Performance
Memory utilization	—	S	S	P
Computer resource utilization	—	S	S	P
Problem reports	P	S	—	S
Software size (lines of code)	—	P	S	S
Software size (units)	—	P	S	S
Personnel stability	—	P	—	S
Development progress	—	P	—	S
Incremental release	—	P	—	S
Test progress	S	P	—	S
Documentation	P	S	—	—

P = Primary impact
S = Secondary impact

design. If process documentation falls behind, the problem may not be immediately evident but will manifest itself later in development. For example, if testing documentation is inadequate, the entire testing program is suspect and the product cannot be successfully qualified. However, this might not normally be evident until well into formal testing. If support documentation falls behind schedule or is inadequate, the product may not be able to be properly used or supported. (See Section 2.3.1 for definitions of the categories of documentation.)

There are a number of possible indicators from which to choose. Some of them track similar information and similar indications or conclusions can be inferred. The selection of a set for a particular project should be based on the objectives of the project and the importance of the development balanced against the resources required for the collection and reporting process. It is unlikely, even on large, complex projects, that the entire set is used. Table 6-2 shows the relation of these indicators to quality, performance, schedule, and cost. Where no impact is indicated (marked by —) it means merely that the impact in the other areas is more prominent.

6.5   SELECTION AND USE OF ENGINEERING SUPPORT CONTRACTORS

The use of supplemental support contractors is common practice in software acquisition. Typically, support is mustered when the buyer lacks adequate resources or specialized expertise.

The seller too may enlist outside support. In many cases the seller uses or employs third-party resources to supplement the development team for tasks ranging from engineering to program management and control. Software acquisition has become so complex that even large organizations may not have all the resources necessary for a specific project. In considering support it is useful to differentiate between development tasks that may be subcontracted to third party suppliers and the support tasks discussed here. The principal distinction is that support contracts or efforts are undertaken normally to supplement, rather than supplant, management or engineering resources of the buyer or seller.

There are three basic categories of support contractors: services contractors, system engineering and technical assistance (SETA) contractors, and independent verification and validation (IV&V) contractors.

1. A services contractor typically provides "soft" services of a wide variety. From a software standpoint, these include general data-processing services such as maintenance of software and operation of data-processing facilities. Perhaps the most common characteristic of services contractors is that they are not usually involved directly in engineering development. The usual motivation for hiring a services contractor is personnel shortage.

2. A system engineering and technical assistance (SETA) contractor is practically synonymous with a services contractor. The distinction is that a SETA contractor is more likely to be involved in engineering tasks. The term SETA is used within certain customer environments, notably agencies of the fed-

eral government. (It sometimes appears as SEDA for system engineering and development assistance.) Services could range from planning the project or conducting independent testing of the product to providing specialized management functions such as program control (for example, scheduling, cost analysis, technical performance measurement, configuration management) and quality assurance. The primary motivation for hiring a SETA contractor is to acquire skilled personnel not available to the buyer or the seller.

3. An IV&V contractor, or effort, provides a specific form of support based on a well-defined discipline. The IV&V contractor performs the functions of verification (in-depth or technical assessment of the software development process) and validation (assessment of whether the developed system performs all intended mission functions). IV&V is a special topic discussed in detail in Section 6.6.

These distinctions are not critical because the objective of using support contractors is to provide resources that supplement the organization's management and engineering effort. Thus, need is the driving force. Once the need is identified, appropriate services from a third-party supplier can be obtained.

The areas considered for support are broad and depend on specific organizational and project needs. Support contractors have been employed in several capacities:

- Supplementing the engineering force of the buyer, and less often, the seller.
- Providing special expertise to the seller such as database engineering, knowledge-base engineering, and communications.
- Independent testing of the product.
- Management support functions such as quality assurance and program control.
- Off-loading non-critical functions so that a limited work force can concentrate on the challenges at hand.

6.5.1 Identifying the Need

During the planning phases, the buyer should estimate necessary resources and identify specialized areas of concern or risk that might indicate the need for a support contract. The following general areas should be considered:

1. *Technical risk.* Areas of high risk may warrant special expertise to support management of the effort. These areas include database management systems, knowledge-base systems, systems analysis, requirements analysis, and communications.
2. *Independent testing.* The development may have areas of high risk that justify independent testing. The support contractor's testing efforts may not be different from those of the developer, at least not in practice, but the perspective of the tester is more objective. As indicated earlier, the developer's motivation is to demonstrate that the system works; the independent tester is trying to find out if and under what conditions it does not work.

3. *Management support.*   This is a variant of (1), except that the concentration is on management support functions such as program control (a function that provides support for administering control of the overall project), quality assurance, documentation preparation, and training preparation. Incidentally, the issue of contracting out the quality assurance function is contentious. Many managers believe that this function should be integral to the seller organization.

4. *Integration.*   Integration is a function employed to manage the interfaces between separate efforts. This function is required when there are different development projects, perhaps under different developers, for systems that have to interface with one another. Integration includes both engineering and management functions. An example of an engineering integration function is defining and controlling the merging of subsystems that were developed by multiple development efforts. An example of a management integration function is providing configuration control of the interfaces across these subsystems.

6.5.2   Defining the Support Environment

It is extremely important that the role of the support supplier be well defined. The support supplier may have to interface with the buyer, the seller, and the various suppliers employed on the project. Naturally, the extent of such interactions depends on the nature of the effort. If the support supplier is utilized in the early planning phases of the project, for example, to prepare planning documentation, then interaction with other suppliers may be minimal and guidance to the seller not required. If, however, the support supplier is involved in a function such as integration management, the conditions of that involvement have to be carefully defined in order for the effort to be conducted in a productive and non-confrontational manner.

Contracts with both the seller and the support supplier should contain language that defines the role of the support contractor and the conditions governing support contractor involvement. For example, if the support contractor must have access to documentation being developed by the seller, that requirement should be included in the seller's contract agreement with the buyer. The agreements should specify both the documentation the support contractor will have access to and the time it will be made available. If the support contractor will attend meetings at the seller facility, that provision should be included in the seller's contract agreement so they have access to the facility.

The most prevalent problem in these types of arrangements involves a seller who wishes to protect proprietary information. A seller may have no objection to making this information available to the buyer, but may object to sharing it with a supplier who might be viewed as a competitor. The best way to avoid this situation is to employ a support contractor that does not have a market profile that is similar to that of the seller organization.

6.6 THE ROLE AND SELECTION OF IV&V CONTRACTORS

Another mechanism utilized for project assessment is independent verification and validation (IV&V). This discipline has commonly been misused. It has been used as a crutch to apply additional engineering resources to the contract in the manner of a SETA arrangement.

IV&V began in the early 1960s with the development by the United Sates Air Force of early ballistic missile systems. A high degree of confidence was required to assure that these critical systems performed reliably as a part of the U.S. nuclear deterrent force. Because software development was in its infancy and development and testing techniques rudimentary, this independent assessment technique evolved. In its original application, an outside contractor was hired to provide an independent assessment of the software development for the flight vehicles and to certify the software for operational use. Since that time, IV&V has gained in popularity as an aid to development of software on critical DOD programs and in other market areas as well.

6.6.1 Definition

The definition of IV&V has not changed appreciably over the past twenty years. Independent verification and validation is defined as:

> an in depth independent technical assessment of the software development process and an independent determination of whether the developed system performs all intended mission functions.

The key operational word here is independent. In its most rigorous interpretation, independent implies that the IV&V function is totally unrelated to the contractor employed to develop the software. Thus, a separate division of the same company could not be employed to perform this function. On the surface, the different functions of verification and validation appear similar. The purpose of verification is to ensure that the development process is sound. Verification involves the following functions:

1. Evaluation of the processes of development
   - Requirements analysis
   - Design
   - Coding
   - Problem reporting
2. Evaluation of the products of development processes
   - Specifications
   - Configuration management and quality assurance plans
   - Software development plan

- Problem reports
- Code
- Algorithms

Validation ensures that the products of development meet operational requirements. Validation includes monitoring the developer's test program, and complementing it with independent tests. Validation involves the following functions:

1. Assessment of product specifications to ensure that they meet operational requirements.
2. Derivation of algorithms and code to establish benchmarks for assessing performance of the products.
3. Conduct of independent testing of the product against the project requirements (or the statement of need).

One can see that these disciplines utilize techniques employed by other functions (for example, quality assurance and testing) on the project. The operative word, again, is the independent nature of the effort.

6.6.2 Environment

IV&V is independent of, but must be coordinated with, the main contractual effort. IV&V efforts tend to try to prove that the system does not work, while the development contractor tries to prove that it does. Thus, a natural competitive environment exists. This situation, if properly controlled, should enhance rather than disrupt work toward the common goal of delivering a system that meets user requirements.

Without a healthy project environment, the IV&V effort could be hampered by infighting among the participants, especially if multiple parties are involved. Withholding of information, lack of cooperation in testing and reviews, and mutual distrust will reduce the effectiveness of IV&V. In order to help avoid such problems, the contract should define carefully the role of the IV&V contractor, so the incentive is to correct problems before they propagate. The initial development contract should specify the buyer's intent to use an IV&V contractor, define the role and responsibilities of the IV&V contractor, and the objectives of the effort. The following points should be considered for inclusion in the development SOW:

- The buyer's intent to utilize an IV&V function to monitor the development effort and assess the utility of the operational products.
- The specific objectives of the IV&V effort, including, for example, identification of the specific portions of the system to which IV&V will be applied.
- The role of the IV&V contractor relative to the buyer project management team.
- The authority of the IV&V contractor, for example, in participation in reviews, access to documentation, participation in testing, and conduct of activities.

- The tasks in which the IV&V contractor will be involved, for example, testing, reviews, audits, and inspections.
- Incentives for the seller to cooperate with the IV&V contractor.

6.6.3   When to Use IV&V

As stated earlier, IV&V is used typically on projects where, due to the critical nature of the system, additional confidence that the delivered product satisfactorily meets requirements is demanded. The user expects a confidence level of almost 100 percent that the system will perform properly when used. Although impossible to provide such assurance, it is possible to establish that the probability of a major problem that would invalidate the use of the system is low or that the failure intensity of the system is acceptable. Thus, the user can be confident that the product will function properly over the system life cycle. It is impossible in current practice to predict the rate of catastrophic failure. However, the rate of failure (noncatastrophic) is predictable. To put this in the context of applying IV&V, Table 6-3 shows a range of systems to consider for IV&V application. The column headings should be read with the following in mind. The risk characteristic is the primary consideration. If the risk is low, however, high cost may justify IV&V. Thus cost should always be considered as a bottom-line discriminator.

In a manned system in which the software is critical to human safety (such as the flight control software for an airplane), IV&V is well worth considering and may even be mandatory. In a system that may be inaccessible once operational, such as a satellite, IV&V is also worth considering. A subsystem that may be critical to the overall development from a schedule standpoint is also a candidate for IV&V, especially if cost and risk are high. For a complex system, IV&V should

TABLE 6-3   Use of IV&V

Development characteristics	System Characteristics		
	High risk Low cost	Medium risk Medium cost	Low risk High cost
Manned systems	Yes	Yes	Maybe
Unmanned remote systems	Yes	Yes	Maybe
Critical to development	Yes	Maybe	No
Complex system	Maybe	Maybe	Not applicable
Data-sensitive (privacy)	Yes	Yes	No
Commercial (e.g., banking)	Maybe	No	No

be considered, but may be sacrificed depending on its cost versus overall system cost and objectives. In systems that may be critical from a data standpoint, for example, a medical system handling data used for treatment, integrity is important and IV&V worth considering. For other systems, such as a commercial banking system, the use of IV&V will depend on other factors. For example, the privacy of data is a key consideration in a banking system. Therefore, IV&V may be worthwhile.

6.6.4 Cost of IV&V

Two objections to IV&V are often raised. The first is that it costs too much. The second objection is that IV&V is unnecessary when dealing with a conscientious seller whose pride is its established development capability. These are both specious arguments. Cost, except as a bottom-line discriminator, should not impact the decision on whether to use IV&V. Where the critical nature of the effort requires the independent scrutiny of IV&V to ensure the integrity and operational utility of the system, cost is not an issue. IV&V is not used to reduce the cost of the development; it is utilized to increase the overall worth of the development.

The typical cost of an IV&V effort ranges from 10 to 30 percent of overall development cost. The IV&V costs of four projects studied (see Figure 6-15) ranged from 13 to 28 percent of development cost [Radatz, 1981]. In projects 3 and 4, where IV&V was applied across the entire development life cycle, costs ranged from 13 to 27 percent of development cost. In Figure 6-16, the life cycle cost benefit was projected based on the cost avoidance associated with correcting an error during the early development phases versus late in the life cycle. As indicated,

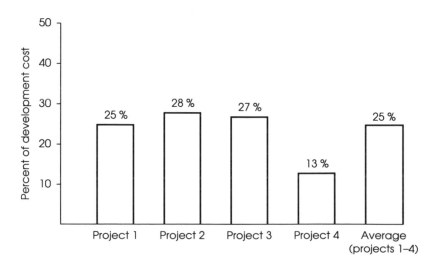

Figure 6-15   IV&V cost comparison

Source: J. Radatz, *Analysis of IV&V Data (R: SED-81319)*, San Pedro, CA: Logicon, Inc., 1981.

Project	Reqmts phase	Design phase	Coding phase	Testing phase	Total savings	Savings as % of dev. cost	Savings as % of IV and V cost
	-------- (Number of anomalies) cost savings* --------						
1	--	--	(72) $497,585	(116) $87,220	$584,805	7 %	27 %
2	--	--	(127) $877,685	(89) $66,920	$944,605	9 %	33 %
3	(10) $76,929	(42) $310,754	(60) $414,654	(27) $20,302	$822,639	29 %	106 %
4	(22) $169,244	(6) $44,393	(56) $387,010	(6) $4,511	$605,158	26 %	203 %

* Cost to fix 90 % of anomalies during testing phase and 10 % of anomalies during operational phase using Wolverton's and Finfer's Data

Figure 6-16 Life cycle benefits of IV&V

Source: J. Radatz, *Analysis of IV&V Data (R: SED-81319)*, San Pedro, CA: Logicon, Inc., 1981.

in projects 3 and 4 where IV&V was applied across the entire development process, the savings exceeded total development cost—in the long run IV&V pays for itself. The second objection, that IV&V is unnecessary because the development contractor is highly reputable and maintains an excellent development environment is defused on several points. IV&V is not undertaken to provide a crutch for the seller. If that were the case, the effort should not have been awarded to the seller to begin with. The seller should not fear the use of IV&V. Remember, the use of IV&V is not to supplement the seller's development effort. It's intent is to provide additional assurance. If such aid is necessary, the use of a supplemental engineering support supplier should be considered.

In the next chapter, Software Management—The Seller's Model, the management environment is addressed from that perspective. Many of the subjects presented here are amplified in the seller's view.

REFERENCES

[Burrill, 1980]: C. W. Burrill and Leon W. Ellsworth, *Modern Project Management*, Burrill-Ellsworth Associates, New Jersey, pp. 329–371.

[Musa, 1989]: J. D. Musa, "Tools for Measuring Software Reliability," *IEEE Spectrum*, Vol. 26, No. 2, pp. 39–42.

[Radatz, 1981]: J. W. Radatz, *Analysis of IV&V Data, (R:SED-81319)*, San Pedro, CA: Logicon, Inc.

CHAPTER 7

Software Management— The Seller's Model

The roles of buyers and sellers during an acquisition have similarities and differences. Although both sides are motivated to do a good job, each side uses different tactics to accomplish its goals. Teamwork and harmony are needed to get the job done, but discord often occurs because each side's performance is rated differently.

Buyers establish the contractual requirements and initiate the acquisition. After choosing a source, they attempt to ensure compliance with the provisions of the contract. Buyers are driven by the need for visibility and control over the project. They are tasked to monitor the effort, keep track of performance, resolve problems, provide direction, regulate changes, and integrate the effort with other efforts.

Sellers accept the requirements and direct the resources necessary to fulfill them within established costs and schedules. They establish and staff the organization needed to achieve the goals of the project and control and direct the resources to accomplish these goals. Their objective, fulfilling all of the terms and conditions of the contract, requires them to deliver an acceptable product on time and within budget. They marshall their forces accordingly.

This chapter focuses on the seller's management model. It responds to and amplifies the subjects discussed in the previous chapter and provides additional insight into these subjects from the viewpoint of the seller.

7.1 PROJECT MANAGEMENT OFFICE ROLES AND RESPONSIBILITIES

The seller establishes a program office to parallel that of the buyer. The seller's project manager is the company's single point of contact with the buyer with regard to the project. This project manager's job is to achieve contract requirements and to keep the customer happy, and he or she does this by making sure the right resources are made available to the job when they are needed. Although this sounds simple, it often is not. The project manager frequently controls a budget and not people, so he or she may have to play numerous political games to get the right resources allocated to the project. For example, establishing working space in a growing company may be more difficult than coordinating people. The project manager may have to horse-trade favors, IOUs, or money to lodge project employees in offices near each other. The project manager may also have to elevate the problem several management levels in order to get a favorable decision that he or she believes is in the best interest of the project. Resolving these problems and issues takes time and effort. It also takes a lot of perseverence.

A good project manager should be invisible to the masses. The majority of people see the project moving ahead seemingly of its own momentum. They know that a project is doing well when the project is making progress, when people are beaming over their accomplishments, and when positive comments are being made.

The roles and responsibilities of the project office and project manager vary as a function of the seller's organization. There are three basic organizations a firm can use to accomplish major projects: matrix, project, or hybrid. Two of these formats are illustrated in Figure 7-1.

In a matrix organization, the project manager acts as the intermediary between the seller and the buyer project manager. Employees' professional skills are nurtured and developed by the functional departments. The project manager controls funding and uses it to bring the needed skills to the job at the appropriate time. Technical personnel get to take their expertise from one project to another and key technical resources can be shared among projects. Competition among projects for personnel resources keeps the organization lean and mean.

The project manager's role in a matrix organization is to identify what has to be done, when, and at what cost. The functional organizations then tell the project office who will do the work and how it will be done as they negotiate schedules and budgets. The project office then monitors the effort and keeps track of progress. The project manager keeps tabs on resource expenditures and tries to direct the staff toward achieving the goals set by the customer.

The problem with matrix organizations is that there are too many bosses. A performer can work for a functional department and two or three project managers at the same time. Accountability for performance and responsibility for schedules are often insufficient because each boss assumes authority, but none of the employees takes responsibility.

In a project organization, all of the needed resources are dedicated to and controlled by a single person, the project manager. The project manager owns the people and makes the decisions on how they are deployed. As he or she fights for the right people for the organization, the inherent advantages and disadvantages of the matrix approach are reversed. Flexibility to provide interesting and varied work assignments is sacrificed for a single focus on finishing the job.

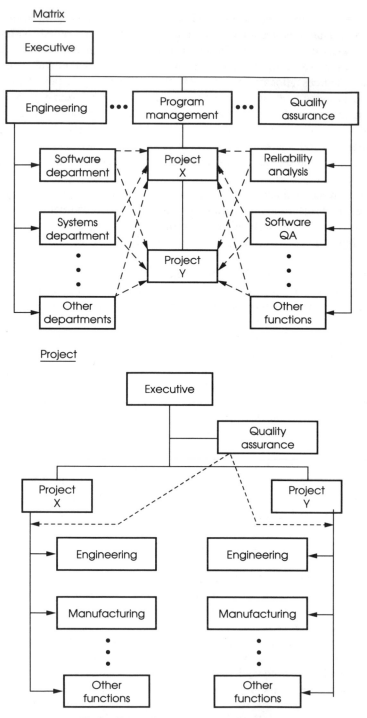

Figure 7-1   Organizational approaches

Neither the matrix nor the project organization is perfect, so most sellers use something in between the two. They may organize functionally, so that projects report at any level of the organization. Independent of how they organize, however, each places a single individual in charge of completing the project. The project manager's sole job is to deliver an acceptable product to the customer on time and within budget. In order to accomplish this, the project manager performs the following tasks:

1. *Interface management.* Project managers are the intermediaries between internal and external organizations. They are given authority commensurate with their responsibilities so that they can get the job done. They coordinate these organizations (such as engineering and product assurance) to ensure that requirements are defined, plans are baselined, expectations are set, resources are available when needed, performance is satisfactory, and problems that occur are settled in a timely manner. They tap the internal resources of the firm to bring in experts that are needed to handle contract negotiations, legal issues, and other problems at the time they are needed.

2. *Project management.* Project managers are also responsible for overall planning and control of the work. They take the requirements and use a work breakdown structure to facilitate the development of an acceptable work plan. They ensure that all contractual requirements are addressed by this work structure and then work with the performer organizations to establish budgets and schedules. They scope the management controls that will be used to ascertain status and to determine progress. They provide leadership and direction for the performers who are striving to achieve their tasks, and they organize the project to get the most out of the staff at their disposal. They encourage communications and teamwork as they facilitate integration of the efforts of all participants in the project. Good project managers have a passion for quality and an ability to get the most out of people. They understand the need for documentation and reviews and try to provide customers with enough information to make them comfortable that the project is being adequately managed.

3. *Resource management.* Project managers also focus attention on managing the following resources, which are allocated during the early phases of the project: people, time, money, equipment, facilities, materials, information, and technology. They perform make/buy analyses and bring in outside resources that are warranted. They coordinate procurements, make sure that delivery does not pose any risks, and maintain a management reserve for contingencies that may arise. They perform periodic cost-to-complete and schedule-to-complete plans so that resource expenditure plans are up to date.

4. *Change management.* Project managers also guard against unwarranted change. They are members of the Configuration Control Board (CCB), in which they assist in assessing the impact of changes on the approved baselines. They negotiate with the buyer on the way these changes affect

the scope of the contract and ensure that configuration management is being soundly implemented. They understand that unwarranted changes can rapidly destroy a project, especially if the schedule is aggressive and the budget is tight. They also realize that changes represent a potential source of additional resources if out-of-scope charges are approved.

5. *Risk management.*   Project managers handle risk by building options in their plans. They establish controls that help them identify and prioritize risks and then develop alternative risk management strategies. By instituting risk abatement programs, project managers try to conquer risks before the risks conquer them.

It is clear that project managers have numerous management responsibilities. They are the architects of project work and the monitors of its accomplishment, but they must rely on the technical people to get the job done. Trust, teamwork, and planning are the keys to success in any project, independent of organizational approach, because motivated people can overcome nearly any problem when structure, control, motivation, and leadership are present.

7.2   PLANNING AND CONTROL—AN ITERATIVE PROCESS

During the proposal stage, the seller's proposal manager develops a "win" strategy that responds to the buyer's technical and contract requirements outlined in the solicitation document. He or she develops a technical approach for doing the job and a top-level management plan aimed at realizing schedule and cost goals. The proposal manager either develops or uses a set customer work breakdown structure (WBS) to structure the software management plan and to create resource estimates for the cost and management sides of the proposal. As the proposal is iterated and negotiations are conducted, he or she finalizes this plan.

A software project manager is assigned upon contract award. This manager's first job is to update the software development plan, the project management plan, or both plans to incorporate any changes that were made as a part of contract negotiations. He or she will have each of the involved organizations submit modifications and budget requests and then will work with each organization to negotiate schedules, budgets, deliverables, and management controls. The primary goal is the integration of the efforts of all of the performer organizations into a consolidated plan; the secondary goal is assurance that software is appropriately sized and funded at the project level. Because many projects view software as a necessary evil, accomplishment of this secondary goal is sometimes a challenge. Software project managers must spend a great deal of time educating their bosses and peers about software so that they can win the battle of the budget. Unfortunately, many nonsoftware managers are ignorant of the technology and afraid of software. This fear factor can make software project managers' jobs difficult as they fight for people, space, facilities, equipment, time, and money.

The resulting plan serves as an initial roadmap through the project. It allows anyone who views it to ascertain what the work is, who is going to do it, and when it is going to get done. The plan helps the project manager do his job by accomplishing the following five objectives:

1. It communicates the work and expectations to those doing it.
2. It establishes a baseline for control over the work-in-process by establishing intermediate goals and milestones.
3. It focuses the efforts of the team toward accomplishment of project-related objectives.
4. It integrates the budgets and schedules so that the impact of slippages can readily be determined.
5. It permits the project manager to exercise control over the many obstacles that can impede satisfactory delivery to the customer.

An outline for a software project management plan developed by the IEEE [IEEE, 1987] is illustrated in Table 7-1. Each of its elements is important because each has an impact on the manner in which the project is managed. Each element must be integrated within the master project plan, especially if a system consisting of both hardware and software is being delivered.

The internal management systems used to put the plan into action within most seller organizations usually revolve around some form of internal contract between the program office and the performer organizations. For each meaningful work package, a budget and schedule are established, based upon the work negotiated between the two groups. The program office establishes the requirements, and the performer organization determines how the work package will be accomplished and who will perform it. In a matrix organization, the contracts are arranged between organizations and are formally documented using a work authorization and delegation system. In a project organization, the contracts are set between individuals, and less formal documentation is used.

The primary planning tool used by the software project manager is the work breakdown structure (WBS) (see Section 3.3). The WBS decomposes the work hierarchically into its component parts so that short, well-defined tasks that will culminate in deliverable products may be defined at each level of the decomposition. Assumptions can be made and risks identified as each task is defined in the accompanying WBS Dictionary. The more detail included within the structure, the better the plan.

Once the WBS has been defined, each of the tasks identified can be scheduled and resources estimated. Tasks can then be interrelated using precedent networks or PERT (program evaluation and review technique), so that the critical path through the schedule network can be identified. Schedules can then be adjusted so that staff levels can be defined and allocated.

The plan, then, serves as the primary basis of control after the project commences. Actual results are periodically compared to estimates so that per-

TABLE 7-1   Software Project Management Plan Outline

Title page

Revision sheet

Preface

Table of contents

List of figures

List of tables

1. Introduction

    1.1   Project overview
    1.2   Project deliverables
    1.3   Evolution of the plan
    1.4   Reference materials
    1.5   Definitions and acronyms

2. Project organization

    2.1   Process model
    2.2   Organizational structure
    2.3   Organizational boundaries and interfaces
    2.4   Project responsibilities

3. Managerial process

    3.1   Management objectives and priorities
    3.2   Assumptions, dependencies, and constraints
    3.3   Risk management
    3.4   Monitoring and controlling mechanisms
    3.5   Staffing plan

4. Technical process

    4.1   Methods, tools, and techniques
    4.2   Software documentation
    4.3   Project support functions

5. Work packages, schedule, and budget

    5.1   Work packages
    5.2   Dependencies
    5.3   Resource requirements
    5.4   Budget and resource allocation
    5.5   Schedule

Additional components

Index

Appendices

This table has been reproduced from *ANSI/IEEE Std 1058.1-1987, IEEE Standard for Software Project Plans*, copyright © 1988 by the Institute of Electrical and Electronic Engineers, Inc., with permission of the IEEE Standards Department.

formance can be assessed according to the plan. Weekly schedule assessment reviews are held to check milestones and deliverables. The rate at which activities occur is analyzed to determine whether schedule variances exist. As unanticipated events occur that require reprogramming of funds and people, reserve resources are allocated. (A detailed discussion of the financial controls used within the seller organization is provided in Chapter 9.) The technical controls employed are similar to those used by the buyer organization. The systems and procedures invoked for problem reporting, configuration management, independent testing, and quality assurance provide indicators for the development process and the products.

Needless to say, planning and control are necessarily cooperative and iterative. As the project progresses, more details become evident, as unanticipated problems and technical risks are uncovered. Software project managers deal with these by replanning and allocating resources. They use the feedback and insight that is provided through project controls to develop more accurate estimates of job completion and then replan the work to take advantage of their better understanding. Plans are really "living documents." They take present knowledge of the project and use it to determine what is required to finish the job. The more that the plan is iterated, the closer it comes to reflecting reality; and the more it reflects reality, the more valuable it becomes.

Good software managers know that planning is one of the most important things that they can do on the project. They take time to develop their plans. When they plan, they say what they mean and mean what they say. Their plans always look to the future as they try to answer the difficult questions: "What will it take to finish this job" and "How will I avoid a recurrence of the problems?"

These software managers also keep their plans current so that the plans can be used as a control device as the project progresses. They understand the repetitive nature of planning and use feedback to keep their plans up to date. They identify contingencies and risks and plan to address them. They do everything they can to predict the future with the understanding that the future is indeed unpredictable.

Good software managers understand the need to make their plans consistent with higher-level plans. They integrate their plans with the others and know how to "work" the system to their benefit.

7.3 ORGANIZATION AND STAFFING REALITIES

Why is planning and controlling a software project so difficult in the early phases of development? The answer is simple: "You don't have time to do it and you don't have time not to do it." Once the project has been awarded, the most pressing problem is getting the people on board and space for them. Managers always fear that they're behind in staffing, and the job always seems to take more time than a manager has available. Recruiting the key people needed to do the job takes time, effort, and perseverance. Keeping them is an even more difficult job. Because the organization is dynamic in the early stages of the project, staffing problems tend to be magnified. Nobody seems to know who is responsible for anything as new people join the ranks daily and fill roles whose responsibilities are somewhat undefined. Getting things accomplished in such an environment seems to take forever.

Good software managers understand these start-up problems and assume as much authority as they need to get the job done. Because it is often easier to ask forgiveness than permission, especially in large organizations, good managers take the bull by the horns and charge ahead, hiring people when they need them, and then bearing the consequences.

Recruiting talented personnel is not a problem for good software managers. The major problem these managers face is the competition with other project managers, who do not want to let key personnel move to other projects. Most of these managers will cooperate with one another, however, when the desires of their subordinates are made known. Good software managers start recruiting the day they start thinking about initiating the project. Because recruiting key people takes so long, these managers will use the organization's informal network to find out if the people they have worked with before are interested in a new challenge. Even before they have planned the job, they know what talents they need in their workers. They also realize that to calibrate, build trust, foster teamwork, and learn to communicate with talented people takes time and hard work. So they prefer to recruit people with whom they have worked in the past. This allows managers to minimize the time it takes to develop a good working rapport.

Good software managers know that about 30 percent of the staff is responsible for over 70 percent of the productivity of their organization. They also know that about 10 percent of the staff is indispensable to 90 percent of the projects. Competition for these key people is keen, so managers may have to use the best available people and build them into a potent workforce. Software managers must resist the temptation to work with the readily available marginal performers and should instead continue looking for people with promise. Yet with such heavy demand for the few key performers, they may have to resort to advising and coaching average workers with internal or outside consultants. Teams must be built so that peer pressures can be applied to mold these avergage performers into a potent workforce.

The people that good software managers recruit must have good technical, social, and communications skills. Managers look for team players who will fit into the organization. They search for people who know how to listen, write, and communicate well with others: They value these nontechnical skills as highly as the workers' ability to perform. These managers realize that one bad worker can be a disruptive force and so will avoid hiring even a talented worker who seems to have a bad attitude. They look for people who can work together and get along with one another.

Good software managers protect their people from the many distractions that plague large organizations. They buffer and protect their people from the organizational politics that are so disruptive to productivity and try to keep their people focused on the project. They encourage workers not to get involved in distracting outside activities (a situation known as fragmentation). These managers understand the need to reduce the typical administrative burdens their employees face and try to help their workers to perform these required services.

People and organizations change throughout the project's life, so good software managers learn to structure their work to reduce the impact of changes on their ability to perform. They learn patience, especially with people who impede accomplishment of the job. After all, that person may soon be promoted and be replaced with a new and more friendly employee. They try to take advantage of the change instead of becoming frustrated by it.

Large organizations hinder effective vertical and horizontal communications. Good software managers will attempt to overcome these barriers: They may participate in software councils to learn from their peers and brief both their bosses and their subordinates to keep them informed. They will also form peer working groups to address problems that transcend horizontal organizational boundaries.

7.4 PROVIDING LEADERSHIP AND DIRECTION

Even with good plans and controls, projects often falter and fail. One major cause of this is the inadequate handling of people on the project by the seller organization. Politics and production dominate, rather than a people-oriented attitude. People may believe that their efforts are not appreciated and feel exploited and used. As a result, they lose motivation and stop trying to do their best.

Good software managers know that people make the project succeed or fail. They foster teamwork and employ a participatory approach to management; and recognizing that people have individual needs, they try to ensure satisfaction. They lead by example with a people-oriented and action-based leadership style. Good managers demonstrate trust in their employees with their actions.

Building synergistic teams into potent forces is a goal of competent software managers. These leaders try to provide rewards that encourage both individual and team performance so that innovation is encouraged and necessary conformance accepted. They provide coaching as the team is forming and structure after it is functioning so that people can do their jobs more effectively. They guide and coach the team leaders, providing encouragement and advice as the project unfolds.

People need motivation to do the best job that they can. They need realistic expectations and help to accomplish their goals. This is the job of a capable software manager. Good managers understand that interesting work, growth, recognition, achievement, responsibility, advancement, and satisfying interpersonal relations are motivators for most people, and they strive to provide these motivators on the job. They must create an electric atmosphere in which people are excited because their work is important to themselves, to their peers, and to the project. They must genuinely care and communicate that care with tact and discretion.

Software managers who are good leaders and delegators understand the need for people to participate in problem solving and goal setting. Giving their people responsibility and providing them with the direction they need to progress is important to these managers. They mediate conflicts and help employees understand the need for rules and the consequences of violations. They also enable their people to check on their own performance and give needed counsel and advice. Good managers provide their people with opportunities to pursue advancement and support their growth when new job opportunities present themselves. They recognize achievements and accomplishments and help people learn from their failures. Helping their people to grow and improve is rewarded when these employees hit the top. Software managers want their peole to be successful, so they do everything possible to place them in a win-win situation.

Good software managers reward competence and incompetence equally. They may be strict, but are fair in all of their dealings with their subordinates. They level with their staff, providing feedback when they do things right as well as when they do things wrong. They listen and admit their own mistakes. These managers are loyal to their people and proud of their accomplishments. As a result, their people are loyal to the managers and will do whatever is asked even when they may doubt the results.

7.5 PERFORMANCE MEASUREMENT AND REPORTING

One key to success in software acquisition is to allow customer visibility in the project: The customer should know the status of the project at any given time. Project managers must work with customers to solve problems. They need to seek customers' advice and counsel and be honest and truthful. Customers should know that these managers need their help. Building trust makes resources on both sides available when needed to develop a workable solution. Project managers must understand that both the developer and the customer have similar objectives—developing a system that meets the user's requirements within the designated time frame.

Software projects don't get into trouble all at once; instead, they get into trouble a little bit at a time. Good software managers believe the management indicators and use them to pinpoint problems in order to solve problems in a timely manner. They don't wait and let things get out of hand, but act, resisting temptations to both overreact and underreact.

Good software managers know that most people want to treat the symptoms of the problems and not their root causes. For example, schedule slippages may occur because there isn't enough time allocated to do the job. These managers try to isolate the causes and seek remedies for them, and they educate those responsible about the effects of their actions. They are aggressive in whatever they do, but avoid promising to do too much. They are realists who understand that action precedes solution.

The need to measure, control, and report progress to management and customers is clear to competent software managers. They are believers in metrics and rely on them to provide insight into quality as well as progress. They use management indicators to provide evidence for their claims of quality and progress, both positive and negative. If problems exist, they report them and explain what they are doing about them. If they need help, they ask for it. Finally, if problems are happening outside of their control, they try to find out who has control and work with them to remedy the situation.

Control is vital to good software managers. Managers need to know where they are in the project and what it will take to deliver the product. They understand their problems and have plans to address them and are not afraid to admit that they have troubles or have made mistakes.

Higher-level managers' thirst for information can often engulf software managers in data. These managers must help their bosses and their customers understand what data they need and what the costs are. As a consequence, much of the data they generate must be reduced and summarized in order to communicate its meaning to management. The software manager knows the data must be related to industry norms to make sense. For example, productivity of 140 SLOCs/PM (source lines of code/person month) might be related to the same application's domain norm of 100 SLOCs/PM to convey the message that project personnel are very productive. Software managers also know that a hard number like a productivity figure may be abused. They are therefore extremely careful to qualify their metrics as they report them to management.

The pressures to provide increasingly more information, especially late in the project when schedules begin to slip, must be resisted. Able managers understand that generation of data takes time and effort and takes key staff away from the project when they are most needed. They also understand that the quality of data counts, not its volume. Of course, they must provide what is required by the contract and their own management systems, but they avoid providing meaningless paper generated to satisfy those who are looking to build a "Pearl Harbor file" should the project fail.

7.6   REVIEWS AND AUDITS

The software manager identifies the reviews and audits to be held in the software project management plan. The reviews and audits selected respond to their customer's requirements and the seller's internal needs to manage the work-in-process. Each takes long hours and hard work, so each must have proper planning. Reviews and audits are of the following five types:

1. customer reviews and audits
2. quality reviews and audits
3. project reviews
4. management reviews
5. peer reviews

A review is a meeting in which technical or management material is presented. The meeting, whose purpose is to obtain feedback into the status of the project, can be formal or informal. Depending on the nature of the review, the buyer may or may not be invited to attend. An audit differs from a review because an external person is in charge of conducting the meeting. The purpose of an audit is to have an objective evaluation of the product, process, or project at strategic points during the acquisition and obtain an independent opinion. It can be conducted using internal or external auditors.

7.6.1 Customer Reviews and Audits

Customer reviews and audits are held to keep the buyer informed, to demonstrate progress, and to obtain concurrence. These reviews and audits are typically held at strategic points in the acquisition process that are fixed by contract requirements and described in the software development, in project management plans, or in both. The buyer often brings in the customer and third party suppliers such as IV&V or SETA contractors to augment the workforce and to provide an objective and independent assessment.

Typically, five customer reviews and two formal audits are held during the acquisition life cycle for software. These have been discussed before and include the following:

1. A requirements review is held to assess the completeness, consistency, technical adequacy and stability of the software's functional, performance, interface, and quality requirements.
2. An architectural design review (or preliminary design review) assesses the technical adequacy and stability of the software architecture and the test approach to be used to buy-off the software system.
3. A detailed design review is held to assess the adequacy of the design and to determine if it is stable enough to initiate coding.
4. A test readiness review is held to assess the adequacy of the testing done to date and to determine whether the software system is ready to start formal testing.
5. An end-product acceptance review assesses the adequacy of the end-product and determines whether it fulfills all of the requirements contained within the then active contract (e.g., the original contract and any changes).
6. A functional configuration audit is held to confirm that the end-product contains the required functionality.
7. A physical configuration audit confirms that all required deliverables are current and that they have been produced according to the form and content requirements of the contract.

These reviews vary in form and content depending on the size, risk, and schedule of the effort. For some quick reaction capabilities (that is, those in which speed is crucial), the buyer and seller may hold impromptu meetings that fulfill the intent of these meetings. On larger efforts in which many organizations and personnel are involved, communications is a more severe problem. Here participants may take weeks to prepare for, conduct, and recover from reviews.

Many people ask how often such meetings should be held. The answer is simple—as often as they are needed to get the job done. For example, meetings need not be frequently scheduled if operations seem to be going extremely well. If, however, unexpected problems were occurring, these meetings should be scheduled more frequently.

7.6.2 Quality Reviews and Audits

Most buyers require an independent organization to conduct reviews and audits to evaluate the quality of the seller's products and to ensure that products fulfill contract requirements. Such reviews and audits are an outgrowth of the buyer's desire for the seller to police itself regarding contractual compliance issues. Such constant self-inspection allows the buyer to concentrate resources on other matters.

Under a total quality management (TQM) approach to quality, the quality organization should teach the performers how to engineer quality into products using a process that can be certified and controlled with statistical techniques (see Section 10.3). Most people in industry agree that inspection does not guarantee quality software. As a consequence, new and innovative approaches are being used by quality organizations to engineer quality into the products during product development.

The following three types of reviews and audits are used by quality organizations whenever the costs and benefits associated with them are warranted:

1. *Quality reviews (circles).* These are meetings in which quality personnel act as facilitators for quality improvements. They can become part of a peer review in which quality personnel moderate the meeting or can be used in separate meetings in which the team gets together to make suggestions that lead to higher quality (circles).

2. *Quality audits (evaluations).* In these periodic audits, quality engineers review interim deliverables (e.g., both documentation and code) to ensure that they meet accepted standards. If the deliverables do not qualify, some form of quality deficiency report is generated that must be closed out before the item is shipped. Quality evaluations may be held as well. These audits concentrate on the technical integrity of the product and on inherent quality goals.

3. *Quality inspections.* These periodic spot assessments of the process or products determine levels of quality. Such assessments can be done manually with a review or automatically using statistical sampling methods and metrics. The major purpose of such inspections is to make sure that the processes established for quality engineering within the firm are not breaking down.

Better quality often accompanies process improvement, but the costs of conducting quality reviews and audits comes along, too. Performers must take time away from other critical tasks to prepare for these reviews and then have to resolve any discrepancies found by the reviewers before they can begin their work again. These reviews can become counterproductive when they are conducted by personnel who act as antagonists instead of teachers. Project management must guard against such situations by forcing the quality managers to use experienced professionals who understand their roles and have the necessary people skills to get the job done right the first time.

Obviously, planning is required to determine the roles of quality assurance personnel so that employee involvement during acquisition can be observed and bounded. Organization temperament is another factor that influences the selection of the quality approach employed by the project.

7.6.3 Project Reviews

Most project managers conduct periodic reviews of their projects to examine status, progress, performance, and problems. Such reviews are very useful when they get the project team members together, get them talking, get them listening, and get them focused on the issues that count. The project manager must schedule reviews when they are needed and get the right people to attend them.

The frequency and content of these project reviews vary. Normally, such reviews are held monthly, but it is not unheard of to have daily reviews when critical milestones approach and decisions must be made quickly to preserve the schedule. Scheduling of project reviews depends on getting the necessary people involved when they are needed. Scheduling too many reviews is as counterproductive as scheduling too few.

Key staff from inside the project (e.g., team leaders and lead engineers) are normally invited to attend the review. Customers and outsiders from other seller organizations are invited only when required by management or contract or when they can make a contribution. The reason for keeping attendance down is simple: effectiveness. Too many new players hinder the efficiency of meetings because each participant must be brought up to date. Time is wasted and meetings become tutorials. Remember, a review must pay for itself. Of course, sellers are also reminded to keep the buyers happy as they implement this business philosophy of limited review participation.

There may be times when sellers do not wish the buyers to attend. For example, sellers may have some specific business issue to resolve that may not involve the customer. They might want to develop a consensus opinion. In such cases the project manager may call an impromptu project review and not advise the buyer. The reverse situation is true as well. For example, the buyer may be discussing strategies for keeping the cost down and may not wish to advise the seller of his game plan prior to negotiations.

7.6.4 Management Reviews

Most sellers set up a series of internal reviews for their projects that are held to appraise management of the status of the contract and to assess and resolve potential problems of the internal organization. Depending on the firm, these reviews can take any of the following three forms:

1. *Upper management briefings.*   These are periodic briefings (normally quarterly or semiannual) conducted to keep upper management aware of what

is happening on the contract. Internal company issues (for example, availability of space and acquisition of capital equipment) are discussed at these meetings as project personnel ask senior management for their advice, help, and commitment.

2. *Steering committee reviews.* These periodic briefings are conducted to keep a group of upper managers aware of the status of the contract. Steering committees are formed when a contract crosses multiple business areas or involves a strategic direction of the firm (such as diversification or expansion). Direction is provided so that the project manager can focus on what management believes is important.

3. *Peer management reviews.* These are periodic briefings conducted to a council made up of peer project managers. Such councils identify problems and tactics that have worked to solve problems on other projects. In addition to project problem solving, such councils identify common infrastructure problems. These are disposed to upper management for resolution. For example, a committee might be formed to recommend improvements in the firm's configuration management system if several projects are having similar problems in that area.

Buyers are typically not invited to attend these management reviews. The purpose of these reviews is to involve the firm's management in the project; the buyer gains because collective wisdom is a product of the reviews. Of course, sellers' project managers have to take the brunt of any criticism and deal with internal politics. They also have to shield their workers from undue interference of their own management. Sometimes, this becomes a difficult task because others in the organization may be trying to make it seem that the project is failing.

7.6.5 Peer Reviews

The final type of review is considerably more technical than managerial. A peer review is a meeting in which design or programming team members review one another's work. Management representatives are typically not present because the review aims to get the team members themselves working together to reduce defects. Peer reviews come in the following four varieties:

1. *Walk-throughs.* In these informal reviews, the software engineer introduces members of the development team to a segment of design or code that he or she has written. The other team members ask questions and make comments about technique, style, and possible errors. The responsible software engineer then takes the advice and uses it for product improvement.

2. *Inspections.* These are formal reviews in which a moderator leads a team of software engineers through a segment of design or code. The reviewers ask questions and comment, and rework is summarized and published as part of the inspection minutes. Discovered defects are analyzed and checklists are prepared to prevent their reoccurrence. A follow-up ensures that the rework has been satisfactorily accomplished.

3. *Round-robin reviews.* In this type of review, each member of the team writes a position paper relative to the material being reviewed. These papers are then circulated until a consensus is reached. If agreement cannot be reached, a meeting is held to resolve the dispute. Round-robin reviews counter leader domination by taking the persuasive effect of personalities out of meetings.

4. *Walkbacks.* These are informal reviews in which someone other than the software engineer explains a segment of design or code to members of the development team, including the author. Other team members ask questions and make comments about technique, style, and possible errors. Then, the originator provides the necessary clarifications and improvements in the product.

There are many good references on how to conduct peer reviews [Yourdon, 1979], yet certain myths concerning management need to be dispelled. These include the following two major fallacies:

1. Management should not attend. Although a peer review should not degenerate into a personnel review, there are times when it makes sense to invite management to attend. For example, when team leaders are asked to perform design duties in addition to managing teams, they should be invited to the design meetings despite the fact that they have supervisory powers. Meetings provide them the chance to learn what the rest of the team is doing to realize the design, and are essential to team-building and communications.

2. Walk-throughs add at most an hour to your schedule. It is true that walk-throughs should last at most an hour, but this time allocation pertains only to the meeting itself. It takes several hours to compile and distribute walk-through packets and several hours to generate the walk-through minutes. Then it may take several days to accomplish the needed rework identified in the walk-through. Although it is still a cost-effective way to improve quality, walk-throughs and other forms of peer reviews do require additional hours and effort.

As one can easily conclude, many different reviews and audits need to be scheduled during any project. Remember, as the project gets bigger, the number of reviews will grow nonlinearly.

7.7   CONFIGURATION MANAGEMENT AND LIBRARY CONTROLS

The seller must also implement a configuration management system that meets the requirements of the contract and ensures product integrity. Most sellers do not implement such a system from scratch, but instead adapt an already existing set of policies, procedures, practices, and tools acceptable to the specifics of the contract. This adaptation is often the cause of many trials and tribulations, and it requires time and inventivity. For this reason, buyers often pay sellers to produce a configuration management plan.

Most seller firms have some form of formal configuration management system. This system, encompassing both hardware and software, has normally evolved over the years. The hardware system revolves around control of drawings and bills of materials. The software system is separate from the hardware system and is interfaced to the hardware system through an appropriate entry into the bill of materials at the assembly level. A discrepancy or anomaly reporting system has also been developed that takes user-identified defects and relates them back to the hardware and software.

Many firms have more than one configuration management system. The reason for this is simple: Different organizations have developed their own systems at various times to meet unique requirements on different contracts. Many disparate forms, procedures, and tools are used, which make it difficult to enforce standardization of configuration management across organizations. These firms may also have more than one set of configuration management archives. As contracts with differing requirements were serviced in the past, alternatives were devised that were increasingly more efficient than previous methods.

The need to adapt these systems becomes paramount as more projects start using incremental software development models. New baselining concepts should be inserted to handle incremental deliveries and status accounting requirements as more versions of software are produced. In addition, the movement of most firms to workstations forces firms to consider distributing their working libraries onto the machines the software engineers use to generate their work products.

It is therefore imperative for the project to develop a workable configuration management scheme. This scheme must build on their existing systems to fulfill customer requirements for configuration identification (for example, baselining), configuration control, configuration status accounting, and configuration audit. Interfaces between this system and those used for problem reporting, hardware configuration management, and archival control also need to be developed. Strategies for hosting the library on the software development environment need to be implemented along with methods of integrating systems so that the working libraries interface with those used for formal configuration control. If the project is big enough, it may have to sponsor such improvements. If not, the project manager may have to lobby for some other group to do the work.

7.8   QUALITY ASSURANCE AND METRICS ANALYSIS

Sellers must also implement an independent quality assurance organization to ensure that the requirements of the contract are satisfied. This organization's role has to be well-defined so that it does not upset the apple cart as it works with the engineering and project organizations to complete the job. Depending upon the criticality of the application, different levels of quality assurance may be practiced. Different tools and techniques may be used as various practices are invoked by the client organization. For example, the project may require independent quality assurance as well as independent verification and validation. A conscious planning effort should be undertaken to structure the work so that the two organizations coordinate to minimize duplication, maximize utility, and minimize interference.

Most sellers have some form of quality assurance organization. The roles of these organizations vary greatly across the industry, but most are limited in their capabilities. In a recent survey of the state of the practice of software quality assurance within the United States, most surveyed firms (more than 100 aerospace and commercial firms were included within the survey) were woefully lacking in the area of software quality assurance [Reifer, 1987]. The specific areas of criticism pertinent to this discussion include:

1. Upper management paid only lip service to quality. Quality was often sacrificed for productivity or schedule performance.
2. The quality organizations were staffed with junior people, many of whom had no real software development experience.
3. The quality organizations were undertooled and undercapitalized.
4. The quality organizations relied on inspection. They neither promoted building quality into the product nor taught those producing the product how to achieve software quality.

The purpose of citing this indictment of current software quality assurance practices is to caution the reader that radical changes may be required for an organization to meet the requirements of a TQM program. A more proactive role may be in order for the quality organization, whose role should be the teacher that facilitates engineering quality into production of goods.

7.9 RISK MANAGEMENT AND CONTROL

The last topic to be covered in this chapter is risk management and control (see Section 6.2.3). Risk refers to factors that occur that increase the possibility of loss or injury. Risk management refers to the process used to identify, analyze, prioritize, contain, and control risk. Twelve software risks that are common to most projects are listed in Table 7-2.

Typically, if one does not manage risk, risk manages to jeopardize the project. A proactive approach is the best way to deal with risk situations. Two simple approaches for achieving this desire include:

1. *Top ten list.* Every month the software manager should attempt to identify the ten top risk items that could endanger achievement of the project's cost, schedule, and technical goals. Based upon this analysis, a matrix could be constructed that prioritizes risk based upon its potential impact and discusses possible approaches to minimize the probability of occurrence.

TABLE 7-2   Common Software Risks

People

    1. Personnel shortfalls
    2. Fragmentation

Resources

    3. Unrealistic schedule
    4. Inadequate budget

Requirements

    5. Developing the wrong functions
    6. Poorly defined requirements
    7. Gold plating
    8. Continuing change (feature creep)
    9. Too little user involvement

Receivables

    10. Other projects don't deliver as promised
    11. Legacy does not live up to expectations

Technology

    12. Technology shortfalls

Adapted from Barry W. Boehm, *Tutorial: Software Risk Management,* New York: IEEE Computer Society Press, April, 1988.

2. *Risk advisory council.*   On large and complicated jobs, the software manager may organize a council to help assess risk and to decide on risk management or containment strategies. The council should meet monthly. It should be chaired by the software manager, and the customer should be invited to participate. Its work product should be a top ten list that summarizes the topics of the meeting. It should focus on reaching consensus and on identifying what is important.

Good software managers know that risks need to be managed, but the risk items are often outside of their control. These managers can only elevate the problem and convince their bosses that certain risks should be addressed. That is why a risk advisory council is often a good idea. If the customer agrees that the risk threatens, management has no alternative but to try to resolve the issue.

The following is a hypothetical example. Systems engineering is failing to define the software requirements in a timely manner. Every day that they are late, the software falls further behind schedule. A strawman specification is prepared to crystallize the issue, but systems engineering says nothing about it. The project manager is in a quandary: If he elevates the problem, he loses favor with the systems engineers; but if he doesn't, the project suffers. He raises the issue at the council meeting and talks about the cost and schedule impact. The council gives the problem first priority on the top ten list. Systems engineering then has no alternative but to buckle under and define software requirements. The project manager volunteers to work as part of an interdisciplinary team to help develop the requirements specification.

The next chapter will discuss issues relative to the team and will address the respective roles of the buyer and seller with respect to these issues. The theme of the chapter is building a team approach.

REFERENCES

[Boehm, 1988]: Barry W. Boehm, *Tutorial: Software Risk Management,* New York: IEEE Computer Society Press, April.

[IEEE, 1987]: IEEE, *Software Engineering Standards,* Washington, DC: IEEE Computer Society.

[Reifer, 1987]: Donald J. Reifer, Richard W. Knudson, and Jerry Smith, *Final Report: Software Quality Survey,* American Society of Quality Control, Milwaukee, WI.

[Yourdon, 1979]: Edward Yourdon, *Structured Walkthroughs,* 2nd ed., Englewood Cliffs, NJ: Prentice Hall.

CHAPTER 8

Software Management— The Team Approach

This chapter discusses issues that concern the buyer's and seller's management environments, roles, and responsibilities. It then discusses topics concerning building a team approach: the theme of this chapter. The necessity for building a sound team environment, ways to foster communications and trust, and rewards and punishments are all included in the discussion.

A most important ingredient for the success of a software project is an environment of communications and mutual trust between the buyer and seller. Many buyers believe that sellers are knowledgeable and experienced in development and that they should be left to their own devices. Too often the buyer relies totally on the contract as a management vehicle. The buyer's approach is to consider problems that arise to be the seller's problems and to expect contractual pressure on the seller to solve them. The adage, "Hold the contractor's feet to the fire" has been a common management mistake. When a problem occurs, the seller is therefore always to blame. This intractable approach has proved unworkable time and again.

The contract represents the best written communication for the requirements of the effort at the initiation of development. It is a only a document, however, and cannot take the place of effective management by the buyer and seller. The objective of the development is not the exercise of the contract—it is the delivery of a viable capability. To achieve a successful delivery requires communication and cooperation by both the seller and buyer—in other words, it calls for a team effort.

The degree of interaction between buyer and seller depends on the nature of the effort and the type of contract utilized. When the requirements are well-defined and the risk of development is low, a firm fixed price contract might be used. In this low-risk case, interaction between the buyer and seller is necessarily minimal. In a high-risk development, requirements may be fuzzy, and a more flexible type of contract might be employed as a cost reimbursable type. Here close interaction between the buyer and seller is mandatory because the risk is shared.

Thus the interaction between the buyer and seller must be consistent with the contract utilized. The buyer's contracting officer representative (COR) cannot stray outside the bounds of the contract vehicle to provide direction that is out of the contract's scope. The buyer, however, must promote a viable communications environment with the seller. This chapter discusses ways to manage this interface and to promote buyer/seller teamwork.

8.1 KEY PLAYERS AND THEIR ROLES AND RESPONSIBILITIES

Most large software acquisition projects involve several organizations: the user, or ultimate customer of the developed system; the supplier, or seller of the system; and the contracting agency, or buyer. Figure 8-1 illustrates a typical buyer/seller model

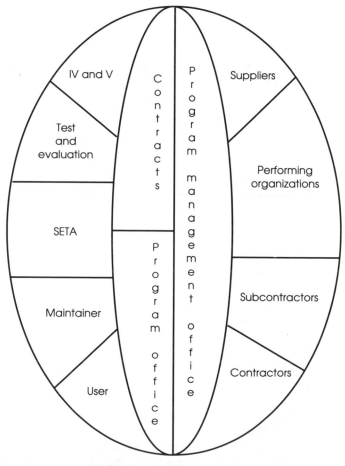

Figure 8-1 Buyer/seller model

with all its contingents. Each of these organizations and the personnel in them have their own expectations and perspectives of the management and development process. These views are not universal: they vary within each group depending on the role of the group and the motivation of the individual within it.

Buyer management is based on the terms, conditions, and requirements of the contract vehicle. The buyer defines operational requirements in conjunction with the user, specifies contractual requirements for the conduct of the project (such as configuration management), monitors implementation, assesses development process, and validates that the product satisfies contractual requirements. The seller responds to these contractual requirements by directing contractual resources to accomplish the project. Thus managers of both the buyer and the seller have the same objective—completing a project that meets requirements within the allocated resources. Disagreements occur because each side has different motivations.

The buyer strives to protect the user by accomplishing the goals of the project within the budget, but it endeavors to get the most out of the contract. In this attempt to maximize gain, the buyer may be over-zealous in interpreting the contractual requirements. This may be seen in the detail of documentation, the rigor of testing and reviews, and the use of automated tools. Before receiving the contract, the seller attempts to reduce the risk of development by paring down requirements or, alternatively, increasing cost or schedule projections. After contract award, the seller tries to settle requirements disputes by negotiating increases to the scope of the effort. This brings increased development resources and therefore brings increased revenue and profit. Disagreements over requirements can often be subtle: For example, the sides may dispute the degree of detail in a specification or the rigor of testing. These differences in viewpoint are more obvious when examined in individual project functions.

8.1.1 Planning

In planning for the project, the buyer must "sell" the project within its own organization. In concert with the user, it defines requirements and prepares and consummates a contract. The planning process usually shortchanges engineering and management decisions that must be made prior to contract award. This is due to political issues related to selling the project, budget preparation and approval, and definition of requirements. Although these are important considerations, planning for the management of the project is also important and should not receive short shrift. This situation arises owing to a lack of understanding of what's involved in preparing a statement of work and the fundamental management decisions that must be made while it is being done.

The seller's primary concern is contract award, particularly in a competitive environment. Contract performance is the next worry. The seller's planning process involves considerations similar to the buyer's, but different in perspective. The seller must first decide whether it can successfully compete for the specific opportunity. This decision depends on the technical capability of the seller, available staff, possible competition for the effort, and available bid and proposal funds. The seller marshals marketing, business development, and engineering forces to assess the opportunity and make a bid decision. The seller usually has limited information to use in this decision process. Thus intensive information gathering is an important activity. If this group of experts decides to make a bid, the upcoming proposal becomes the focus of activity. In the seller's desire to win, every effort is made to present the best picture of the seller's ability to develop the system. Resources must be applied and management commitment exacted as the proposal is prepared and then submitted.

Once the contract is awarded, resources are drawn from different functional organizations to perform and manage the project. When a lengthy lead time from proposal preparation to contract award exists, the nucleus of the development team (which participated in the proposal preparation process) dissipates into other projects leaving a skeleton project organization that must be populated once the project is awarded. This causes the majority of engineering resources to come into a project cold, without preparation. The buyer can avoid this planning pitfall by properly preparing the statement of work, requiring review of the draft SOW by the seller community, and sticking to a tight procurement schedule.

8.1.2 Engineering

The engineering staff is motivated to build the best product it possibly can. The ideal workers, however, are not always available when they are needed, and there is always a conflict over resources. It is not uncommon to have staffing difficulties either in recruiting the desired number of personnel or in tapping the appropriate expertise. In addition, engineers tend to increase complexity and add features that are nice to have but are not completely necessary. These features contribute to cost and complexity, compounding both the buyer's and seller's management task. This added-function "creep" may be exacerbated in a matrix organization in which engineering personnel are assigned to the project manager from an engineering function. These personnel still owe loyalty to the engineering organization that has direct control of their career progression and merit raises. If an engineer's performance is graded by his or her engineering manager, the project manager may have difficulty controlling cost and complexity growth. It is important, therefore, to manage requirements carefully through management requirements boards and the normal management processes of development, such as requirements reviews. These activities, properly applied, contribute to an effective communications environment.

8.1.3 Documentation

Documentation is often completely ignored in the planning process. Although numerous standards and guidelines regulate the employment of documentation, buyers are usually not equipped to make decisions about tailoring documentation requirements. The ultimate user, the customer, is even more ignorant about the need for documentation, especially documentation that supports the engineering process. The user realizes the need for customer-oriented documentation, such as user's manuals, but is often oblivious to design specifications, test documentation, and so on.

The seller recognizes the overall requirement for documentation, but owing to cost and competitive considerations, may be reticent about recommending the needed paperwork to the buyer. It never pays to tell your customer he or she is wrong when a competitive award is at stake. Worse yet, during development, sellers may de-emphasize documentation if they fall behind schedule. Nevertheless, documentation remains the single most important aspect of the software development process because it represents the predominant gauge to assess progress.

Although the engineering documentation required by contract is a primary focus of the buyer and seller, many forms of informal documentation also exist that are used by the system developers. Examples of these less-formal references are engineering data developed during the analysis process to document design tradeoffs and risk analyses, the outputs of tools used during the development process, the results of informal testing, and the results of peer-level reviews and walk-throughs. Documentation prepared using informal procedures remains an important part of the legacy of the project and should be archived in development folders or notebooks that are accessible to the buyer. The review and inspection of these development folders provides visibility into the engineering process. This is particularly important when long periods of time separate formal reviews, a common practice in projects that span several years.

The buyer is well advised to ensure that the contract vehicle provides the opportunity to review informal documentation. The seller may try to limit the scope and number of these reviews because of cost and schedule impact. Too many meaningless reviews should be avoided because they detract from accomplishment of the contract's overall goals. If the seller is interested in the integrity of the development process, it will accommodate this management requirement and cooperate with the buyer to make these development folders readily available. A seller's reluctance to expose the development process to scrutiny signals danger to the buyer and detracts from an effective communications environment.

8.1.4 Configuration Management

The configuration management process is second only to documentation in its importance in software development. An inadequate or poorly handled configuration management process is an early indicator of trouble. If the configuration management process is only partially effective, the development process will suffer, leading to slipped schedules and increased development costs.

Although users are probably not involved or conversant with configuration management, buyers should be and should recognize its importance. Buyers, however, may not have a full appreciation for an effective life cycle configuration management process. Configuration management requirements are usually placed into the statement of work without any real understanding of their important aspects or of their proper evaluation in the seller's proposal. Sellers, on the other hand, may recognize the importance of CM, but may not have an effective configuration management process in place. They may not have the use of a robust, automated configuration management tool essential for modern configuration management practice. Quite often the seller may not be willing to develop or buy tools because capital funds are unavailable. Configuration management resources are often cut back during the contracting process in order to save money and develop a more competitive proposal. This is unfortunate, because a good configuration management system contributes immeasurably to an effective communications environment because it preserves the integrity of the products and helps manage the work-in-process.

8.1.5   Quality Assurance

Quality assurance, which is possibly the most misunderstood area of the management process, has suffered from being viewed as a useless appendage to the development process populated by inspectors who are always looking for foul-ups. The buyer's statement of work normally requires that the seller institute a quality assurance program. As was the problem with configuration management, however, the buyer often does not understand how to place effective requirements into the statement of work. Evaluating the seller's response is an even greater enigma for many buyers. The seller views quality assurance as a necessary evil, or worse, as an internal inspection pain. During negotiations, resources for QA often get cut or decreased, yet QA requirements are not. The sad fact is that industry has not really accepted the need for a QA program. In this negative and uninviting environment, the quality assurance workers are hard pressed to effectively perform their jobs.

On small contracts, the need for a quality assurance program is typically deemphasized or even eliminated with the sellers encouragement. This is an ill-advised reaction to quality assurance. The issue here is not whether quality assurance is required for the project, but whether the buyer and seller understand its value and know how to tailor it to small projects. A seller recommendation to eliminate the quality assurance program is probably evidence of its inability to effectively implement such a program. It may also be an admission that it has no quality assurance function or that the function is spread too thin.

Quality assurance is a necessary part of the engineering process, because it assures the integrity of the development process. It is a constructive function whose proper employment contributes to the ability of the buyer and seller to manage the quality of the development project—its processes and products. Effective quality assurance depends entirely on a good communications environment.

8.1.6   Software Tools

Software tools are becoming a popular addition to software development as tools become increasingly user friendly and integrated with software engineering environments. The availability of modern tools (such as those in modern CASE sets) is making a dramatic improvement in software engineering practice.

Generally, the buyer is primarily interested in tools if they are required to be delivered with the system so that the buyer can perform maintenance. The buyer often does not understand the requirement to automate the development to improve quality and productivity and may not adequately evaluate this requirement in the seller's proposal. The seller may want to invest in tools, but will have little incentive to do so unless the buyer demands it. Tools increase overhead expense and contribute to a higher bid price. The contract requirement for an automated development environment will motivate the seller to provide one that is responsive to the needs of the project or risk the possibility of being deemed nonresponsive to RFP requirements.

8.1.7   Testing

Testing is a given in software development, but it is neither understood nor effectively practiced in a typical development process. Testing is often viewed simply as the process that follows code development. It is actually, however, a process that begins with the requirements specification; continues through design, code development, and integration; and culminates, from a development standpoint, with the successful delivery of the system. It is a joint managerial and technical process that is supported by reviews of the products of development, documentation of the various testing phases, and informal and formal testing. Qualification requirements are defined in the software requirements specification and match performance requirements one for one. If a requirement cannot be tested, its worth should be seriously questioned.

From the buyer's viewpoint, testing demonstrates that the product meets requirements and works to the user's (customer's) satisfaction. The customer, therefore, emphasizes the operational assessments of functionality, performance, ease of use, and maintenance. The buyer's motivation is the need to ensure that the product fulfills the provisions of the contract. Thus emphasis often rests on qualification, or system-level testing designed to demonstrate that the acceptance clauses of the contract are fulfilled.

The seller is interested in demonstrating that the product works. This demonstration proves that the system meets the requirements of the statement of work and helps the seller gain acceptance for the product. It is incumbent on the buyer to ensure that a sound test program exists that includes the participation of the ultimate user. A poor testing program will erode communications and become a constant sore.

8.2   BUILDING SYNERGISTIC BUYER/SELLER TEAMS

Building an effective relationship with the seller should begin with the buyer's project team and its approach to managing the effort. If the team does not understand software development, its members will be defensive about problems that arise. People who are placed in positions that they are not equipped to manage tend to insulate themselves. Thus the first step in building a sound communications environment is to educate the project management team about the goals and what resources are needed to realize them.

8.2.1 The Contract

In the selection of a contractor, the buyer must consider whether a sound rapport with the seller is possible. Placing a requirement in the solicitation that the seller should exhibit good communications and an ability to work effectively with the buyer and its representatives is not effective: It is parenthood, not management. Certain methods can be employed, however, to judge whether a sound communications environment is achievable between the parties concerned.

1. *Ability of the seller to perform.* If the seller is not experienced in software development, the chances are good that communications and rapport during development will suffer simply because the seller will become defensive and will try to hide problems. In some cases the objectives of the effort may preclude or detract from the requirement for a sound software management capability. For example, in a high-risk development the seller may be selected more for technical capability. Or the seller may select a team member who is unschooled in an acquisition environment, but who possesses a key technical talent. This situation may not be evident in the seller's proposal.

2. *Organization.* The buyer should solicit information about the seller's method of organization and about the communication processes that the seller employs to manage projects internally. The buyer may inquire about management of the seller's internal projects to gain insight into the communications process that the seller routinely employs. The capability to manage subcontractor efforts should also be examined to determine whether the seller has experience with and set procedures for subcontractor management.

3. *Experience.* A most revealing characteristic is the experience that the buyer has had with the seller on previous projects, or the experiences that other buyers have had with the particular seller. Past experience can certainly be considered an evaluation criterion. In some large organizations, a history of poor performance with a particular seller can even lead the organization to blacklist the seller from competition for subsequent development projects. Blacklisting is generally a poor practice, one that is justifiable only if unethical practices have been used by the seller. It has been used in some cases for the wrong reasons: For example, the buyer may not recognize the high risk of a development effort and may attribute failure to the seller rather than to an invalid development concept. The inadequacy of the buyer's management team may have led to or even caused project failure.

It is always easy for the buyer to ignore its responsibility for this situation and to ascribe the failure to the seller. Unusual circumstances usually cause the biggest problems for a project. For example, the requirements for the project may be indeterminate at contract award, yet the buyer may insist on a firm, fixed price contract. If the seller is anxious enough (or greedy enough) to accept that condition, serious problems may result. In another example, the development may be of very high risk, yet the buyer may not recognize the technical risk of development and may treat the project like a production process. These conditions will normally turn even a good communication environment into a defensive and backbiting situation. In a final example, the buyer may overmanage the contract, forcing the seller to produce many meaningless reports and attend many unnecessary meetings. The buyer then blames the seller for the consequences.

8.2.2 The Development

Throughout the development project, interaction between the buyer's and seller's organizations is paramount for building and maintaining sound communications and a team approach. If the project environment has been well founded, both the buyer and seller should work as a team that has a positive view for the project. Although this may sound trite, there are effective actions to take and signals to look for that can aid in the project's success.

Project Leaders Both the buyer's and seller's project leaders should have positive attitudes, with mutual respect for each other and rapport. If this is missing, the project may be soured at the start. Senior oversight management should understand the importance of this situation and correct it if it occurs. The seller is typically sensitive to buyer needs and expectations and wishes to ensure that the seller's project leader is acceptable to the buyer. The buyer, on the other hand, sometimes believes that the onus for cooperation is on the seller, because the buyer is the customer, or the agent of the customer (user). Actually, nothing could be further from the truth. The buyer, like the seller, must recognize its responsibility to ensure that personnel selected to head the project are appropriate and that personality conflicts do not exist. To use a cliche, the art of communication is a two-way street, and both sides must recognize their respective responsibilities to ensure that it is effective and sound.

Personality Conflicts It is not uncommon to find severe personality conflicts on a project. When this occurs in a key management area in which two people interact on a routine basis, progress can be delayed. This type of conflict is not a buyer problem or a seller problem—it is a project problem. Affixing blame is not going to solve the problem. The personnel involved must be replaced or their interaction must be supervised to control the situation.

It is difficult to supervise the interactions of personnel who are in management positions. Removing the problem employee or changing his or her role may be the only recourse. It is also difficult to remove personnel who are crucial to the technical effort, but the interaction among these key technical personnel is susceptible to control.

Crowd Control Formal review meetings can be extremely volatile, especially when key issues are being discussed or when differences of opinion exist among personnel. The latter situation is the most prevalent problem. Remember, contentious issues should be identified and resolved before a meeting takes place. If an issue is left unresolved, then the conditions are ripe for disruption at the meeting.

It is always easier to settle disputes outside of a crowd, because large meetings make communications more difficult: People may be afraid to speak their piece in front of a group or may become trapped into defending organizational positions. Neither situation is conducive to problem solving.

Although it may seem odd to avoid resolving issues at formal meetings, these meetings are set up for other purposes. Ad hoc meetings are normally scheduled to resolve issues. The primary purpose of formal reviews is to communicate the status of the project to a large number of involved personnel—the customer, buyer and seller management, and seller organizational team, including technical and support employees (such as quality assurance personnel). If contentious issues are raised and their resolution is attempted, the meeting can quickly degenerate into detailed technical discussions that subvert original meeting objectives.

The primary mechanism for controlling this situation is a strict agenda. The meeting agenda should clearly define the objectives of the meeting and identify open issues consistent with the purpose of the meeting. Thus the manager can take steps before the meeting takes place to divert problems. If conflicts cannot be resolved before the meeting, they should be identified at the meeting with a report on the ongoing activities for resolution. However, the meeting leaders should avoid any attempt to solve the issue at the meeting itself. Other sources of contention are the many onlookers who believe their worth is judged by the volume of discrepancies they note at the meetings. Remember that it is quality, not quantity, that should be stressed.

Personnel Stability   Another vital issue is the stability of project personnel. There are two aspects to stability: first, the normal outflow of specialists when their work is finished; second, attrition. For an example of the first situation, systems analysts are usually employed during the architectural and design phases of the effort. As the project proceeds into coding and subsequent testing, however, their value diminishes, and their numbers are cut or their labor-hours reduced. Employing analysts is expensive, so this reduction is a normal way for the seller to manage the costs on a project. The phasing of personnel should be addressed in the seller's proposal, the project management plan, and the software management plan. This type of personnel fluctuation is not usually a stability problem.

The other issue, a dilemma for stability, is the loss of personnel owing to attrition—that is, leaving the company, retirement, and so forth. A company may pride itself on an attrition rate that falls below 5 percent. Company attrition is an indicator of the overall stability that a company enjoys, but the stability of the project itself is more important to the seller.

The buyer should track the seller's stability of both overall project personnel and key personnel. (Section 6.4.6 suggests indicators that may be used for this function, specifically for tracking key personnel in the project.) A rapid loss or fluctuation of project personnel, regardless of the experience of the company, usually indicates a future problem. The issue to investigate is the resolution of the problem.

It is the responsibility of the seller's project manager to manage undue fluctuations in stability. If an adverse trend is indicated, perhaps through an indicator such as mentioned above, the buyer would want to meet with the seller to discuss the situation. The manager may be aware of the situation and may have already taken steps to remedy or alleviate the problem. If he or she has not acted, however, then the buyer has to ensure that appropriate steps are taken to remedy the situation. In extreme cases a formal plan may be required to manage instability. In any case the following actions should be considered for managing personnel instability:

- identification of key tasks and the distribution of personnel for those tasks
- attention of seller management to the overall problem and actions that they may take to alleviate the problem
- mechanisms to track the problem, including reporting the problem to the buyer project manager
- hiring new personnel to promote overall seller personnel stability
- subcontracting a portion of the effort to a third party supplier
- acquiring temporary resources from a services oriented supplier

If the project manager cannot remedy the situation, higher-level seller management should be consulted. The key is to attract management attention before the situation progresses.

If the situation deteriorates in spite of management's help, the buyer has to consider extraordinary steps such as termination of the contract. Of course, this step should not be considered merely on the extraordinary fluctuation of personnel. It should also be based on contract performance. This gets tricky: If the contract cites a firm, fixed price delivery, the buyer has little choice but to wait out the effort, even if the probability of success is low. Cost-type contracts give the buyer more latitude. If costs start to rise before the seller meets key milestones, the buyer can take action to control cost growth. In either case, however, the buyer should build into the contract provision for termination at various milestones. Even if this provision is made, the problem will not be easy to manage. The seller is usually motivated to keep the contract going at all costs and may innovate schemes to show how the objectives of the effort can still be met or may blame failure on extraordinary circumstances.

Key Personnel Stability   One of the buyer's central concerns is the stability of key personnel on the project. The buyer usually requires that the seller identify key employees in the proposal and may place restrictions into the solicitation that limit the seller's prerogative to remove these personnel from the project. This is a poor practice. Although it is good management for the buyer to request identification of key personnel as a consideration for contract award, it is unreasonable to demand control of the seller's right to allocate personnel. There are exceptions: If the award was predicated on unique expertise, the absence of that expertise could lead to a contract default situation. To manage this situation the buyer can place replacement criteria into the contract that allow the buyer to review the seller's replacement expert and negate it if he or she does not meet the buyer's stated qualifications.

The buyer normally contracts a seller based on the seller's development capability in a specific applications area (such as banking). The seller company is accountable for fulfilling the requirements of the contract and should be allowed to manage its own work force. Placing unusual personnel restrictions into the solicitation creates an environment supporting false claims about personnel stability in the proposal and sets the wrong stage for a team effort based on trust. Often the proposal manager may not have the authority in the organization to agree to commitment of certain personnel, yet he or she may be forced to include the resumes of the desired employees in the proposal. Sellers cannot predict unusual circumstances and should not be asked to make undue promises about personnel.

Personnel stability, however, *is* important. This is especially true in research and development efforts in which the basis for award to a specific seller is the presence of key technical specialists or scientists. Loss of these personnel to another project may not be the fault of the seller, but it has a definite impact on the project. This situation must be managed. If the seller cannot arrive at an appropriate alternative solution, the purpose of the contract may become invalid.

Appropriate mechanisms for managing or maintaining key personnel stability are as follows:

- Identify areas or technical specialties that the buyer believes to be important to the project.
- Employ a priority list for critical skills.
- Require that the seller identify persons in these target categories and mechanisms that the seller will employ to ensure that they are available for the project.
- Require that the seller notify the buyer COR when a change will occur in critical personnel assignment and tell the buyer how the seller will manage the change.

Remember, personnel changes cannot be avoided, but they can be managed in a cooperative manner.

8.3 COMMUNICATIONS AND TRUST

Any project should have a healthy environment of trust and communications—one of solving problems, not affixing blame; of facing issues squarely, not avoiding them; of communicating directly and effectively instead of relying on contract mechanisms or paper alone; of accepting responsibility rather than transferring it; of supporting informal networks, not relying on formal mechanisms alone. Software projects are people intensive. They require good communications in order to build the proper environment that can solve problems and develop an effective product. The environment must be based on a concept of faith and trust. Where that exists the chances of success are good; where it does not, the probability of success will be low.

Trust, as defined by Webster's New World Dictionary, is the "firm belief or confidence in the honesty, integrity, reliability, justice, etc., of another person or thing." There is no foolproof formula for building trust into a project relationship. That trust must exist on both sides; its characteristics, however, will be evident throughout the project. The following questions can help the buyer and seller identify trust in the project's proceedings.

1. Do both sides meet commitments? Do they respond to each other's telephone calls and requests for information in a positive manner?
2. Is the provided information reliable? Does it accurately reflect the project situation?
3. Is the environment conducive to problem solving? Do both sides approach a problem from the standpoint of solving it instead of affixing blame?

Building good communications mechanisms is a more concrete thing. There are many mechanisms, such as the following, that can be used to ensure that good communications exist.

Informal Networking   This is the basis for good communications in any organization. The adage, "Ask the secretary if you want to know something" attests to this. There is nothing that management can do to eliminate an informal network, but there are ways to impede it. For example, requiring formal communications for every interaction between buyer and seller personnel stems from the misguided notion that control over communications is essential to effective management, and it hinders successful informal communication. Control is vital to those formal structures of the project, but it should never be applied to informal contacts. Restrictions that prevent informal contacts among personnel impede communications and lead to distrust.

Electronic Communications   One mechanism that serves to enhance communications is the use of local area networks and electronic mail. Tying the buyer and seller together with a computer network and implementing an electronic message system are excellent ways to promote communications, especially over large distances. These networks serve formal as well as informal communications and reach many people in an efficient way. They also allow personnel at different levels to interact without the physical barriers that sometimes prevent or formalize communications (barriers like doors and secretaries).

Project and Telephone Lists   These simple mechanisms can be highly effective. Answering the telephone and returning phone calls promptly are extremely important to good communication because they build trust and confidence. Both gestures indicate that the person cares and is interested in the caller's problem or quest. It is even more important to answer phone calls despite the apparently insignificant role of the caller. Delegating a phone call to a third person is a bureaucratic ploy that says the caller is not important enough to talk to the called person. It is a detriment to confidence and trust in the project environment, especially because the person delegated to return the phone call may not have the authority or ability to adequately respond to the issue.

Minutes and Reports   Reporting the minutes of a meeting is a good way to increase overall communications on the project. Minutes signify that a meeting was important and recognize the contributions of the personnel involved. It also communicates to those who were not present the details and results of the meeting. It is extremely important, however, that minutes be reported promptly. Publishing minutes long after the meeting is over, when the reported activities have been overtaken by project events, simply supports bureaucratic procedure and does not promote communications.

It is also a mistake to formalize the minutes so that they contain unnecessary detail. The essence of a meeting may be captured in few words—in fact, the fewer words the better. Adding words merely delays the report and increases the cost of the project. It may look great in the development library, but it does not serve a useful purpose.

Newsletters   Although the high cost of a newsletter may not be consistent with the size of every project, its use is worth considering. In many cases existing company newsletters may serve the purpose. It may be difficult to portray current, active events in a newsletter that is published on an infrequent basis, but significant actions and accomplished milestones that are reported contribute to an environment of trust. Project personnel should be proud of their accomplishments, so publicizing achievements promotes confidence and contributes to effective communications and trust.

8.4   REWARDS AND PUNISHMENTS

Rewards are more important than punishments. After all, punishment is associated with failure and may detract from the objective of delivering an effective and responsive system by emphasizing mistakes rather than achievements. Punishment should only be used to correct a situation in the project or to prevent a similar situation from occurring in the current project or in a future one.

Everyone likes to be rewarded. However, people respond to different types of awards. Although some people are satisfied that they are employed, are making a decent salary, have suitable vacation time, and have commensurate benefits, most workers require more. People want to believe that they are contributing to an important endeavor. They also want to believe that they are valuable to that endeavor and that the project could not be better accomplished by any other organization. Rewards contribute to trust by building confidence in the organization and in the project. They recognize personal effort and say "good job" to those who have excelled. Organizational and personal awards are the two general award categories.

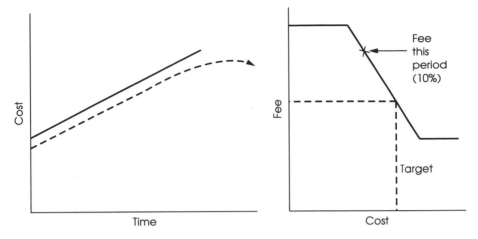

Figure 8-2 Maximizing fee (cost)

8.4.1 Organizational Awards

The most common organizational awards are the various incentives on the contract. The following sections discuss some of these incentive programs.

Cost A cost incentive places a portion of the profit into an incentive program. (See Chapter 5.) Typically cost, schedule, or a combination of both are the objects of incentives. The cost incentive offers a share in the profit that is allowable on the contract. This encourages the seller to underrun cost while meeting project objectives in order to achieve maximum profit. (See Figure 8-2.) If the seller performs on target—that is, within the original expectation of contract cost—the declared percentage is awarded. Similarly, as shown in Figure 8-3, schedule can be used as a basis for fee incentive. If the schedule is exceeded, the payment bottoms out. However, if the seller delivers ahead of schedule, it can achieve maximum profit.

A cost incentive could be counterproductive to the objectives of the buyer. If the seller realizes that it may overrun, and therefore lose fee, it may opt to increase the cost of the effort by continuing the effort long after the projected end date. For example, consider the case of a project with a contract cost of 12 million dollars and a fee range of 8 to 15 percent. At 8 percent, profit would be $960,000 and at 15 percent it would be $1.8 million. If the seller realizes that it is going to severely overrun schedule, it can opt to continue accruing labor hours, thus increasing revenue. At the floor fee of 8 percent the loss would be $840,000 (the difference between the possible fee of $1.8 million and the floor fee of $960,000). By expending at a rate of $400,000 per month they could make up the loss in less than three months, accruing additional revenue after this point. Thus the basis for the cost incentive is somewhat offset by the ability of the seller to continue to accrue cost and to achieve increased revenue expectation despite the reduced fee.

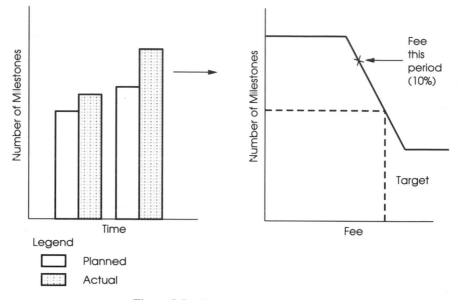

Figure 8-3   Maximizing fee (schedule)

The method used to negate this possibility is the use of negative incentives (penalties or punishment). If the seller does not meet cost projections, schedule projections, or both, the fee can take on a negative connotation. As the cost or schedule is exceeded, the fee becomes negative. Thus the seller begins to pay fee back to the buyer, thus reducing the effect of increased revenue. The preferred incentive structure rewards the seller for good performance, not for poor performance. In addition, a stop work notice can be used to halt the project at a reasonable point so that the buyer can protect the budget.

Award Fee   The use of award fee incentives somewhat offsets the disadvantage of the cost incentive structure. This places the incentive directly on performance. Award fee is a prenegotiated amount of money based on the importance of the effort and awarded on the successful completion of a significant delivery milestone. Thus the award may be based on the successful implementation and operation of a system within schedule. In order for the award fee to be successful, it has to be based on a well-defined event. (It has been used, for example, for the launch of a missile or the first flight of an aircraft: two unmistakable events.) If the event's occurrence cannot be easily proved, the use of an award fee is questionable because the event may be staged.

The advantage of the award fee is that the success of the event is clearly under the control and authority of the buyer. Thus the buyer defines the event up front at contract award and determines whether the seller has met the requirement of the event. The seller can contest the success of the event, but experience shows this to be uncommon.

8.4.2 Personal Awards

From a buyer's viewpoint, personal awards help establish a healthy project atmosphere. They contribute to a feeling that the project is important and that efforts are worthwhile, and they grant individual fulfillment. The buyer is well-advised to promote a personal awards program.

Likewise, the seller should have a corresponding program. A personal awards program is even more important to a seller organization. The buyer is the customer—it is buying something and ultimately enjoys the use of the system, usually unseen by the seller. The seller is the provider. The seller's personnel are removed from the operational use of the subsequent product, which decreases visibility of the actual use of the product and contributes to a lack of fulfillment.

Although the buyer is not normally involved in the seller's personal incentive program, it can certainly promote the program. The buyer can ascertain whether the seller has a personal incentive or awards program and subsequently encourage it. The most important characteristic of an awards program is equality. Recognition should comply with the following guidelines:

- It should be consistent with the expected norm across the industry for similar efforts.
- It should be consistent within the program.

An example of a poor incentive program is a case in which the buyer and seller recognized a cost-saving reduction that had been jointly submitted by two employees—one from the buyer and one from the seller. The buyer's employee is given a monetary award, but the seller's person is awarded only a certificate of recognition. This injustice, or inconsistency, will be felt by the entire seller organization and may contribute to a decrease in morale.

The seller should establish a sound personal awards program to provide a sense of operational fulfillment. Seller personnel want to believe that they are contributing to a useful system that will provide society with value. They want to build a good system and to believe that each employee individually contributes to that objective. A personal awards program should recognize these two accomplishments:

- An employee's personal achievement contributes directly to the success of the program.
- An employee's personal achievement marks a step in the person's professional career.

The buyer should investigate the seller's understanding of the benefits of an awards program and the use of such a program within the seller's organization. A personal awards program contributes to the overall communication between buyer and seller project personnel by fostering the feeling of trust that is important in a positive and productive project environment.

The next chapter gives an interesting and pertinent change of pace. Cost issues and answers is the subject.

CHAPTER 9

Cost Issues And Answers

This chapter deals with cost and the ways it is estimated, confirmed, priced, controlled, projected, and managed. It also looks at the relationship of cost and technical performance so that problems can be identified while there is time to remedy them.

There are four steps in cost estimating: estimating resources, costing, pricing, and accounting. During the first step, both the buyer and the seller estimate the time and labor required for development. The cost must then be set using agreed-upon rates and economic factors. Next, price is established based upon the principle of supply and demand. Finally, control over cost and schedule is exercised once a contract has been established.

9.1 DEVELOPING A REASONABLE COST ESTIMATE

Both the buyer and the seller need to develop reasonable effort and duration estimates as they plan and execute an acquisition. The buyer's estimate supports the development budget, allocating funds consistent with the projected expenditure of resources and the evaluation of the seller's cost estimate. The seller's forecast provides the estimate of resources needed in order to meet solicitation requirements and prepare a winning bid for the competitive procurement. The buyer and seller must be as accurate as possible with their estimates because their performances will be evaluated against these cost targets and profit and loss will be dictated by them.

The quality of an estimate is directly related to the quality of its source information. The volatility of this information varies as a function of time and the firmness of the requirements. During the early stages of an acquisition, uncertainty of requirements results in low-confidence estimates. As time progresses, uncertainty decreases and estimates dramatically improve in confidence.

The primary techniques for developing estimates are summarized along with their relative strengths and weaknesses in Table 9-1. Each of these methods is briefly explained as follows:

1. *Analogy.* The estimate is based upon comparative analysis of similar acquisitions whose cost, schedules, and characteristics are known, understood, validated, and documented. The similarities and differences among systems are investigated using past experience as the basis of the estimate. Parameters such as relative product complexity, staff experience, and management burden are used to adjust forecasts. A modified estimate is then produced based upon the results of this analysis.

2. *Bottom-up.* The estimate is derived by dividing the work into its elementary units using a work breakdown structure (WBS) (see Section 3.3). The effort and duration for each of the units in the WBS is estimated using techniques like analogy or parametric models. The effort is then summed across all work packages to arrive at an overall projection.

3. *Expert opinion.* The estimate is derived by polling experts. Each expert uses a different method or tool to develop a forecast. The experts are assembled with a facilitator who attempts to develop a consensus estimate based upon their expert opinions. This is a time-consuming approach because it often takes several passes before agreement is reached. It is most applicable in systems that are dependent on new technologies or are in unprecedented systems.

4. *Parametric models.* The estimate is developed using mathematical formulas that model the statistical relationships among effort, duration, and the parameters that directly influence them. The parameters of interest are called cost drivers because their variation directly influences overall effort. The models are typically automated using software programs. They are repeatable, allowing estimators to perform sensitivity and domain analyses. A variety of models exist that can be used by different estimators to provide a check on one another. (These will be illustrated in Table 9-2.)

5. *Top-down.* Often called design-to-cost, this estimating technique allocates an effort bogey to the various work packages contained within the WBS. Each work package activity is then successively refined to determine whether or not the bogey provides sufficient resources for accomplishing the work package. If it does not, project requirements are modified and the allocation process iterated. Detailed problems that could escalate costs are overlooked as estimators attempt to determine whether the job can be done for the money allocated.

6. *Price to win.* The estimate is developed based upon what the seller thinks it will take to win the job. Often, the seller's price may be less than his cost. The seller may be economically motivated to bid into the project because of the possibilities of large follow-on contracts or economic leverage. Naturally this situation is advantageous to the buyer, as long as the seller can perform and deliver as promised.

TABLE 9-1 Cost Estimating Methods

Method	Strength	Weakness
1. Analogy	Based on past experience, so effort can be substantiated	Only as good as past experience: doesn't work without it
2. Bottom-up	Based upon a detailed assessment of the work that needs to be done	Overlooks the work needed to coordinate and communicate between groups
	Gets people who will do the work to commit to the estimates	Extremely time-consuming and expensive to develop estimates
	Promotes a deep understanding of the work to be done	May overlook incidental activities conducted on a project
3. Expert opinion	Based on consensus reached using different people and different methods	Only as good as the experts employed
	Different estimators cross check one another to ensure that something was not inadvertently overlooked	Time-consuming and expensive to reach consensus; sometimes creates a false sense of security
4. Parametric models	Based upon mathematical formulas that can be calibrated to actual experience	Calibration to the past not necessarily indicative of the future
	Estimates are objective and repeatable	Factors are subjective; accounting for exceptions to the norm is difficult
	Models take many factors into account as the estimate is generated	
5. Top-down	Based upon an assessment of the global properties of the system	Fails to identify details and to work low-level issues that may escalate costs
	System-level focus applied to the project as effort is allocated	Provides no detailed base for justification and iteration
6. Price to win	Based upon an assessment of how much the customer has to do the job	Most times, too aggressive

Parametric models have gained considerable popularity as the complexities of acquisitions and systems have increased. The reasons for this phenomenon are numerous and varied. First, models embed the knowledge that estimators have gleaned over the years in the form of parametric estimating equations. Many of the relationships that exist between variables in these equations are nonintuitive. Second, models embed the experience that estimators have recorded in a form that can be validated. Models can be calibrated to reflect actual experience. Auditors can verify results and certify that the models, when properly calibrated, accurately generate past performance. Past experience can therefore be used to justify estimates that are based upon more than just engineering judgment. Finally, models embed mathematical relationships that allow their users to investigate risk. For example, cost drivers can be varied and their effect on effort and duration evaluated. Sensitivity analyses can then be conducted to determine to which parameters effort and duration are most sensitive. The consequences of alternative management and technical decisions can also be assessed, as tradeoffs among effort, duration, and other factors like size are investigated using statistical techniques.

Popular parametric models used within the community for software cost estimating, the software packages that implement them, and their pertinent characteristics are summarized in Table 9-2.

All of these models assume a relationship between software effort and size that takes the following form:

$$\text{Effort (in staff months)} = a * b * (size)^p$$

where a = calibration coefficient

b = cost driver coefficient (sum of several different parameters whose variation directly affects effort)

$size$ = estimate of how big the job is in either source lines of code or function points

p = power law or regression curve coefficient

Effort estimates are extremely sensitive to size estimates. Therefore, care should be taken to ensure that the effort and duration estimates are based upon a sound forecast of how large the software will become.

Two different size metrics are used in these equations: source lines of code and function points. Source lines of code is a design-based size metric typically determined by projecting the number of physical lines of source code (for example, carriage returns or terminal semicolons) that will be delivered upon conclusion of the job. Estimation of source lines is typically done by analogy, based upon past experience with similar applications. Function points are a specification-based size metric typically determined by using properties of a requirements specification (such as number of inputs, number of outputs, number of operational modes, and so on) to generate the size estimate. Function points is the preferable method because it allows cost to be related directly to requirements within a specification.

TABLE 9-2 Popular Cost Models

Model	Packages	Characteristics
1. Ada-COCOMO	COSTAR COSTMODL	Parametric model for Ada with power law stabilizing at 1.04; 18 independent cost drivers; validated using five projects
2. COCOMO	COSTAR PCOC REVIC SECOMO	General-purpose parametric model with three modes of operation; power law varies between 1.05–1.20; 16 independent cost drivers; validated using hundreds of projects; simplest and most popular model
3. Jensen	System-3	General-purpose parametric model with nonlinear power law; 19 independent cost drivers; roll-up model part of the package; validated using numerous projects Popular model for military systems
4. PRICE S	PRICE S	General-purpose parametric model based upon heuristic relationships; validated using hundreds of projects; interfaces with a variety of hardware and life cycle models Popular model for many systems
5. Putnam	SLIM	General-purpose parametric model with nonlinear power law; 12 independent cost drivers; modified Rayleigh distribution used for allocating resources; validated using hundreds of projects Popular model for business systems
6. SoftCost-Ada	SoftCost-Ada	Parametric model for Ada with power law stabilizing at 0.95; 28 cost drivers, many of which are conditionally related; based upon an extensive analysis of Ada project experience; validated using over 100 projects
7. SoftCost	SoftCost-HP SoftCost-NASA SoftCost-R	General-purpose parametric model with linear power law; 32 cost drivers, many of which are conditionally related; size expressed in source lines of code or function points; validated using hundreds of projects Popular model for real-time systems

Of course, source lines of code may be the only alternative when no specification exists and analogy is the only means to derive the size estimate.

Other forms of mathematical models are used during this phase for hardware and life-cycle cost estimating. These models relate effort to independent variables like weight, size (that is, the number of boards in a hardware chassis), and volume. They relate the effort and duration to the physical configuration of the hardware to estimate its cost.

Both the buyer and the seller use these cost models throughout the acquisition cycle to get a handle on the effort involved. The seller uses the models to generate an estimate for effort, duration, and risk for the job. The buyer uses them to estimate the resources needed and to confirm the fact that the seller's estimates are reasonable. For example, the buyer may require the seller to complete a parametric form that captures data of interest on cost drivers as part of the solicitation. The buyer then uses these data to calibrate their cost model, which is then used to develop "should-cost" estimates for the effort. The buyer will use these estimates as a baseline for negotiations during the source selection phase. After all, they were generated using the seller's data and should represent what the seller believes it will take to do the job. The seller might counter the buyer's arguments about effort and duration by defending the forecasts of size or the different ratings for the parameters used to adjust the model. In any case, it simplifies negotiations when the buyer and seller use the same model to derive their estimates.

Deciding which estimating method or model to use is a difficult task. Each has its own merits and deficiencies. Probably the best advice we can provide is summarized as follows:

- If possible, use two different estimating methods or models so that one can be used as a check on the other.
- Use whatever method and model the customer uses as one of the selections. That way, the customer will understand the assumptions that bind the estimates.
- Pay considerable attention to definitions. Before venturing forth with a forecast, make sure that the manner in which each parameter of interest is quantified in the estimating equations is well-defined and understood.
- Invest the time to develop better size estimates. Technology exists to reduce the uncertainty in this variable around which cost estimates revolve. Remember, an error in size is considerably amplified when cost is estimated using nonlinear power laws.

9.2 COSTING—HOW IT IS DONE

9.2.1 Effort Estimating

The estimates developed identify how much effort (for example, in staff-hours or staff-months) is needed to accomplish the job within the allotted time period. They do not account for different labor, overhead, and inflation rates. That is typically done in a cost-reimbursement-type contract when the job is costed using rates negotiated between the buyer and the seller prior to or during the source selection. These rates allocate allowable costs to specific cost accounts. Rates that must be established to generate a responsive cost proposal include the following:

- *Direct labor rates.*   The average salary paid per hour for the seller's employees is computed by labor classification (such as senior engineer, engineer, and technician). These rates are normally provided on a quarterly schedule to reflect changes that occur because of such factors as attrition and raises.
- *Labor overhead rate.*   The cost to the firm of providing a skilled labor pool is represented as a fixed percentage of the direct labor rate charges (for example, costs in this category include benefits like vacations, holidays, medical leaves, and premiums; facility and equipment; supplies; mandated taxes like social security; indirect labor; services and management charges; and fringes). This is commonly referred to as the burden rate.
- *General and administrative rate.*   The costs associated with the general administration of the business (like accounting, bookkeeping, legal, and research costs) are allocated as a fixed percentage to the burdened labor rate charges.
- *Inflation rate.*   This is the rate at which the value of the monetary unit declines, owing to increases in the cost of living, decreases in industrial capacity, and other economic phenomena.

As an example, let us assume that a 12-month software job was estimated to take 360 staff-months of labor to complete. To estimate cost, an average direct labor rate would need to be developed using the following labor mix as the basis of computation:

Labor category	Number of staff-months	Average monthly salary	Total cost
Senior software engineer	12	$4,200	$ 50,400
Software engineer	240	3,300	792,000
Software manager	24	4,500	108,000
Software quality assurance engineer	18	4,000	72,000
Software configuration management engineer	18	3,000	54,000
Software technician	24	2,000	48,000
Secretary	24	1,800	43,200
Total	360	$3,243	$1,167,600

Using this mix, the average cost of a staff-month of effort becomes about $3,243 ($1,167,400 divided by 360). Of course, no one on the project really receives the average salary (unless by coincidence) and adjustments must be made when actual charges are accrued and compared to the estimates. Such adjustments make a good cost accounting system a necessity for firms doing business under cost-reimbursement-type contracts.

Continuing with the example, assume that a 100 percent overhead rate and a 30 percent general and administrative (G&A) rate have been negotiated. The average cost of a staff-month would now be computed as follows:

Direct labor rate	$3,243.00
Burden rate (100%)	$3,243.00
Burdened labor rate	$6,486.00
G&A rate (30%)	$1,946.00
Average cost/staff-month	$8,432.00

On fixed-price contracts, the rates charged vary as a function of the market. Many buyers do not care what the cost/staff-month charges are. They only care about the bottom line and that they get proper value for their money. Therefore, costing may be done using some fixed rate in which overhead and G&A rates do not have to be discussed or substantiated.

9.2.2 Federal Government Regulations

The Federal Acquisition Regulations (FAR) and Public Law 87-653 required contractors to submit cost and pricing data for government contracts and subcontracts in excess of $100,000. Contractors must also certify that as of the date of agreement on price, the data is accurate, complete, and current. This is the case unless the contract is exempted because of lack of competition or establishment of a fair market price for a commercial item based upon an advertised catalog listing.

For defense contracts, several different agencies may become involved in rate determinations. For example, the Defense Contract Audit Agency (DCAA) may audit the contractor prior to contract award to determine what its actual direct, overhead, and G&A rates were during the previous year. Based upon these results and future hiring plans, the DCAA will work with the contractor to establish standard bidding rates. Using this information, the buyer may negotiate more favorable rates based upon economic arguments. For example, the government may argue that equipment should be purchased as a capital expense and amortized across all contracts as an overhead expense. The buyer, however, may argue that the expense is peculiar to a project and should be a direct charge.

The General Services Administration (GSA) may become involved if the item is a commercial product for which the contractor wishes to barter a discount for increased volume of sales to the government. If GSA can negotiate a favorable price, it will list the product in the GSA catalog. It is much simpler for a government buyer to order an item from the GSA catalog at the discounted price than to write a separate purchase order or to contract for it.

Independent of rate determinations, the buyer must make sure that the budget is approved and integrated with the Department of Defense (DOD) Planning, Programming and Budgeting System (PPBS). The PPBS runs on a tightly controlled schedule. If the acquisition is not synchronized to it, money may not be appropriated when it is needed. A wise buyer will ensure that the paperwork is completed in time to get through the PPBS signature gates. Many of these signatures must be coordinated at higher management levels when the dollar values involved exceed certain thresholds established by DOD directives. This increases approval and payment times.

As the contract unfolds, the buyer will monitor the contracting firm's performance and use fee to motivate it to keep a lid on costs. The DCAA may periodically audit the contractor during the contract to determine the actual rates and to adjust payments accordingly. This can occur even after the contract has been terminated.

The most interesting arguments in rate determinations deal with allowable and nonallowable costs. As we saw in Section 5.5, the FAR dictates what costs can or cannot be charged to a contract. For example, overhead expenses for advertising that are not needed to fulfill a contract requirement are nonallowable. Advertisements taken for public relations purposes are therefore excluded from the overhead calculation. Advertisements needed to recruit personnel for the contract team, however, are allowable and are included in the burden rate. These subtleties can be the cause of argument, debate, and negotiation. Both the buyer and the seller are well-advised to be honest and fair in all their dealings with each other. Rate determination should be done in a cooperative atmosphere and should not be treated as a form of warfare.

9.3 PRICING

Pricing is the art of figuring how much to charge the customer for the job in the face of competitive market forces. If the seller charges too much, it might not win the job. If it charges too little, it may go bankrupt. The buyer and seller want to settle on a price that rewards initiative, provides adequate reserves, and compensates the seller fairly for all work performed as part of the contract.

Most people mistakenly think that the price must exceed the cost for the seller to make a profit. Although it seems logical, this situation does not always hold true. A seller can set the price below the cost and still make money under certain circumstances. For example, assume that a seller has 20 software engineers. Ten of these engineers charge their time directly to contracts, and the other 10 charge all of their time to overhead. The seller undertakes a new job priced at a loss so that the 10 engineers on the overhead payroll can charge their time directly to the new contract. The effect of taking these engineers off overhead actually makes the job profitable because the overhead rate will decline and compensate for the loss. Thus the incremental contribution of this job to overhead and profit proves that taking the contract at a seeming loss was a wise financial decision.

9.3.1 Pricing Strategies

Typical pricing strategies used by the seller to win a job involve many factors and complexities. Setting a price that is attractive, overpowers the competition, lies within the buyer's budget, and responds to marketplace pressures such as demands for the best people, resources, and cash can be a trying experience. The law (and in federal government procurements, the FAR) may also constrain pricing decisions: For example, it is illegal to arrange a price based on industrywide collusion.

One of the following three methods is often employed to price an offer:

- *Full cost pricing.* Prices are proportional to the full cost of the item being acquired and are set to derive the same percentage profit margin across all related projects. An acceptable range of profitability is set, below which the seller will not take the job. The buyer and seller use predefined guidelines to establish the profit margins allowed on the acquisition.
- *Investment pricing.* Costs are shared and prices are set based upon some equitable investment formula. Both the buyer and seller share the potential risks and benefits associated with the acquisition. For example, the buyer may allow the seller to retain commercial marketing rights for a software product developed at the seller's expense if the seller prices the development software on a cost-sharing basis.
- *Promotional pricing.* Costs are not fully recovered by the offered price either to "buy into" a development or to account for the incremental contribution of the job to overhead and profit (as in the preceding discussion). Losses are written off by the seller as promotional or marketing costs.

Pricing a job just to make money is not in itself sufficient cause to justify the continued viability of a seller. The financial strength of a firm stems from its capability to manage assets like retained earnings, cash flow, and growth (or stability) and its ability to deliver quality goods and services to its customers. An attractive price alone may not be enough to ensure that the seller will keep its commitments in the real world. Preservation of assets may be more important to the seller when there is a need to guard against inflation, nontimely payments, and tax problems that result from factors independent of the contract.

Acquisition managers are advised to investigate the financial health of the seller and, if necessary, include protection against matters that may affect payments and cash flow in their contractual and pricing strategies. Lines of credit, swing loans, and other forms of financial insurance should be utilized to protect against default once the job has been awarded. In addition, copies of the source code may be kept in escrow to guard against nonavailability due to financial problems or bankruptcy.

9.4   COST ACCOUNTING PRINCIPLES

Most buyers require sellers to use generally accepted cost accounting principles to develop bids and keep track of costs when contracts involve progress payments or reimbursed costs. Such principles provide for separation of allowable and non-allowable costs in overhead and G&A rate computations. Various bookkeeping practices should be employed and ledgers maintained to ensure proper segmentation of the costs charged to a contract. Other accounting practices should be used to ensure that charges are auditable and can be traced to their sources. A good bookkeeping system should provide traceability from the approval of the contract charge (for example, the issuance of a purchase order or the submission of a signed timecard) to the actual incurrence of the charge (that is, when the charge is posted in the ledger using either a cash or accrual basis). Other types of accounting systems should be developed to demonstrate to the customer that the estimated costs included within a bid are based upon experience and are reasonable and credible.

The accounting function is responsible for collecting, summarizing, analyzing, and reporting financial information pertinent to the acquisition. The buyers and sellers use this information to ensure that resources are obtained and are used effectively and efficiently to fully satisfy the goals of the contract. The following seven principles guide the accomplishment of the cost accounting function within most firms:

1. *Money measurement.*   Accounting records are made of only those facts that can be expressed in monetary terms. Intangibles (such as goodness of management) are not taken into account.
2. *Business entity.*   Cost accounts are kept for business entities, not for the individuals associated with them. The buyer and seller may have to determine the financial status of multiple entities to determine overall performance relative to a contract.
3. *Going concern.*   Accounting assumes that the business will continue to operate indefinitely. Indicators of financial health are evaluated, but the failure of the business is never considered.
4. *Cost.*   Resources owned by a business are assets. Assets valued at cost are entered on the books for the amount paid for them. As time progresses, however, the real value of these assets may not reflect book value because of factors such as depreciation and devaluation. This is especially true for computer assets, because their real value goes down rapidly as new equipment is introduced. The accounting systems, then, may not accurately report the true market value of the assets of a firm and its real financial health.

5. *Dual aspect.* Accounting systems are set up to account for both assets and equities. They are not devised to measure or monitor contract performance. The claims of parties against the assets of a firm are called equities and are expressed in the form of liabilities (creditor's claims) or owner's equity. All assets of a business are claimed by someone, so assets must equal equities.

6. *Accrual.* Assets are valued on the books as they are derived or expended. As an expenditure is made, it is debited. When income is derived, it is credited. Many conventions exist for handling abnormal situations (such as prepaid expenses) in which the bookkeeping rules are not obvious.

7. *Materiality.* The accounting system does not attempt to record events that are so insignificant that the effort of recording them is not justified by the usefulness of the results.

It is important to understand that two sets of books may be used on a project. One set is used for control, and the other is used for taxes. The set used for control may be based upon an accrual basis, and that used for taxes may use the cost principles of accounting. Auditors, however, favor having the seller use the same system for both purposes.

9.5 COST ACCOUNTING AND CONTROL

9.5.1 Cost/Schedule Control Systems Criteria

The control of the cost of major acquisition contracts has been a continuing concern within the Department of Defense. Over the years, DOD managers have been effectively aided by the DOD cost/schedule control systems criteria (C/SCSC) and the cost performance report (CPR). The buyer requires the seller to provide cost data via a standard report so that the program managers on both sides can determine cost and schedule performance using earned value techniques. To ensure uniformity across projects, the seller's management system must be validated against a set of predefined criteria. These criteria require the seller to break down all known work for the next six months into detailed work packages using a work breakdown structure (WBS) that is typically supplied with the contract. A monthly budget for the contract is then developed based on the start and stop dates of these work packages and on the budgets assigned.

At the close of each monthly reporting period, the seller must be able to report the dollar amount of the budgeted cost of work scheduled (BCWS) for the period. In addition, the seller must be able to provide a report of the budgeted cost of work performed (BCWP). Regardless of the actual cost of the work, the BCWP includes only the budgeted amount for each element of work that the seller has completed. As Figure 9-1 illustrates, the difference between the BCWP and BCWS is the dollar value of the schedule variance (SV).

The criteria also require the seller to be able to accumulate actual costs expended during the current reporting period. This actual cost of work performed (ACWP)

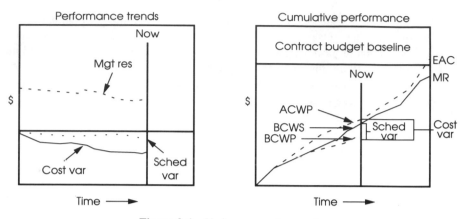

Figure 9-1 Variance report example

reflects actual, not estimated, costs. The difference between BCWP and ACWP is the cost variance (CV).

The C/SCSC requires the seller to analyze any significant variances to determine what action is required. Such actions must be contained within the CPR. Small variances are often lost as costs are accumulated up the WBS. Large variances, however, are generally not overlooked. At this time the WBS becomes an invaluable tool because it can be used to pinpoint trouble areas as the variance analysis progressively moves down the tree structure to the guilty cost accounts. The CPR also summarizes and periodically reports the status of all budgeted, actual, and estimated costs on the contract. An example of a variance report is shown in Figure 9-1.

9.5.2 Cost/Schedule Status Report

It has become apparent in the DOD that this concern should be extended to the cost control of nonmajor contracts (for example, development contracts less than $25 million or production contracts under $100 million). As a result, the cost/schedule status report (C/SSR) was established to meet the needs of all managers for cost and schedule information on nonmajor contracts in which the government assumes or shares the cost risk. The C/SSR is a standard data item with certain negotiable elements. Unlike the C/SCSC-CPR approach, the C/SSR requirement does not establish minimum standards with respect to the contractors' management systems. Neither does it involve the evaluation, acceptance, or rejection of the contractors' internal management procedures, except in cases in which compliance with contractual provisions relative to the report is questioned.

Although C/SSR appears to be a scaled-down version of CPR, some differences between the two reports should be clearly understood. The C/SSR requires neither cost performance reporting by functional organization nor incremental current-period reporting. In addition, C/SSR does not require the baseline and staff-loading reporting required by CPR. The most important difference between the CPR and C/SSR involves the definitions of data elements in BCWS and BCWP. For CPR reporting, BCWS and BCWP must be the actual result of the direct summation of work package budgets. The C/SSR permits the determination of these values through any reasonably accurate and mutually acceptable means. Table 9-3 provides definitions of C/SCSC and C/SSR terminology.

TABLE 9-3 Compilation of C/SSR and C/SCSC Terminology

1. *Actual cost of work performed (ACWP).* This is the cost actually incurred and recorded for performance measurement purposes in accomplishing the work performed within a given time period.

2. *Authorized work.* This is the effort that has been defined and is on contract plus any work for which contract costs have not yet been agreed upon and for which written authorization has been received.

3. *Budgeted cost for work scheduled (BCWS).* This is the numerical representation (in dollars) of the value of all work scheduled to be accomplished in a given period of time.

4. *Budgeted cost for work performed (BCWP).* This is the numerical representation (in dollars) of the value of all work scheduled to be accomplished in a given period of time.

5. *Contractual work breakdown structure (WBS).* This structure portrays the work to be performed as a tree in which the limbs represent the major activities and the branches identify the detailed tasks or work packages to be performed.

6. *Estimated cost at completion* or *estimate at completion (EAC).* This sums up the actual direct cost, indirect costs allocable to the contract, and an estimate of cost (both direct and indirect) for the work remaining.

7. *Management reserve (MR).* This is an amount of the allocated budget withheld for management control purposes, rather than designated for the accomplishment of a specific task or set of tasks. It is not part of the performance measurement baseline.

8. *Performance measurement baseline.* This is the cumulative total of all work packages within the contract (i.e., those synonymous with the cumulative BCWS at that same time).

9. *Significant variances.* These differences between planned and actual performance require further review, analysis, or action. Appropriate thresholds should be established for the magnitude of variances that will require variance analysis.

10. *Total allocated budget.* This is the sum of all budgets allocated to the contract. This budget should reflect the negotiated contract cost plus the estimated cost of any authorized unpriced work.

11. *Undistributed budget.* This is any budget applicable to the contract that has not yet been distributed to a CWBS element at or below the lowest level of reporting to the buyer.

9.5.3 Basic Objectives of C/SSR and C/SCSC

The basic objectives of C/SSR and C/SCSC are the same:

- objective, integrated cost/schedule reporting on contracts
- standardized cost and schedule performance reporting on contracts
- compatible cost and schedule data independent of contract type

These objectives are extremely important when the effort has a high degree of cost risk. The buyer may invoke either C/SSR or C/SCSC within the solicitation. The systems proposed to collect, normalize, and validate the data required to make the C/SSR or C/SCSC work must then be evaluated during the source selection. The buyer must include appropriate enabling clauses in the contract. Once the contract is let, the seller has 30 days to correct any deficiency in the system and to make it work to the satisfaction of the buyer.

9.5.4 Variance and Trend Analysis

The following information, derived from an analysis of C/SCSC and C/SSR data, can provide the buyer and seller insight into cost and schedule trends and variances:

1. *Cumulative contract performance status.* These time-phased cumulative plots of BCWS, BCWP, and ACWP from the beginning of the project show how cost and schedule vary against the performance measurement baseline. BCWP can be compared with BCWS to determine the schedule status of the project. The ACWP indicates the actual cost to perform the work indicated by the BCWP. ACWP can be compared with BCWP to determine if costs exceeded budgets. These plots do a good job of showing what the status of work is as a function of time throughout the term of the contract.

2. *Performance variance trends.* The schedule variance, SV, is the difference between BCWS and BCWP. The cost variance, CV, is the difference between BCWP and ACWP. The performance trends of a contract at any organizational or WBS level can be shown by these variances plotted on a monthly and a cumulative-to-date basis.

3. *Variance analysis.* When variance trends exceed predefined limits over several periods of time, a variance analysis should be performed to analyze the problem. A narrative report should be produced to set bounds for the problem, trace it to its source, and recommend corrective actions. If appropriate, management reserve should be allocated to fund the corrective action program.

9.5.5 Earned Value

Those who are not involved in DOD contracts may not be interested in C/SSR and C/SCSC concepts. These methods require sophisticated project management systems in order to capture, analyze, and report cost and schedule status and variances.

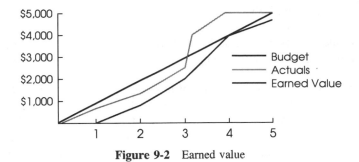

Figure 9-2 Earned value

They create a large administrative burden and generate a lot of paperwork. Yet these concepts have served as useful models for commercial sector developments. Many popular project management packages provide support for these concepts under the feature name "earned value determination and reporting."

Earned value is a way of relating milestone completion to cost and schedule status. The best way to explain this concept is to offer an example. Assume that five tasks are budgeted at $1,000 each and are scheduled to be completed within one month. When completed, these five milestones will earn $1,000 each. This means that no credit is received for either starting a task or for work in process. Figure 9-2 shows that at the end of the first month, about $600 was expended with no earned value. In other words, the milestone was not completed. Although the project has underspent, it is behind schedule and potentially in budget trouble. At the end of the fourth month, $5,000 has been spent against a budget of $4,000, and $4,000 worth of earned value has been achieved. In other words, the project is on schedule, but has spent more than the authorized budget. Note from the figure that this is a fixed-price task and that only $5,000 will be spent at the end of month five.

This trivial example illustrates the power of the earned value concept. Think about applying it to a larger job in which tens of tasks are in progress during any time period. Then think of using the concept to provide early indications of trouble as actuals are summed according to the WBS by tasks and are compared to budgets and earned value. Add to these concepts the power of schedule networks and critical path analyses, for example, and it is easy to see why a computer-based project management package is an indispensable tool to a program manager.

9.6 TECHNICAL PERFORMANCE INDICATORS

Identifying cost and schedule progress without tying it to technical performance is a mistake. It does not do a business much good when its staff delivers an inferior product to its customers, even if the product is on time and within budget. The rework of costs and schedules, bad will, and demoralization that occur as a result make such premature delivery a very unwise business decision.

Many buyers require the seller to use other more technical measures of performance to supplement earned value, C/SCSC, or C/SSR reporting. Although they are related to cost and schedules, these measures are selected to provide early warnings of technical problems that earned value measures do not catch. When it is feasible, these measures should be applied at the work package level. The five most used measures are the following:

1. *Size growth.* This is a measure of how the size of each computer software configuration item (CSCI) grows as a function of time. It is very revealing because cost and size are directly related, as the cost model discussion showed. If growth goes unchecked, cost will too, because someone will have to program these new lines. Often, the buyer requires the seller to baseline the original size estimate. The seller will re-evaluate the estimates periodically and report how the new forecasts compare to the old ones upon which the budgets were predicated. (See Section 6.4.6.3.)

2. *Staffing rate.* This is a measure of how well the buyer and the seller staff the project. A staffing curve is fit to the schedule, identifying the numbers and categories of the people needed. Actual staffing is then compared to these needs and is reported periodically. Attrition and turnover are also incorporated into the plots so that problems can be determined. (See Section 6.4.6.4.)

3. *Change rate.* This is a measure of the stability and maturity of project requirements. If these requirements are shown to be subject to frequent change, the project may suffer false starts and wasted effort. Every attempt should be made to solidify the requirements and to baseline them as soon as possible during an acquisition. The metric of Chapter 6 (Section 6.4.6.3, Figure 6-9) may be used to track this or a requirements metric as shown in Figure 9-3 may be used.

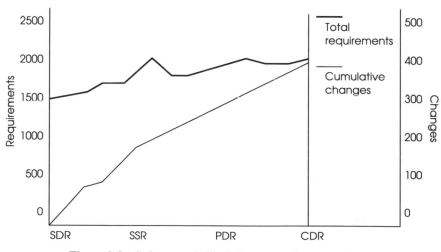

Figure 9-3   Software volatility/software requirements changes

4. *Rework rate*. This measures the number of times it takes to get a product right as it is being developed. The goal, of course, is to do it right the first time. If minutes of reviews indicate a high degree of rework, project managers should try to find out the cause. High rework rates indicate that people are wasting effort because they don't understand how to get the job done.

5. *Error rate*. This is a measure of the discrepancies that are found as the software is integrated and tested (for example, with engineering testing and beta testing) as a separable product from the hardware. High error rates indicate that the product is immature and that its quality is questionable. (See Section 6.4.6.2.)

9.7 COST MANAGEMENT STRATEGIES

The buyer and seller can use a variety of different methods to estimate, confirm, price, control, project, and manage cost. Independent of the method that is selected, costs must be managed once budgets and schedule are established for the contract. Otherwise, they might run out of control and escalate unacceptably.

The consequences of cost overruns are severe. First, the buyer's and seller's reputations become tarnished. This affects each side's ability to trust the other side's competence. Distrust is like a cancer that destroys teamwork and causes the work to stop flowing. As the cancer spreads, more and more therapy is needed, and the costs skyrocket. Second, schedules may have to be extended if money is not available until later years. Customer dissatisfaction may result because the buyer's schedule needs are not being accommodated. Third, if money is a problem, the acquisition may have to be diminished or canceled. Finally, morale deteriorates as pressure is applied to the team to correct the situation with hard work and unpaid overtime.

The buyer and seller typically treat the symptoms and not the cause of the cost problem. Although this strategy may provide temporary relief, it does not fix the underlying problems. For example, the schedule itself may be impossible. Unless schedule relief is offered, added effort alone will not be able to correct this problem. The reason for this is simple: Effort and schedule are not interchangeable commodities on a software project (the famous Brook's Law) [Brooks, 1975]. As another example, size growth may plague the project if realistic estimates are not developed at the start of the project. Instead of adding effort based on requirements, the team may attempt to limit the size to some arbitrary number.

All of this leads to the conclusion that cost must be managed throughout the acquisition. To accomplish this, a workable infrastructure should be devised and a strategy for cost management should be implemented that revolves around this infrastructure. The engineering life cycle models discussed earlier in the text are the infrastructure models most organizations use. They define what needs to be generated, when, and by whom in order to get the product out. They identify the steps in the process, the products, and the reviews and relate them to the people and organizations that are responsible for their orderly accomplishment.

Buyers and sellers can institute three main strategies to manage costs:

1. *Exception management strategy.*   This strategy imposes a system of internal controls on every activity undertaken to support the contract from inception to death. The cost accounting principles reviewed earlier are implemented through a management system that provides an auditable trail through every cost decision. The buyer expects the seller to manage cost and sets variance thresholds that, when exceeded, elevate the problem to a buyer-seller team for review and solution. In other words, a control system is implemented that involves the buyer when exceptions to the norm occur. This is a typical strategy employed on commercial contracts in which multiple suppliers provide goods and services (for example, the development of a commercial airplane like the Boeing 757 aircraft).

2. *Cost consciousness strategy.*   This strategy imposes a system of external controls on every activity undertaken to support the contract. The cost accounting principles reviewed earlier are implemented through a management system that provides a paper trail through every cost decision. Technical and cost decision making are separated so that no collusion occurs. Reports abound, and audits are plentiful as independent reviewers continuously survey the books to ensure that no liberties have been taken and that reported statistics are correct. This is the typical strategy employed on government contracts. It often causes friction and costs a great deal to implement because it requires many watchers who contribute marginally to the effort.

3. *Gating strategy.*   This strategy imposes a system of controls on activities that occur between major milestones or gates in the project's lifecycle. Internal to the gate, the seller manages cost and reports exceptions using an auditable system. At gates, the buyer and seller review actuals and projections and make decisions relative to the next phase of the development. Actual costs and costs-to-complete are reviewed along with the phase products. This is a typical strategy employed on commercial contracts in which interim progress and market conditions govern whether it continues to be profitable to develop a new product (such as the development of a new communications switch).

   Each of these strategies has advantages and disadvantages. Selection is normally governed by the customer through contractual requirements. Independent of the strategy chosen, costs must be managed throughout the development so that growth can be controlled.

9.8   BUILDING A COST AND PRODUCTIVITY DATABASE

A database of cost and productivity data is an invaluable planning tool. It enables the buyer and seller to better calibrate their cost models, understand their past performance, evaluate cost trends and drivers, and generally take advantage of lessons learned, especially as they impact costs and schedules.

To understand their past costs and productivity, most organizataions build a historical database containing their experiences. To construct this database, the buyer and seller must capture data of interest during all phases of an acquisition. In order to do this, they must define metrics and identify data needed to support their long range goals. For example, cost model estimates and actuals would have to be collected, normalized, and analyzed to devise the updated calibrations needed to achieve the goal of improved cost estimation accuracy. To achieve this goal, a system that captures this data automatically would have to be developed in order to consistently collect reliable data. The most useful data tends to be subjective because it reflects lessons learned. Therefore, both hard and soft data need to be collected and put into this database.

The primary means for collecting these data are reviews (for example, design reviews, code walk-throughs and management meetings) and instrumentation built into the software support environment. A post mortem review is also valuable because it enables the team to get together and discuss what they did right, what they did wrong and, most importantly, what they would do differently if they had the chance to begin the project again.

A variety of statistical techniques are used to analyze the hard data in these databases. For example, regression analyses (such as least squares fits of data) are used to establish relationships between variables such as size in source lines and effort in staff-months. After these analyses are completed, norms can be established based upon actuals and used as the foundation of accounting and control over estimating, costing, and pricing.

This chapter was intended to introduce cost estimation and management strategies and techniques. Hopefully, the information and advice provided will enable firms to develop estimates and realize them in a manner that satisfies the intent and content of its contracts. In the next chapter we switch themes by discussing a subject that is extremely important to acquisition projects: quality management.

REFERENCES

[Brooks, 1975]: F. P. Brooks, *The Mythical Man-Month: Essays on Software Engineering*, Reading, MA: Addison-Wesley.

CHAPTER 10

Quality Management

Quality has become a critical software issue, particularly in large, complex, and costly systems. Poor quality can manifest itself in different ways. The software may have a high failure rate or be difficult to use or maintain. A product can meet all operational requirements yet still be of poor quality. For example, the time to fix errors could be excessive, resulting in user work-arounds and high maintenance costs.

Traditionally, quality management of software was addressed through the software quality assurance program. This program was carried out by the seller's software quality assurance function. As software became more important to society, it was natural to turn to a quality program modeled on the existing one for hardware. The hardware quality program involves checking, or inspecting, the processes of production and the products that evolve. There were problems with copying that approach. During software development, software quality assurance personnel were forced to inspect the processes of software engineering, something that they were unprepared for. Software quality assurance required an in-depth knowledge of software engineering techniques, and personnel were not trained to accomplish this task. Software engineering was difficult enough for early developers. Software quality assurance tools and techniques were primitive when available. The practice has since improved. With an improved discipline, trained and experienced personnel, and better tools, quality personnel are in a better position to manage quality.

Today quality is in transition from an approach that relied solely on a quality assurance function to a quality management concept that places the responsibility on all—the buyer and seller management, project management, and the engineering team. This change is reinforced by the concept of Total Quality Management (TQM). Basically, TQM says that quality is everyone's responsibility. Thus the responsibility for quality is shared throughout the buyer and seller organizations, and they are assisted by the software quality assurance function in the pursuit of that goal.

This chapter discusses how to specify quality requirements, how to implement a quality program, and how to assess quality. Software quality is placed in context with modern practice. The proper place for a quality assurance program, what that program entails and how it is managed, and what techniques may be used are addressed. Along the way we develop a larger view, which focuses on building quality into the product through a sound engineering process.

10.1 SOFTWARE QUALITY

Quality is not a well-defined term. One DOD standard (*DOD-STD-2168*) defines software quality as "The ability of a software product to satisfy its specified requirements." Yet if those requirements did not specify quality goals, the product has little chance of achieving quality. Indeed it is common practice to invoke a quality assurance program without having quality requirements. This situation has arisen because of a poor understanding of quality and the engineering practice to implement it. Progress has been made both in the definition of quality and the use of measures or metrics to assess it.

There are different interpretations of quality. One person may think that a quality automobile is one that will not break down on the road. Another may think of quality in terms of the car's handling or performance characteristics. Still another view may be that low maintenance costs represent quality. All these views are correct—there are many ways of defining a quality automobile. The same is true of software. Some believe that software with a low failure density is quality software, while others prefer a product that is maintainable.

Simply to require a high-quality product is ineffective. Implementation of a quality assurance program without specific quality requirements, while current practice, is not as effective as specifying requirements for the software product.

A concept of quality factors has been developed in work sponsored by the United States Air Force [Bowen, 1985], which provides insight and definition for software quality. The work defines 12 quality factors. Each of these factors has a specific connotation for quality (Table 10-1). Understanding these factors and their application provides the basis for defining quality requirements for the project. Selective use focuses the project on specific requirements, for example, maintainability.

The factors are grouped according to performance, design and adaptation. Performance requirements deal with, for example, how well does the system make use of memory? Design requirements examine the ability of the design to verify performance requirements. Adaptation requirements deal with the ability of the system to allow for or accommodate change. That is, how easy is it to convert to a new computer (hardware) system?

Naturally, the assignment of factors to these categories is somewhat arbitrary. A selection could be made of specific factors to the exclusion of others and

TABLE 10-1 Software Quality Factors

Acquisition concern	Quality factor	User requirement
PERFORMANCE	Efficiency	Resource utilization
	Integrity	Security
	Reliability	Confidence of operation
	Usability	Ease of use
DESIGN	Correctness	Requirements conformance
	Maintainability	Ease of repair
	Verifiability	Ease of verifying requirements
ADAPTATION	Expandability	Ease of upgrade of capability or performance
	Flexibility	Ease of change
	Interoperability	Ease of interface to other systems
	Portability	Ease of transporting to other systems
	Reusability	Ease of conversion to another application

Source: Bowen, T. P., G. B. Wigle and J. T. Tsai, *Specification of Software Quality Attributes, RADC-TR-85-37,* Vol. 1–3, Boeing Aerospace Company, 1985.

independent of the acquisition concern provided by the taxonomy. For example, if efficiency of resources and maintainability are the most important requirements for the project, they should be emphasized or selected as the only quality requirements. During project planning, appropriate quality requirements should be defined for inclusion in the statement of work. Later, an example is presented to show how these quality factors may be employed to define quality requirements.

One of the deficiencies of quality factors is that, in some cases, they are difficult to define and therefore to verify. It is fairly simple to define efficiency requirements, for example, by the percentage of utilized memory or response time of a display device. It is difficult, however, to define flexibility. One can stipulate that the system be designed to accommodate change. However, it is difficult to implement and verify this requirement. This requirement usually results in the use of structured code disallowing the use of programming statements such as GO TOs that increase implementation complexity. Verification may be performed by measuring the average manhours over time to implement changes to the software. Software engineering practice has not yet evolved to the point where this particular requirement can be implemented effectively. Thus, in the selection and specification of quality factors, the manager has to ensure that requirements for quality, like operational requirements, are amenable to specification, implementation, and verification.

Quality has to be specifically defined according to the needs or requirements of a particular project. Because requirements for projects differ, quality requirements will vary. In order to specify quality, therefore, one must understand what is important to the project and select and emphasize the pertinent requirements.

A banking system can be taken as an example. In the initial planning process, managers decided that they want a system that is easy to use, will not break down, and can be expanded as the banking business prospers and grows. The three most appropriate quality factors are reliability, expandability, and usability. Now the task is to determine how to measure or verify that the developed system meets those requirements.

The first, reliability, is the easiest. There are models available, based on failure density, that can be applied [Musa, 1989]. In fact, a simple fault density metric, measuring the number of detected faults in a system per unit line of code over some period of time (for example, in CPU or clock time) can be used. Expandability is more difficult, but there are techniques that can be used. For example, the user can require that new data added to the system will be accommodated without revising system hardware or software. The user can stipulate that system performance will not degrade as new data is added. The tester can use dummy data to test these requirements.

Usability is even more difficult to assess, basically because it is more subjective. In this case, the user may require average training times based on a certain degree of user proficiency. It will be difficult to measure this before the system is complete, and even after it is delivered. During the course of the training program, the buyer may bring in users to determine the adequacy of training and, indirectly, the usability of the system. In this case, the buyer will have to create measures to determine the extent to which this requirement is met. These may be subjective because they stem from opinion.

10.2 QUALITY ASSURANCE PROGRAM

The perception in the engineering community is that if the engineering process is sound and trained, experienced personnel are attached to the development, a quality assurance program is unnecessary. After all, if the process is perfect, one should not have to check on it. The problem, of course, is that the process is not perfect. Quality assurance is as necessary for software as it is for hardware. A proper quality assurance function plays an important role in the management of the project. In traditional practice, quality assurance is implemented by or through the seller's quality assurance function.

We have seen that quality is not a precisely defined term. Our view is that each project must define the quality requirements that are important to the project and then manage to those requirements. The traditional quality assurance function must support this activity.

A quality assurance program is based on the following definition of software quality assurance:

> A planned and systematic pattern of all actions necessary to provide adequate confidence that the item or product conforms to established technical requirements [IEEE, 729-1983].

Notice that this statement does not define quality; it describes the quality program. The definition of software quality is:

1. The totality of features and characteristics of a software product that bear on its ability to satisfy given needs; for example, conform to stated specifications.
2. The degree to which software possesses a desired combination of attributes.
3. The degree to which a customer or user perceives that software meets his or her composite expectations.
4. The composite characteristics of software that determine the degree to which the software in use will meet the expectations of the customer [IEEE 729-1983].

Thus, a quality program is a set of activities that presumably provide, or assure, a quality product.

The quality program is a planned set of activities designed to collect objective evidence that technical requirements have been established, that products conform to established technical requirements, and that the delivered products can perform the intended operations for the specified period. The software quality assurance function performs this by:

- Preparing quality assurance plans for the development that define the goals of and detail the activities of the QA function.
- Participating in the development process—monitoring process activities to ensure that they conform to planned project activities and meet established standards.
- Evaluating the products of development to ensure that they conform to preparation standards and meet the project's requirements.

The quality assurance function is the monitor for both the buyer and seller for the conduct of the quality program. It must perform its activities in concert with the rest of the development process with minimum interference.

10.2.1 Establishing Requirements

Planning for a quality assurance program is the first step. Quality requirements must be considered in planning documentation such as the project management plan and detailed in project specifications. These may be stated in any number of ways, whether using quality factors, general requirements for the quality assurance program, or a combination of both.

A typical quality program is based on general functional requirements for the quality assurance organization such as quality audits and documentation inspections. Requirements for the program are described in the SOW or referenced to a quality assurance standard. The SOW should require at the minimum that the contractor develop a quality assurance plan for the development project.

10.2.2 The Quality Assurance Plan

The quality program begins with the preparation of the software quality assurance or evaluation plan. This plan is normally prepared by the seller after contract award or project go-ahead. A plan should be prepared for each specific project. Although a seller may have a standard plan or approach, the plan must be customized to the specific needs of the project, including, for example, special quality requirements and organizational considerations. The elements of the software quality assurance plan are:

1. *Identification of the system.* A short description or hierarchy of the organization or taxonomy of the software system. This serves as an introduction and focuses on the specific products of development.

2. *Quality objectives.* These should be objective statements and requirements for the quality assurance program. If quality factors are used, methods for verifying factor attainment should be defined. The plan should describe how the function will ensure that the processes for attaining the factors are implemented. It should describe the procedures for assessing achievement.

3. *Organization.* A description of the organization responsible for carrying out the quality assurance function. The plan should specify the authority and responsibility of the organization and relate it to the project organization. It is particularly important to ensure that the quality function retain independence of operation. It should include the relationship to other contractor efforts involved in managing or evaluating the software product (for example, IV&V and SETA contractors).

4. *Resources.* A description of the resources available and necessary for performing quality assurance on the project.

5. *Quality assurance procedures, methods, and tools.* The techniques that will be applied for the quality assurance activity are described. Examples include inspections, reviews, and audits. The techniques should be described in enough detail to be implementable, or reference to specific documented procedures should be given.

6. *Quality assurance activities.* This section should detail the specific activities that will be performed by the quality assurance program for the project. Quality assurance activities are normally organized into process- and product-related activities. Process activities ensure that the specific development processes conform to accepted and described practices. Product activities are attuned to the evaluation of the specific products of the development, for example, design specifications. The following are examples of activities that should be considered for inclusion in the program:

   • Process-specific evaluations. These would cover the conduct of project activities such as design reviews and walk-throughs.

- Evaluation of project activities. These might include configuration management, a software development library, as well as documentation and data preparation, distribution and control.
- Product evaluation. Products include design documentation, test plans, and user manuals.
- Evaluation of subcontractor products and the subcontractor quality assurance program.
- Recording results. This should describe the methods for documenting the results of quality assurance activities and the procedures for implementing corrective actions.
- Other activities that may be considered for inclusion are review activities and quality assurance in testing and acceptance inspection.

7. *Schedule*. A schedule of the quality assurance activities to be performed on the project. This should be related to overall development activities.

A software quality plan may not be required for every project, particularly if the project is small or not appreciably complex. That does not mean that quality assurance should be ignored. In situations that do not warrant a quality assurance plan, it is sound practice to describe the quality assurance program in the project plans, that is, the software development or project development plan.

10.2.3 The Quality Assurance Organization

The seller quality assurance organization is chartered to conduct the quality assurance program through auditing the processes of development and inspecting the products of development. The organization must be effective. It must have the authority and responsibility for conducting the program and not be subject to undue influence from the developing organization. Project plans should identify the relationship of the quality assurance function to the project and ensure that appropriate resources are budgeted to efficiently implement the program. Figure 10-1 shows an example of a typical contractor product assurance organization.

On small projects it is typical for the contractor to embed the quality assurance function in the project development organization. That may work, but only if sufficient resources are allocated for the performance of quality assurance activities. This situation is prevalent in smaller contracting organizations, which seldom have an institutionalized quality assurance organization. In this situation the buyer must determine whether the quality assurance program is real and not just the result of an ambitious seller trying to meet RFP requirements. On large projects the quality assurance function should be independent of the development (project) organization. With most large contractors, this is the norm. Typically, the quality assurance function is in a technical services or product assurance organization as shown in Figure 10-2. One of the dangers of having a totally independent organization is that the developer may ignore quality assurance or view it as an inspection function. The buyer has to remain cognizant of this possibility and take action to ensure that quality assurance remains a viable function that contributes in a positive manner to the project.

10.2.4 Tools, Techniques, and Methods

The primary tools, techniques, and methods used by the quality assurance organization include the following:

1. *Reviews.* The quality assurance function conducts reviews as a part of its responsibilities, and quality assurance personnel also participate in project

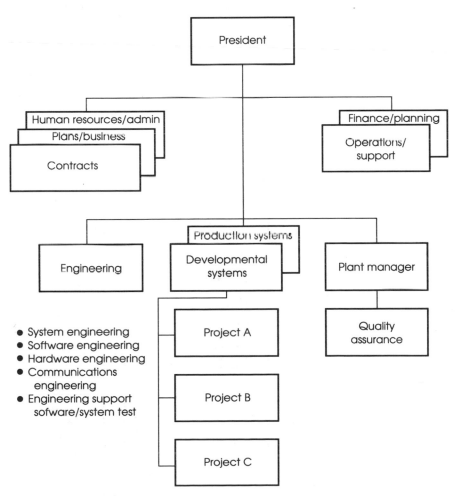

Figure 10-1 Typical contractor organization

reviews. This participation has two purposes. The first is to assess the quality of the review process. The second is to assess the specific products of the review.

2. *Inspections*.   An inspection is a narrow activity, normally conducted on a nonparticipatory basis. Typically, these activities involve the review of specific documents. The inspection is not normally technical. The quality assurance function rarely has the capability for conducting technical activities. The review should be made against specific criteria for the preparation of documentation such as standards or formats for the documents.

3. *Audits*.   An audit is very much like an inspection but is related more to reviewing a process or is devoted to resolving a specific problem. Thus the objective is fairly focused. Audits are normally conducted on a participatory basis with project personnel. An example of a quality assurance audit involves the examination of procedures for conducting reviews.

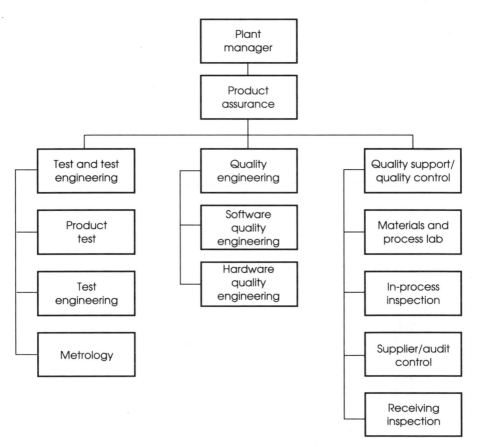

Figure 10-2   Product assurance organization

4. *Tools.* In current practice, most quality assurance activities are manual functions best performed by manual techniques. However, there are exceptions. Certainly the assessment of a specific quality factor is amenable to automation. Factors such as efficiency can be measured by performance monitors. Automation can be of great assistance in the performance of process audits. A tool such as the Expertware POWER™ tool provides an automated capability for managing an audit checklist, automatically recording results, preparing trends, and providing or preserving historical data.

10.3 TEAM APPROACHES FOR BUILDING IN QUALITY

The best way to build quality into the development effort is through a sound, well-planned software engineering program. The concern for quality should not be limited to the quality assurance function within the contractor organization. Quality is the responsibility of all—the buyer, seller, and quality assurance organization. The quality assurance organization has the responsibility to check on the quality program, but it cannot make a quality product. Quality is not obtained simply by invoking a quality program. The project manager and his or her team have to accept their responsibility for developing a quality product, meeting the quality goals that have been set.

This situation has been reinforced by disciplines such as verification and validation (see Section 12.3) and the introduction of new concepts such as Total Quality Management (TQM). Total quality management was developed by an American, W. E. Deming, and is common in Japan. The basic premise is that quality is the responsibility of each individual. TQM requires cultural change; that is, it is implemented by techniques that change the culture of how systems and products are developed. It provides a view that the individual plays a key role in improving the process of development and attaining quality in the resulting products. This concept is taking hold in the United States. The DOD has a major initiative to introduce TQM, and many contractors are following that lead [Schwartz, 1990]. TQM has the promise to change the manner in which government and industry approach their everyday tasks across the spectrum of activities they are involved in. For more information on TQM, consult the Additional Reading list at the end of the chapter.

10.4 ASSESSMENT—THE ROLE OF METRICS AND MANAGEMENT INDICATORS

The use of metrics is being applied increasingly to quality assessment. Metrics are not only a technique for assessing quality. They are applied to project management and engineering activities as well (See Section 6.4.6). In Chapter 6, a number of high-level metrics called management indicators were introduced. Here, the concept of metrics as a means for assessing quality is presented.

Metrics are a method for measuring the characteristics of the software with the objective of predicting performance. One of the early methods for characterizing software is Halstead's Software Science. This method measures two basic characteristics of the software—the number of distinct operators and the number of distinct operands. Using these characteristics, one can calculate aspects of the software such as length (the sum of the total number of occurrences of operators and operands), volume, and vocabulary.

Another method is McCabe's Complexity Model. This method uses classical graph theory to describe the complexity of software. The method counts the number of edges in the program (e), the number of vertices (n), and the number of connected components (p). Using these measures, the cyclomatic number of the program can be calculated by

$$V(G) = e - n + 2p$$

This method is intended to provide a relative figure for assessing complexity.

Measures such as these, while useful for understanding the characteristics of the software product, must be related to the attainment of specific requirements. For example, if an objective is a simple design to foster maintainability, low complexity is desirable.

One approach to providing a methodology for relating metrics to quality requirements is the work referenced in Section 10.1 [Bowen, 1985]. This work describes a series of metrics for evaluating the quality factors based on the software quality model shown in Figure 10-3. The taxonomy for quality factor maintainability is shown in Figure 10-4. The figure shows the five criteria that define factor maintainability. Each criterion is further described by a number of measures, or metrics, as shown in the figure (that is, CS.1, CS.2, and so on). When combined, the metrics provide a quantitative score for each criterion. The criteria scores can then be combined to form an overall score for the quality factor.

There are serious problems with the use of this methodology. First of all, it depends on the collection of an extensive amount of data for the hundreds of metrics

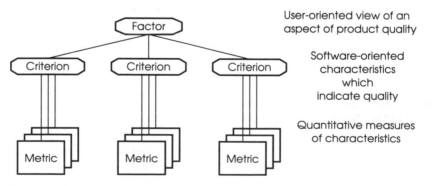

Figure 10-3   Software quality model

Source: Bowen, T.P., G.B. Wigle, and J.T. Tsai, *Specification of Software Quality Attributes, RADC-TR-85-37*, Vol. 2, Boeing Aerospace Company, 1985, pp. 2–16.

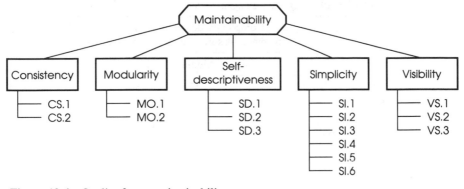

Figure 10-4   Quality factor maintainability

Source: Bowen, T.P., G.B. Wigle, and J.T. Tsai, *Specification of Software Quality Attributes, RADC-TR-85-37*, Vol. 2, Boeing Aerospace Company, 1985, pp. 2–14.

required to support the methodology. Second, there is no experiential baseline score that provides the manager with a gauge for satisfactory behavior and compliance with requirements. Third, the cost of collecting the measurement data has impeded introduction, thus contributing to the lack of experiential data. This is especially problematic if one wants to employ the entire methodology with all the quality factors, criteria, and metrics required.

In spite of the difficulties, metrics play an important part in modern practice for evaluating the processes and products of development. In fact, there has been good experience with the use of quality factors in Japan and to a limited extent in the United States. In data collected applying these factors over a nine-year period, a cost reduction of 35 percent in full-scale development and 51 percent after 12 months of operation was observed [Marine, 1988]. The cost of using this system was attributed at 3 percent of development cost per quality factor. Needless to say, this cost may deter many managers because the up-front development cost is usually very critical in a competitive evironment. The reported results, however, could do much to convince managers to take the chance of trying quality factors.

10.5 ASSESSING THE COST OF QUALITY

The cost of a quality assurance program clearly depends on the requirements of the development effort. If the effort is a prototype, quality may not be an important factor. If the development has implications for human safety, for example, an avionics system on a commercial or military aircraft, the demand for a quality product is great. Quite often the desire for quality is high, but the will to pay for it is not. Quality, and the cost of quality, is an integral part of the development effort. Not only must quality requirements and a quality assurance program be planned and implemented, but the cost for the quality program must be budgeted up front and the program monitored to ensure that resources projected for quality assurance are expended.

TABLE 10-2 Quality Program Costs

	Complexity/development risk (Percentage of software development cost)		
Size	Low	Medium	High
Small <$500K	1%	2–3%	3–5%
Medium $500K–2M	2–3%	3–5%	≈5%
High >$2M	2–5%	≈5%	5–10%

K = 1 thousand
M = 1 million

The cost of a quality program will depend on the nature of the program. For a traditional quality assurance program, costs range from 5 to 10 percent of overall software development costs. Table 10-2 provides a guide for managers on expected costs for traditional quality assurance based on complexity, risk of development, and size of effort. Naturally these costs will vary, depending on the rigor of the effort. That must be left to the planners of the system acquisition. The quality program should be laid out and then costed.

The percentages in Table 10-2 vary, depending on the characteristics of the project. For example, if the project is small but of a highly complex nature, the upper bound of 5 percent should be used (from the intersection of small size and high risk).

The most common danger is that the quality program will not be fully implemented after the contract is awarded. What could and often does happen is that in the bidding and pricing process the contractor, in order to be as competitive as possible, will shave costs but not requirements. Thus, the quality assurance function is forced to reduce manhours but not quality requirements. This is clearly not in the buyer's interest. At contract negotiation, the buyer should be particularly attuned to this situation. Remember, you get what you pay for. Or in the words of that common adage, "You can pay me now or you can pay me later."

What is the cost of quality? A better question is, What is the cost of not having a quality assurance program?

10.6 SUMMARY

In order for a quality assurance program to be successful, a cooperative effort between the developer and contracting agency is essential. The program has to be properly thought out and planned early in the project, certainly before the RFP is issued. There must be management commitment on both sides. The buyer should be aware that cost reductions by the contractor to become more competitive, particularly in so-called best and final offers, usually imply a cutting of resources to programs such as quality assurance.

A common problem is that the quality assurance program is not seriously integrated into the project management and development process. The quality assurance process is conducted but has little affect on the development. The buyer has to continually evaluate the quality assurance function to ensure that it is beneficial. This can be accomplished at project reviews. However, a much better solution is individual review of the quality function, perhaps through audits, and informal contact with quality assurance personnel.

Although a contract is a formal agreement, a successful software manager will rely on informal contact with the customer. Formality often breeds bureaucratic intransigence and secretiveness. The organization takes over and tends to force a conservative position in interactions between the buyer's project management team and the seller's development team. Management of software development is a two-way street, requiring cooperation, push and pull on both sides, and good communications. Good communications require a certain degree of informality.

It usually falls to the buyer to ensure that the quality assurance function is sound. Thus, the buyer acts as the quality assurance function for the seller's quality assurance program. If the contracting agency does not review the quality assurance program at periodic intervals and utilize the program to assess development progress, it is easy for the seller to ignore quality assurance. Remember, the development manager, preoccupied with trying to manage the project, may not understand how to make quality assurance work for the goals of development or may even view it with annoyance. It is better to not expend the resources for a quality assurance program than to pay for one that is merely pro forma.

On the whole, a good quality assurance program is an effective management mechanism for the development effort. For quality assurance to be effective, it must be based on a sound set of verifiable requirements. The use of metrics supplies the management team with the means for quality assessment. A quality assurance program, however, is not a cure-all for quality problems—that results only when the entire team is focused on that objective.

In the next chapter we discuss a variety of special acquisition topics: innovative contracting approaches, cost-sharing and back-ended payments, reusability/modularity, reliability warranties, subcontract management approaches, data rights, maintenance transition, and productivity.

REFERENCES

[Bowen, 1985]: T. P. Bowen, G. B. Wigle, and J. T. Tsai, *Specification of Software Quality Attributes, RADC-TR-85-37,* Vol. 1–3, Boeing Aerospace Company.

[DOD, 1979]: *Department of Defense Standard 2168,* Defense System Software Quality Program, August 1.

[IEEE, 1983]: IEEE, *ANSI/IEEE Std 729-1983, IEEE Standard Glossary of Software Engineering Terminology,* New York: The Institute of Electrical and Electronic Engineers, Inc.

[Marine, 1988]: G. E. Marine, "Integrating Software Quality Metrics with Software QA," *Quality Progress,* November, pp. 38–43.

[Musa, 1989]: J. D. Musa. "Tools for Measuring Software Reliability," *IEEE Spectrum,* Vol. 26, No. 2, pp. 39–42.

[Schwartz, 1990]: K. D. Schwartz, "DOD Hopes Quality Control Can Save Time, Money," *Government Computer News,* January 8, p. 40.

ADDITIONAL READING

Deming, W. E. *Out of the Crisis.* Cambridge, MA: MIT Center for Advanced Engineering Study, 1982.

Deming, W. E. *Quality, Productivity and Competitive Position.* Cambridge, MA: MIT Center for Advanced Engineering Study, 1982.

Department of Defense, *Draft Total Quality Management Guide.* DOD 5000.51-G, August 23, 1989.

Humphrey, W. S. *Managing the Software Process.* Reading, MA: Addison-Wesley, 1989.

Pressman, R. F. *Making Software Engineering Happen.* Englewood Cliffs, NJ: Prentice Hall, 1988.

CHAPTER 11

Special Topics in Acquisition Management

Software acquisition is a broad and complex subject. In this chapter, we discuss several topics, not to provide a detailed treatment, but to help the reader develop recognition and a degree of understanding of the issues involved.

11.1 INNOVATIVE CONTRACTING APPROACHES

Requirements definition represents one of the most difficult issues and risk areas in software development. Many methods have been proposed to alleviate or eliminate this problem, from requirements definition contracts to concepts of "evolving" software through a series of incremental system deliveries. Although these methods have potential advantages, there always seems to be a contract bottleneck. The buyer wants the contract to be based on a definitive statement of requirements so that the effort can be realistically costed. Herein lies a potential fallacy. Project costs are based on requirements that may not represent the system that the user desires or the system that will be delivered. This is because requirements collection is not a rigorous discipline. In most cases, the work environment is dynamic. There will be a changing set of users due to retirements, promotions, and hirings. Work procedures are continually evolving as new methods are introduced. Changing markets demand new user services. These are natural situations that must be accommodated. One strategy is to use a contracting approach whereby a series of incremental contracts are phased over the development.

The effort could start with a requirements definition contract. This initial contract might be awarded on a fixed-price basis. Any seller selected for the effort can continue into the next and subsequent phases. This would ensure continuity of the work force. If the seller's performance was unsatisfactory, the next increment can be recompeted. Each subsequent phase would be negotiated based on the results of the previous phase contract and the defined work for the upcoming phase contract. Thus, the effort results in a series of contracts, perhaps with several competitive sellers initially, narrowed down to one for the development and subsequent operation and maintenance phase (Figure 11-1). The buyer's advantage in this approach is that the process can be altered before major commitment of resources is made. Each contract can be based on a more definitive set of requirements. This makes budgeting and pricing for future increments more realistic and manageable.

The disadvantage, of course, is that the buyer is faced with a series of contract actions. Most buyer contracting organizations try to avoid this situation in the interest of holding down the organization's work effort. Contracting organizations are always overworked. This leads to a paradox—the contract cart is driving the development horse. A solution to advanced software development in a dynamic requirements environment is negated to avoid increasing administrative effort. If aggressive and innovative software development approaches are to be taken, contracting organizations will have to be more flexible and take greater responsibility for the ultimate success of the acquisition.

The series of contract efforts could result in the delivery of successively enhanced operational versions, or increments (Figure 11-2). The delivery of each increment allows the buyer to test the operational implementation as it proceeds, thus avoiding the front-end requirements definition dilemma. The trick is to deliver a usable increment of the system before requirements based on new personnel and work processes invalidate the requirements statement. Coupling prototypes into the concept adds another positive dimension. Prototypes afford rapid development and testing of requirements. A prototype is typically developed to test concepts, refine

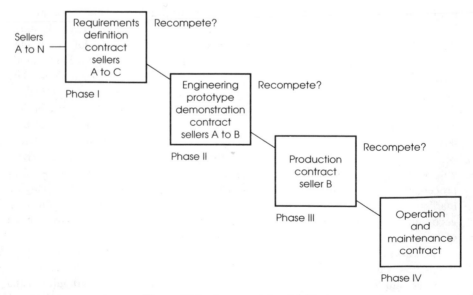

Figure 11-1   Incremental acquisition

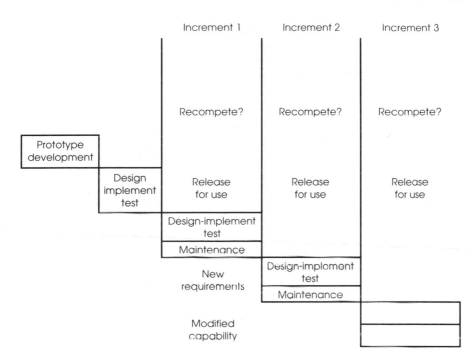

Figure 11-2   Incremental delivery

requirements, and reduce risk. It is not intended for operational use. It is not a fully operational system meeting all requirements nor does it have the required support materials (such as documentation and training). Each incremental delivery must be accompanied by appropriate training and user documentation so that the system can be used effectively.

11.2   COST-SHARING AND BACK-ENDED PAYMENTS

This book has so far discussed conventional contracting strategies. Yet many innovative approaches are being used within industry to have the buyer and seller share risk and to provide the seller with positive incentives to control costs. Some risk is involved in each approach. The potential rewards offered to both parties therefore tend to be greater. Let us look at several of these schemes to see how they work.

As a first example, let us explore the world of cost-sharing. All parties in such buyer/seller relationships make investments, share risks, and share in potential rewards. Take a hypothetical telecommunications firm that wants to subcontract the development of a TCP/IP protocol emulator. There may be no takers when the company tries to contract for the software at a fixed price. In working with several potential vendors, one means to generate interest might be through the negotiation of commercial rights to market the package. In return for a fixed-price arrangement and the rights to use the package within the buyer's organization, the firm gives the vendor limited rights to sell the emulator on the open market. In addition, the firm promises to add a year's maintenance contract at a fixed level of support to sweeten the pie.

There is some risk that the seller will overrun the contract and have to incur some cost. Future sales could compensate for such losses, and the maintenance contract ensures that there will be continued support for product enhancements after the emulator is introduced. In addition, the firm would serve as both a beta test site and reference (hopefully) for the product. The buyer's risk is minimized with the establishment of a fixed price for a reasonable time period. Also, the price of maintaining the product might be reduced in the future should commercial sales take off.

Other forms of cost sharing are practiced in which the buyer provides the seller with limited rights to the product or business futures for concessions on price or risk. Research and development costs can be shared so long as they lead to some form of increased profit. All in all, such arrangements work best when both the buyer and seller benefit over the long term.

The Air Force's Advanced Tactical Fighter (ATF) represents another case study in acquisition innovation. To bring the ATF in on budget, the Air Force altered its procurement rules and the way it conducts business. Instead of holding a design competition, the Air Force pushed for competitive prototype fly-offs between contractor teams from large aerospace companies. By so doing, they forced the contractors to put up their own development money to fund their aircraft. The Air Force also issued general performance guidelines to the contractors and did not insist that they meet the government's detailed design specifications. Instead, they were issued simple guidelines that basically said, "Bring the jet in under budget." In addition, the Air Force baselined the cost and stated that any resulting cost savings due to contractor innovations would be shared.

Another form of innovative acquisition approach is through back-ended payments. Instead of reimbursing the seller's allowable costs and making progress payments, the buyer holds the majority of payment in reserve until the seller either delivers a product or meets a major milestone (such as completion of a major test or delivery of a partial capability). Under such an arrangement, the buyer's risk is minimized because the seller must generate products in order to get paid. Of course, such a situation is offered only when the buyer has added some form of sweetener, like increased profit or business futures, to the pot. Whatever the formula employed, it must be made attractive to both the buyer and the seller. It must also be administratively tractable; that is, payments must be tied to something easily measurable. It must reward risk and be fair and equitable.

Let's look at another example. A factory is being automated and the buyer is concerned about the seller's performance. The seller is proposing an innovative and complex system. The buyer wants it but is afraid that it will not be delivered on time. The buyer suggests a back-end payment scheme to put pressure on the seller to deliver according to the agreed-upon schedule. The seller wants to get a first customer for the product to reduce development risk. The fees the buyer will pay will offset the development costs. Risk is high, but so are the potential returns. The buyer and seller work out a back-end payment arrangement that is keyed to major delivery milestones in the factory. In return for concessions, the buyer promises to allow the seller's prospective clients to see the system in operation. Both sides benefit from this agreement.

Other new acquisition approaches exist and have been tried for software and software-based systems. Each tries to have the buyer and seller share risks and rewards. Each tries to insert flexibility into a process that is often inflexible.

11.3 REUSABILITY/MODULARITY

Two general categories of software reuse may be encountered. The first involves the use of previously developed software in a way that is similar to its original application. This is the case in precedented systems where the new system may be an upgrade of or an analog to an existing system. The second involves packaged software units that can be put "on the shelf" in a software library or repository and called into use as components in a new software application. Although these may seem similar, there are distinct differences. The most notable difference between the two is that packages in the latter case can be used by parties not involved in their production. A seller, or set of sellers, builds reusable packages intended for general application and made available to a wide body of developers. There are ongoing efforts to develop reusable packages, including a DOD project based on the Ada higher-order language. There are serious business issues, however, that preclude the sharing of software across sellers. For example, a seller may desire to retain a package for its own use to increase its competitive posture. It will be some time before this concept gains widespread use in software acquisition.

The first case normally applies to a seller that has focused on a specific applications area such as banking, logistics, or training. Over the course of developing these systems, the seller acquires applications area expertise and usually has a number of systems to draw from for similar applications. The combination of experience and the accumulation of large amounts of developed software (algorithms, designs, and code) allows the seller to rapidly develop similar systems. This environment is depicted in Figure 11-3.

The buyer would naturally like to take advantage of reusable products. Reusable software has many advantages. It allows software to be rapidly prototyped. There have been cases of prototype systems developed in a matter of months with productivity rates in excess of 1000 instructions monthly. Of course, these rates do not result in a production quality system. They do afford the seller the capability to respond rapidly to user requirements. The reusable components can then be customized with the development of other software that may not be in hand to develop a production quality system.

Reusable software permits rapid evaluation of requirements. Thus the conduct of development can be better controlled through a better definition of requirements and

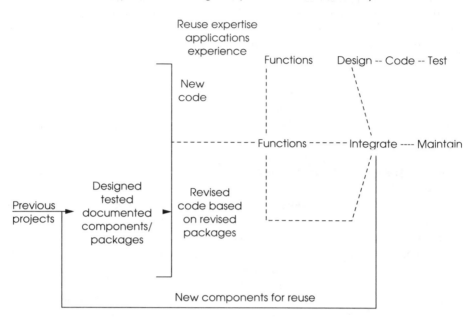

Figure 11-3 Reusable development environment

up-front effort. The more applicable reusable components are to the development, the more the expected cost can be limited.

With reusable software, there are disadvantages as well. The most prevalent problem is that reusable components are often considered proprietary to the seller. This raises the issue of ownership of the completed product. Also, components may be written in a language unacceptable to the user, resulting in a mixed system (that is, software delivered in several languages). In order to simplify the maintenance environment, components may have to be rewritten in a common language acceptable to the user. Documentation may have to be rewritten if it exists at all. The final problem is the level of trust a potential user places in the package. If the software bombs, users become reluctant to try reuse again.

With buyer-furnished software, the buyer has a certain degree of responsibility for the performance of the system. The buyer must share responsibility for failure if the system does not perform as required. Even if the reusable components are not the cause of system performance degradation, this may be difficult to establish. In this situation, the seller may try to shift a portion or all of the blame of failure to the buyer. One way to circumvent this occurrence is to make the reusable components available for evaluation during the proposal preparation period. This allows the seller to inspect the products to determine their suitability based on the seller's approach. The seller may accept responsibility for the buyer-furnished software or propose alternative approaches. Whenever feasible, the buyer should not direct the use of buyer-furnished components, but require their evaluation by the potential sellers as possible components for the development.

Although reusable components present some problems, their use provides an overall advantage to the buyer and should be employed whenever practical. After all, they do represent potential cost and schedule reduction.

11.4 RELIABILITY WARRANTIES

A great deal of attention has recently been focused on warranties for software-intensive systems. For example, the DOD Appropriations Act of 1984 contained a provision requiring written guarantees for weapons system procurements. Effective January 1985, the FAR was revised to require that weapons systems of cost greater than $100,000 should:

- conform to the design and manufacturing requirements delineated in the contract
- be free of all defects in material and workmanship at the time of delivery
- conform to the performance requirements delineated in the contract

If the item fails to meet any of the three criteria, the contractor will be required by the DOD to correct the failure at no additional cost or to pay reasonable repair costs.

Similarly, such warranty protection clauses have been put into use within the telecommunications industry to guard against poor quality. Properly executed, warranty clauses can focus attention on the level of quality the buyer expects from the seller. There exists, however, uncertainty and misunderstanding among buyers and sellers alike relative to the proper specification and execution of such warranties. This section tries to clarify warranty concepts so that readers understand how they could be applied to provide incentives to build quality systems/software at minimum life cycle cost.

There are basically four forms of warranties invoked contractually:

1. *Commercial warranty*—fixed-price warranty where the seller's liability is limited to replacing faulty parts with a like item in working order. The seller does not assume any other form of liability whatsoever.
2. *Extended warranty*—fixed-price, extended duration commercial warranty where the seller fixes all legitimate failures at no additional cost to the buyer throughout the life of the contract.
3. *Reliability warranty*—fixed-price, extended duration specification warranty where the seller fixes only legitimate failures in excess of an allowed number based on specified reliability at no additional cost to the buyer throughout the life of the contract.
4. *Performance guaranty*—fixed-price, extended duration guarantees where the seller agrees to meet specific performance requirements. In case of failure, the seller is held liable for free maintenance and/or redesign and retrofit at no cost to the buyer. Performance measures could include such items as mean

time between failure (MTBF), response time, speed, accuracy, range, and resolution.

The first type of warranty is straightforward and has been used for years in software contracts. Literally, it is a "let the buyer beware" warranty where the seller is liable only for replacement parts.

The second type of warranty has also been applied widely to software products through what is called a maintenance contract. Most operating systems and commercial software packages fall under this heading. The seller repairs or replaces the failed version with a new release that fixes the problem. Interim solutions are permitted (for example, patch tape) so long as the software's advertised functionality and performance are preserved. Of course, the buyer waives all right to hold the seller liable for damages outside the seller's control. Timeliness of repair and responsiveness of the seller are sometimes inadequate.

The third and fourth types of warranties are much harder to implement on software projects. The interpretive problems involved in measuring and determining the seller's compliance make administration of such warranties very difficult. As a result, such warranty clauses have not been used much in software contracts.

11.4.1 Warranty Specification

Let us look at several ways buyers have utilized such warranty clauses to provide sellers with incentives to control life cycle costs.

1. *Extended or reliability improvement warranty.*   Buyers have used an extended warranty on contracts where the seller performs software maintenance services over an extended period of time at a specified level of repair (that is, anticipated change and bug rates) on a fixed-price basis. Thus the buyer provides the seller with an incentive to improve quality because engineering change proposals (ECPs), which reduce the seller's repair and support costs, are not allowed. To maximize profit under a contract where repair levels are set beforehand, the seller must achieve high reliability so that the maintenance effort is less than originally estimated. The buyer must not renege on the obligation should the seller achieve better than anticipated reliability levels.

2. *Reliability warranty.*   Buyers have used reliability warranties on contracts where the seller commits to providing a certain level of system or software quality as part of the contractual requirements. Quality is measured somewhat qualitatively using the indicators discussed in Chapter 6. As a consequence, administration of the warranty clauses is difficult because only limited "hard data" are available to determine incentive or penalty payments. Often an award fee type contract is used during acquisition to reward the seller for meeting contractual warranty requirements. A maintenance contract with an extended or reliability improvement warranty is then used to focus attention on preserving the quality as the system is operated, extended, and enhanced in the field.

Independent of the approach taken, both the buyer and the seller need to agree that the risks and rewards associated with the warranty are fair. In addition, an approach to administering the warranty needs to be negotiated as part of the contract. Both parties need to do their homework to ensure that warranty provisions are understood, reasonable, realistic, realizable, measurable, and enforceable.

11.4.2 Warranty Implementation

The implementation of a warranty involves considerable effort. A monitoring system, using appropriate metrics, must be established. The buyer and seller must coordinate and negotiate warranties with subcontractors supplying software and institute measures to determine whether or not the subcontractors are in compliance with the contract provisions. The buyer must work with the seller to set in place a way to measure end-product acceptance. Procedures and operating instructions must be established to document the work-in-process that occurs as a result of the warranty provisions of the contract.

It should be noted that final negotiated warranty clauses are not always firm. Phrases are constantly reworked, reinterpreted, and renegotiated. Many warranties are overcome by events. They are never enforced because the software requirements are in such a state of flux that it is impossible to administer warranty provisions. Windows of feasibility change because new software standards, methods, or technology is introduced in the midst of the contractual effort. Nothing is fixed in concrete.

In the real world of warranty implementation, most software firms shy away from such provisions because they fear the negative consequences will outweigh the positive. "Why should we subscribe to such provisions? Can't we waive these requirements? After all, they are impossible to measure," they argue. Few, if any, buyers have forced the issue: "If I can't administer a warranty easily, why invoke it contractually?" All these arguments have merit. It takes a lot of courage for the buyer and seller to agree on a warranty clause for software. Yet warranties will become more popular as the software process becomes more measurable. The industry will likely see increasing pressure to apply them in the near future.

11.5 SUBCONTRACT MANAGEMENT APPROACHES

As previously discussed, the contractual environment is often more complicated than a single buyer and single seller relationship. On the buyer's side, there is also a user or user community that the buyer usually represents with respect to the acquisition. Depending on how active the user will be in the management of the acquisition, this arrangement can present problems such as changing requirements, especially as the effort proceeds. It is common for the user to become smarter about project requirements as the development progresses. On the seller's side, the contractual environment is often a team arrangement of several subcontractors, or third-party suppliers, that have negotiated agreements with the seller. Other suppliers may be involved, directly under contract to the buyer. For example, the buyer may be conducting a fly-off between several prime contractors, or the buyer may be employing an outside contractor to provide engineering support or IV&V. Thus the contracting environment is often more complex than it may seem (Figure 11-4).

The complexity of the contracting environment complicates the buyer's management task. The buyer cannot assume it is only to manage the prime contract, relegating the management of third-party suppliers to the prime contractor. Although unable to interfere contractually with the seller's prerogative to manage the contracting team, the buyer must recognize that it exists, understand the pitfalls that it may present, and understand how to achieve control and visibility of the total effort. Here are some of the issues that concern both the buyer and seller as a prelude to understanding management actions that help to provide a viable contracting and project environment:

1. *Partition of work.*   Often the prime seller dictates the terms of the agreement to the subcontractors. Although a prerogative of the seller responsible for the overall development, this can work to the detriment of the effort. The seller commonly attempts to assemble the best team in order to win the contract. After contract award, however, the team can be altered. The seller may wish to increase its proportion of the effort in order to attain more direct labor charges. This can result in reduced technical effort. Presumably, the third-party suppliers are selected for their special technical abilities. Substitution detracts from that rationale and could result in a degraded technical capability.

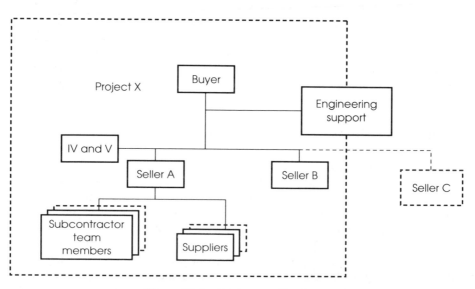

Figure 11-4   Contract environment

2. *Price*. The prime seller can dictate the pricing arrangement to the subcontractors. For example, assume that the third-party supplier bids a cost-plus, fixed-fee contract to the prime seller, while the prime seller bids a fixed-fee contract to the buyer. The price that the prime seller places on third-party supplier tasks could be much more than the effort is worth. If the contract effort is a task-ordering agreement where the seller "buys" individual tasks at prenegotiated rates, the seller could be inhibited from ordering the high-price tasks assigned to the third-party supplier, thus deflating the third-party supplier's prospective piece of the overall effort.

Another price issue involves the pressure that the prime seller can put on the third-party supplier during cost negotiations. The prime seller could pressure the third-party supplier to reduce the price of tasks without negotiating a reduction in performance requirements for those tasks with the buyer. Thus the third-party supplier is placed in a difficult position. If it resists, it could be eliminated from the contracting team. If it complies, it will face a severe cost/performance dilemma after contract award—forced to cut costs and still meet the requirements of the contract. Such arrangements are seldom visible to the buyer but become evident during contract performance.

3. *Communication and visibility*. In a complex acquisition the buyer's primary interaction is with the prime contractor. Subcontractor efforts are often hidden from the buyer's management team in order to protect seller control over the development team. Although this is quite natural, it does present visibility problems for the buyer. Critical portions of the effort may have been assigned to a third-party supplier. Unless the buyer management team has insight into these efforts, it may not be aware of developing problems. Experience shows that the prime contractor will attempt to shelter a subcontractor's efforts, resulting in decreased buyer visibility.

The buyer should ensure contact with third-party supplier personnel. The buyer should not be insulated from the suppliers. To create contact, the buyer should have third-party personnel participate in appropriate project activities (such as reviews, testing, quality assurance, and configuration management). For example, the seller configuration management plan should describe how the various suppliers involved in the project will participate in configuration management control board activities.

Communications can also be fostered through informal contacts. Although the buyer must take care not to interfere with the authority and responsibility of the prime seller, informal contacts may be used to gain insight and visibility outside the formal management processes. Another means of closing the communications gap is through the use of networks. An electronic message system connecting all the participants in the project allows the management community to communicate freely in both an informal and formal manner.

4. *Management mechanisms*. The prime seller may impose its own management mechanisms, terms, and conditions on the subcontractors (such as accounting procedures and management reporting). The prime seller may require that the subcontractor collocate personnel at the seller's location,

regardless of where the work would be more effectively accomplished. There may be legal issues such as access to proprietary information or data rights to software products that the subcontractor brings to the overall effort. These issues compound the management environment.

In some cases, it may be extremely difficult or impossible to impose direct management controls over the subcontractors. There are techniques that may be applied, however, that help the situation.

The buyer should require that the same management requirements placed on the seller's contract be utilized for all subcontractors. For example, management indicators, reviews, and configuration management controls should be consistently applied throughout the project environment. The management environment should be as homogenous as possible. If the buyer does not impose this requirement on the seller, the seller is left to its own devices, and management controls on subcontractors could be weak or nonexistent. This will promote a management schism between the seller and third-party suppliers. Visibility and control are weakened, and information needed by the buyer and seller to effectively manage the project will be limited. There is a caveat: if the third-party supplier is small, the seller must be careful not to overburden it with management procedures. Management controls must be consistent with the management capability of the supplier and commensurate with supplier-assigned tasks.

The buyer should ask for either the seller's subcontractor management plan or procedures manual, or at the least a description of how the seller manages subcontractors. Each prime contractor should have a set of internal management procedures for dealing with third-party suppliers. If it is impractical to provide these to the buyer, they can be summarized in the seller's proposal. These procedures should be described in the seller's project management or development plan. The buyer must take responsibility for promoting a good management and communications environment.

11.6   DATA RIGHTS

The allocation of rights to software and technical data represents an important issue governing use of the products that are developed or delivered under the contract. Rights are equally important to the buyer and seller. The buyer wants to ensure that it has sufficient rights to enable it to use, maintain, and reprocure software and data. The seller wants to ensure that its proprietary rights in software developed at its own expense are protected in order to maintain its competitive advantage. There has also been increasing concern about protecting the right to commercialize software which has been developed at government expense.

Software developers rely on several types of intellectual property protection for their software, including copyright, patent, and trade secret law. Copyright is still the most popular form of copyright protection, although the scope of copyright protection continues to be litigated. Trade secret law is the second most commonly used form of intellectual property protection for software and is often used in combination with copyright protection. The use of patent protection for software is also increasing.

When a software developer develops a product, much like an author writing a book, he or she may claim a copyright in the software. According to the Copyright Act of 1976, the owner of the copyright to a particular software product has five exclusive rights, three of which are particularly relevant to software:

1. The right to reproduce the work (make copies).
2. The right to prepare derivative works (based upon the existing work).
3. The right to distribute copies of the work to the public by sale, transfer of ownership, or through rental or lease.

Although, as a general rule, only an author of a work is entitled to claim a copyright in it, under the copyright law's "work-for-hire" doctrine, the copyright in a work made by an employee in the scope of his or her employment is owned by the employer. The doctrine also recognizes several categories of specially comissioned works that are considered works for hire. Since software usually does not fit into one of these categories, the copyright in specially commissioned software products is owned by the developer, in the absence of a written agreement providing for a different alocation of rights.

11.6.1 Government Rights in Publicly Funded Software

Since a considerable quantity of software is either developed under federal government contract or licensed to the federal government, the government procurement regulations are relevant to any discussion of software procurement. The general policy provisions and standard contract clauses found in these regulations govern all transactions by which software and its documentation are acquired by the government.

Data rights are a software issue because government regulations have historically treated software as data. Under the current regulations the government claims unlimited rights in software developed at public expense, which includes the right to

1. Use the software in whatsoever manner they choose.
2. Duplicate the software to make additional copies.
3. Revise the software to correct errors or create derivative products.

There is some confusion about what constitutes unlimited rights in data. Some argue that "unlimited rights" implies ownership of the data, whereas others argue that it is merely a broad license. Anything less than these rights would be limited or restricted rights. The owner of a product assigns certain limited rights to a product when it is marketed—usually to allow copies for the purpose of creating backup copies for protection and limiting the use of the product to a specific computer or set of computers or to a specific set of personnel. These limited rights are quite common for software that is commercially available. However, for customized software, they are probably insufficient.

The DOD supplement to the Federal Acquisition Regulation (FAR) defines unlimited rights as the "rights to use, duplicate, or disclose technical data, in whole or in part, in any manner and for any purpose whatsoever, and to permit others to do so." The definition of limited rights to data includes the rights to use, duplicate, or disclose technical data, in whole or in part, by or for the government, with the express limitation that such technical data shall not, without the written permission of the party furnishing such data be: (1) Released or disclosed in whole or in part outside the government; (2) Used in whole or in part by the government for manufacture, or in the case of computer software documentation, for preparing the same or similar computer software; or (3) Used by a party other than the government. In essence, these are the minimum rights that the government will seek with respect to software that is not acquired at government expense.

There is also the matter of restricted rights. Restricted rights allow the government, according to the DOD FAR supplement, to do the following:

(1) Use computer software with the computer for which or with which it was acquired, including use at any Government installation to which the computer may be transferred by the Government; (2) Use computer software with a backup computer if the computer for which or with which it was acquired is inoperative; (3) Copy computer software for safekeeping (archives) or backup purposes; and (4) Modify computer software, or combine it with other software, subject to the provision that those portions of the derivative software incorporating restricted rights software are subject to the same restricted rights.

Item 4 provides a loophole in that few commercial vendors will allow a product to be combined or modified unless, of course, appropriate renumeration is provided. Confusion also arises with the preclusion of the government, under the copyright act, from obtaining a direct copyright for software developed at government expense.

In order to ensure the full spectrum of rights afforded by copyright, the government (or customer) may want to include a provision seeking to assert ownership by obtaining a copyright for the software developed for it by the seller. The Copyright Act of 1976, however, prohibits the federal government from directly acquiring copyrights. The government uses a "special works" clause for this purpose. In effect, this clause claims a copyright for the data as a "work for hire." Unfortunately, the use of this clause is inconsistent with the copyright act. A better option for the government is to take a copyright to software developed at public expense by "assignment, bequest, and the like." Within NASA, a special works clause is used that requires the seller to do just that and assign the copyright back to the government. This approach is a better solution to the government's dilemma and is consistent with the copyright act.

11.6.2 General Strategy

Although data rights is a typical problem in government procurements, it is becoming an increasing problem in the civil sector as well. The following steps, therefore, which are suggested as means for the government obtaining rights in the software, provide guidelines in civil sector procurements as well.

1. Determine the purpose of the software product and the need for data to support that purpose (for example, maintenance through a competetive follow-on contract).
2. Develop a preliminary logistics concept that includes the use and maintenance of the software. Provide that guidance to the sellers in the RFP.
3. Provide for predetermination in the data rights clause in the RFP package. This clause should require that the seller identify, to the extent possible, all software that will be developed and used by the seller during development, the rights that the buyer will acquire in that software and data, and ownership of copyright in software.
4. Negotiate a data rights agreement with the selected development seller based on the predetermination data and the logistics plan.

It may not be possible to ascertain the ownership of all the software products at the time of contract award. For example, the seller may decide that a specific software tool that was not identified at the onset of the effort needs to be employed. The buyer must recognize that these cases will occur. The buyer should establish categories of software that may be developed or used during the development effort. The rights to each category could be prenegotiated so that when new products emerge, appropriate rights may be applied. Generally, the products will fall into five categories:

1. Software developed at the expense of the buyer.
2. Software used in development that is considered proprietary to the seller.
3. Software that will be provided by third-party suppliers.
4. Commercially available software provided by the seller (possibly acquired and used by a third-party supplier).
5. Inventions discovered in the course of performance.

The general approach is to ask the prospective sellers to project the software to be applied/used/developed into one of the above categories with the suggested rights that they will assign for that category. If the buyer has determined that certain rights are required, those requirements, by category, could be placed into the RFP and used to evaluate the various sellers' proposals. Insofar as possible, all software that can be identified at the beginning of the project should have its data rights established. At the least, predetermination provides a starting point for establishing rights to data.

The first category should be clear, except where the seller claims to use proprietary methods that will be incorporated into the code of the software. The second and third categories are similar, except that an additional layer of contractual management is involved, the third-party supplier. This category often proves troublesome. The buyer's strategy is to ensure that any software in this category is provided with at least limited or restricted rights. The seller's strategy is to ensure that the negotiated rights protect its competitive position in subsequent market actions and opportunities.

The fourth category does not normally present a problem. Here the buyer wishes to ensure, at the minimum, that the products used will be commercially available to the buyer or customer during operation, maintenance, and support. The real issue is that the seller may acquire these tools/products specifically for the project using project funds. In that case, the buyer must establish that the seller has acquired sufficient rights to enable it to sublicense the buyer the rights needed for maintenance and support. The seller may try to buy these products out of overhead monies in order to retain the rights to the product after operation. If, however, the product was specifically acquired for use on the buyer's project, the buyer should have the right to acquire whatever rights were licensed by the third-party supplier to the seller for the use of the product.

The fifth category is probably the most complex. It is a valid issue but is beyond the scope of this limited treatment.

11.7 MAINTENANCE

Maintenance is a support function that occurs routinely in a software project. Maintenance involves correcting faults, modifying the system to incorporate new requirements, incorporating changes that add capability, and modifications to enhance performance. Support for the system must be planned at the beginning of the project. Decisions about documentation and delivered software (especially support software and test cases) are extremely important if responsibility for maintaining or upgrading the system is to be transferred to a new seller. The buyer may not realize that these preparations must be made or may assume that the support of the system will be provided by the seller. When this occurs, the buyer may be left with a system that will be improperly documented and difficult to maintain.

Such considerations are often neglected at the start of an effort. The buyer normally requires the developer to maintain the system for a period of time after it is delivered and in operation, usually for a period of one to two years. If transition planning is not accomplished, the buyer will have problems downstream. The key transition issues are:

1. Will the seller be required to provide maintenance and support and for what period of time?
2. Will the buyer want to transfer maintenance and support of the system to a new supplier, either at the successful conclusion of the development or at a later time?

3. Will the system be recompeted at a later time to provide for major enhancements or a new maintenance supplier?

4. Will the buyer require that system maintenance and support be transferred to the user organization?

There is a range of possibilities, but the stategies for dealing with each are similar. Appropriate documentation is necessary to support any transition, and the support facility must receive adequate consideration.

As previously pointed out, a wide range of documentation is possible for any given project. Typically, the buyer will require that user and/or operations manuals be prepared to support utilization of the system. The specifications required for the development and programming maintenance manuals are also necessary for proper transition. Other documentation considerations, however, require transition planning actions.

- *Test documentation.* Normally, formal test documentation is required and delivered with the system. There are other data that should be considered for delivery: individual test cases, test drivers, software development folders, and so on. These can be delivered in contractor format to hold down documentation costs.

- *Tools and support products.* Consideration should be given to the delivery of any special tools that have been used in the development. This is especially important if the tools have been developed by the seller. If the tools are provided by a third-party supplier, a reasonable degree of assurance should be obtained that they will be commercially available to either the buyer or subsequent maintenance and support suppliers.

- *Training materials.* These are normally required to support operational use. However, consideration should be given to acquiring these materials to provide for possible recompetition of the system.

The data rights to all documentation, whether acquired or not, should be ascertained at the onset of the project. If this is not accomplished, there will most likely be problems when the buyer later desires to recompete or transfer maintenance. The key decision will be what rights to acquire. For example, rights to a commercially available tool are not important or desirable. However, the rights to a tool generated by the seller are important. As discussed in Section 11.6, the spectrum of rights required is also important. The buyer does not necessarily require what are commonly referred to as unlimited data rights. Unlimited data rights are normally required only when the buyer wishes to ensure that it has the authority to freely give the data to another supplier for uses such as creating derivative competitive products. This is probably an extreme case, as the buyer is not usually in the business to organize a supplier competitive market. It may be used where the buyer's goal is to transfer a technology, such as a compiler for a higher-order language, in order to make it commercially available.

The purpose, or use, of the data is important in determining the extent of data rights required. The buyer may not require the right to revise the software product. Normally, the right to revise software is required to allow revision of the software by a new supplier, especially for the creation of derivative products. A derivative product is one that evolves through the incorporation of changes for correcting errors and adding new capabilities. Unlimited rights, which would allow a new supplier to create a product that may be marketed in direct competition with the original developer, are not, in most situations, warranted.

The following guidelines explain the general principles involved in the acquisition of data rights to support maintenance:

1. *Customer maintenance.* The buyer must acquire all the software necessary to support changes and revisions to the products and the right to modify the products.
2. *Contract maintenance.* The buyer must acquire, in addition to (1) the right to supply the software to a third-party contractor.
3. *Public domain.* The buyer must acquire copyright protection of the software so that it can make the software available to the general public.

Table 11-1 summarizes data rights required by different categories of use.

The buyer must take into account the support facility that the software product will be maintained on, especially if maintenance will be transferred to the user. A software support facility consists of the hardware and software necessary to support maintenance and redevelopment of the software system. Usually this will be synonymous with the facility used to develop the original system. However, because of special tools that may be required to support maintenance actions (for example, regression test tools), the maintenance and redevelopment facility could be different.

A support facility represents a large investment for the seller, and the seller's approach to the development of a system is often based on the software development facility that the seller has in place. It is not to the buyer's advantage to dictate a specific support facility. This forces the seller, unless it already has a compatible facility in place, to take on a costly enhancement effort or to forgo the development opportunity. In some situations, the buyer is forced to mandate a specific support facility. For example, the buyer may be developing a system that will be maintained

TABLE 11-1 Data Rights for Maintenance and Support

Category of use	Rights
Developed software	Unlimited rights with copyright
Commercial tool/product	Commercial (limited) license
Developed documentation	Unlimited rights with copyright
Existing documentation	Restricted rights to use and copy

in a facility as part of a larger system, dictating the requirement for a common buyer or user support environment.

There is a wide range of possible facilities depending on the nature of the development effort and the envisioned concept of maintenance and support. In some cases, where the system involves unique hardware (for example, an air-craft avionics system), the seller has to develop a facility to support that hardware configuration. Figure 11-5 depicts a support facility for an avionics system. In more general applications, say a banking or library management system, the choice of hardware is quite open and the seller has a number of possible host environments. The choice of support concept will therefore depend on the circumstances of the development project. The following are several possible scenarios with accompanying support approaches. In each, the buyer is interested in assuming maintenance support and therefore employs a rigorous approach to obtaining an appropriate support facility.

1. *General system.* This type of system is dominated by a combination of off-the-shelf software and general-purpose, commercially available computing hardware. In this environment, the host support system is identical to the operational system. The developer may build the system on the host facility and then operate it on the same or identical hardware after successful system testing.

OFP   Operation flight program

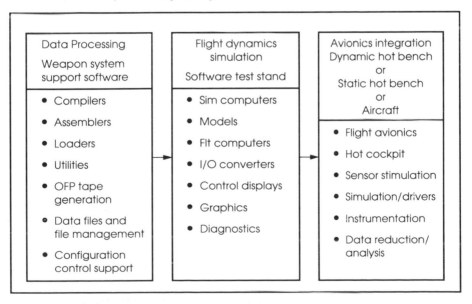

Figure 11-5 Avionics integrated support facility

The buyer should ensure that the system is supported by commercially available software development products that run on a variety of hardware systems. For example, if a DBMS is required, one that has a wide range of host environments is preferred to a DBMS that runs only on one system, or worse, is unique to a specific hardware vendor. The seller normally chooses the DBMS in accordance with program requirements. However, the buyer can control the selection by stipulating that the selected DBMS be available on multiple hardware operating system environments. Another consideration involves the language(s) employed to code the software. Standard languages that have been implemented in a wide variety of systems should be used. For example, instead of specifying an HOL, the specific set of acceptable HOLs that should be considered should be identified. For example, if COBOL is used, ANSI-STD-COBOL should be specified. This will ensure the widest possible applicability of the system if recompetition is envisioned.

2. *Different host/target systems.*   In this scenario, the software is developed on a host system and then retargeted to a different system. The retargeting process takes code written for one computer and produces code that will run on another. This is accomplished through a cross-compiler, which accepts the original language for the system, for example, Pascal, and generates code that runs on the target machine (Figure 11-6). The target system may be unique and not generally commercially available (for example, a control system for automating a production line). Rather than develop the software on the target system, a host facility is used for a variety of reasons.

- The target system may not be available at the onset of development.
- The target system may lack a strong software development environment, making development more costly.
- The target system may not support easy programmer access.

Usually, the host environment will incorporate a target environment, as shown in Figure 11-7. While the host environment will support early development, testing on the target system is necessary to ensure that the system and any changes to it are unaffected by peculiarities of the target system. Testing in the target system can establish whether the hardware and software delivered meet system requirements.

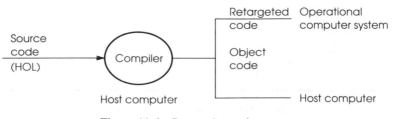

Figure 11-6   Retargeting code

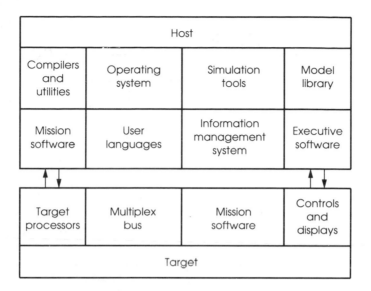

Figure 11-7 Host/target environment

Thus the support concept must take into account the possibility of acquiring a specific target environment if the user wishes to assume maintenance responsibility. This usually turns out to be difficult, and the buyer may become locked into a specific seller for the duration of the life cycle of the system unless specific steps are taken to ensure ownership of the target support system. Note that a target support environment is not necessarily identical to the target system. A support environment includes the target system as well as tools such as hardware- and software-testing devices.

The buyer should ensure that the rights and ownership of the target support environment are clearly established. In a contractor environment, ownership of the support facility becomes complex. The preferred strategy is to have the target environment moved into a buyer location or facility at the onset of operation. Possession is nine-tenths of the law. This will help alleviate problems that arise. The buyer must ensure that data rights to the software be obtained. Possession of the facility alone is not sufficient.

In the case of the host environment, the same stipulations given in (1) are still important. Again, because the host environment is expected to be commercially available, it may not be necessary to assume control at the onset of development. If, however, the buyer support concept is to employ buyer or user maintenance, a complete facility concept should be planned and the host facility acquired with the target facility. The host/target facility can be left at the seller's location until development is complete and operation begins and then moved into a buyer/user location. Splitting the host and target facilities is possible, but not desirable. This situation makes communication among team members more difficult and increases the complexity of end-to-end testing.

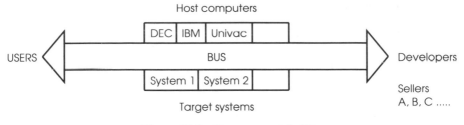

Figure 11-8   Buyer support facility

3. *Buyer facility.* In this scenario, from the very onset, development takes place in the buyer's environment. If the environment is not already in place, the developer may be responsible for assembling the support environment as a task of system development. This strategy should be used when the buyer wishes for some operational reason to house the support facility. It could be that the user may support more than one system in the facility, and the operation of the complete facility is necessary from an overall operational system standpoint. For example, a worldwide financial system may be composed of a number of separate software systems with a number of hardware configurations. This system may be supported by a wide range of contractors (Figure 11-8). The buyer and user desire to ensure control over the overall system, and it is impractical to separate the system simply for the convenience of the various contractors involved.

The disadvantage of this environment is that it places a burden on the buyer/user for the management of a complete facility. The buyer must worry about acquiring not only the hardware and software for the support environment but the physical facility as well. There may be increased costs of development as the seller may have to relocate personnel to the user's facility location. Of course, the seller may develop the system on a compatible host environment at the seller's location and transfer the system to the buyer/user environment after system test and acceptance. This type of arrangement is usually employed in large and complex environments and is not the norm because of its cost.

11.8 PRODUCTIVITY

One of the concerns that managers face is programmer productivity. The manager may want to develop early estimates of development cost and during development gauge the progress of individual programmers. In comparing different programmers' work, the manager should not fall into the trap of using such comparisons as an absolute measure without considering the complexity and quality of the code developed in each particular case. In any organization, there will be "hot shot" programmers able to turn out an enormous amount of code. That is not to say that programmers appearing to have low productivity should be eliminated. The outcome of the project is always more important than individual performance.

Productivity is a measure of the amount of work generated by a programmer over a period of time. It is commonly measured in lines of written code per man-month. The problem with this measurement is in equating it with the productivity expected to achieve the software product. The number of lines that a programmer is able to produce may have little meaning to the overall project. In fact, the number of lines is not a good measure for the planner at all. More realistically, productivity is measured in terms of the number of lines of code delivered (that is, lines of code that have been produced, tested, and documented). In other words, a set of code that results in an acceptable and usable system is the best productivity gauge.

Productivity figures are normally used by computer scientists to compare certain development methods and techniques. For example, early comparisons were made of the programmer productivity rates of higher-order language programming and assembly language programming. Oddly enough, the programming rates were very similar, varying from 100 to 400 lines of code per man-month for fairly complex applications. Since an HOL results in an expansion of source code relative to compiled machine language instructions, the resulting amount of code is much greater. Typically, this expansion is on the order of five to one. It would appear that if one could predict the lines of code required for the system, a fairly good estimate of the development effort could be made. For example, if a man-month costs 10,000 dollars, the cost per instruction, based on a productivity rate of between 100 to 400 lines of code per man-month, would range from 25 to 100 dollars per line of code.

The problem with this approach is the difficulty of predicting productivity rates for different projects. Systems of varying complexity and risk, albeit with the same expected number of lines of ultimate code, can require vastly different efforts. A simple database system can achieve very high productivity rates using off-the-shelf DBMSs with good support tools. In systems where the requirements are not well-defined, the programming rate can be fairly low. Rates for a system to produce real-time applications code for a production control system could range from 50 to 100 lines per man-month. Naturally, more complex systems will entail more expensive development efforts. In any event, such productivity figures, however interesting, are not practical except for gross comparisons of like systems produced under similar development methods.

The techniques for increasing productivity on software development projects must be selectively applied based on the circumstances of the development. The most popular current technique is the use of fourth-generation languages. This technique derives from the use of application generators. These are based on special languages, written in speechlike command statements, that are tuned to specific application areas such as the production of code for accounting systems. When applied, they are able to produce code very efficiently. The code produced may not be as efficient as code developed with more traditional techniques but can be fine-tuned to develop a production-quality system. Often these application generators are used to rapidly produce a system (prototype) in order to understand and refine the requirements for the system.

The common application of these languages is in data-intensive systems where the use of commercially available database management systems is in vogue. Used with DBMSs, they allow the user to rapidly formulate the user interface to a defined database. Thus the user can easily develop a system to utilize data that have been established in a usable data set or database and extract those data.

The use of techniques to rapidly produce code (such as prototypes and fourth-generation languages) is an aid to the development process. Their use is based on system factors such as requirements, schedule, risk of development, and so on. Obviously, if the requirements call for a database system, the use of fourth-generation languages with off-the-shelf database management systems is preferred except in unusual situations where a special-purpose database management system is required to meet system requirements. For example, the data from a real-time system such as radar might require a customized database system. The use of these special database systems, however, is fast disappearing as commercial DBMSs improve in effectiveness and efficiency.

The thrust to automate the programming process is ongoing. In Japan, there are examples of productivity rates of 1000 lines of delivered and documented code. Such cases, however, have occurred under special conditions. The applications area is usually very narrow, applications-tuned programming techniques are utilized, and the programming team is intimately familiar with the application environment. There is also work ongoing to apply programming techniques developed in the area of artificial intelligence, specifically knowledge-based systems, to increase productivity of systems development. This topic will be discussed in Chapter 12.

Future Directions
in Acquisition Management

The driving force in the computer industry has been the explosive advance of technology. Hardware technology has progressed so fast that the ability to keep pace with it has been sorely taxed. It has captured the imagination of a generation of computer technologists and provided the world with systems that have improved human existence.

Thirty years ago we were in what has been called the first generation of computer technology—the large mainframe environment, typified by the IBM 7090 computer. Today we are in a fourth-generation environment and rapidly moving toward a fifth. People are programming on powerful and dedicated work stations with interactive programming capabilities. Computers communicate with one another over vast telecommunications networks. Intelligent systems are being employed in medical diagnosis, oil exploration, and equipment maintenance.

This vastly improved hardware environment has made the jobs of software engineers both easier and more difficult. On the one hand, there is more capability at one's fingertips. On the other, this technology advance has presented a vast potential for applications that is straining the creativity of the software industry. Software technology has been unable to keep pace with the rapid developments in hardware.

This hardware explosion creates many challenges for software technologists and managers. Technologists strive to harness the technology by providing new capabilities. Software managers are confronted with new development paradigms. This chapter examines some of the new software technologies and management techniques.

12.1   ARTIFICIAL INTELLIGENCE (KNOWLEDGE-BASED SYSTEMS)

The knowledge-based system (KBS) is an application of software technology derived from the field of artificial intelligence. Artificial intelligence is often described as a processing technique that conveys the impression of possessing intelligence when solving a problem. A KBS is a system with a database that contains knowledge about a particular subject or domain. The user accesses the system through a speechlike applications language to pose and solve problems.

In the simplest sense, a knowledge-based system consists of three components (Figure 12-1):

- A user interface through which the user may enter problem statements and receive solutions.
- A knowledge base that contains the applications or domain-specific knowledge about the problem.
- An inference engine containing the processing system that associates the defined problem with the knowledge base and develops a solution.

The terms *knowledge-based systems* and *expert systems* have been used synonymously. An expert system is one in which the applications or domain-specific database contains expert knowledge. When the knowledge base consists of a set of rules, the system is said to be rule based. Thus an expert system that uses a set of rules describing expert knowledge is called a rule-based expert system.

Examples of knowledge-based/expert systems that have been built include (1) MYCIN, a system built at Stanford University used to diagnose infectious diseases, (2) R1, a system built by Digital Equipment Corporation to configure Digital Equipment's VAX computer systems based on customer requirements, and (3) DENDRAL, a system built at Stanford for identifying candidate molecular structures based on mass spectral and nuclear magnetic resonance data.

Traditional programming provides a specific data domain and an explicit algorithm to solve a specific problem. If the problem strays outside the algorithm's

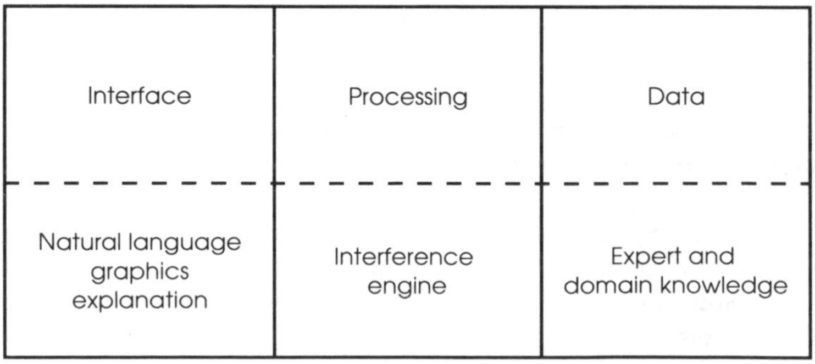

Interface	Processing	Data
Natural language graphics explanation	Interference engine	Expert and domain knowledge

Figure 12-1   Knowledge-based system

ability to solve it or the data changes in such a way that invalidates the algorithm, the program will be unable to arrive at a solution. In knowledge-based systems, the processing rules and data set are structured in such a way that a solution is almost always feasible, although perhaps with a degree of uncertainty. The solution is only as good as the data and rules contained in the knowledge base.

In knowledge-based systems the problem is not rigidly predefined. A problem or application-specific domain is defined (for example, diagnosis of gasoline-engine faults). Then a set of rules is defined about the domain. An example of a rule is, "If the engine is burning oil, it could mean that the rings are bad." This rule is then specified in a logical language and put into the knowledge base along with similar rules on gasoline engine performance. (Clearly, there are other possible reasons for a gasoline engine to burn oil.) The inference engine has to associate the rules with the problem to suggest a cause.

As human knowledge about a domain increases, that knowledge can be added to the knowledge base to increase the expertise of the system. The addition of new data and rules increases the logical capability of the system to solve problems and to do so with a greater degree of certainty. Thus the system can be improved to provide more intelligent answers.

In the evolution of this field, a new vernacular has developed as well as new development techniques. For example, a person who collects or extracts knowledge is termed a *knowledge engineer*. Another term is *logic programming*, which refers to the process by which logical statements are developed for processing by the KBS.

There are some striking differences between the approaches to developing a KBS and a traditional system. In a traditional project, concentration is focused on designing and developing software that will produce answers to a predefined set of conditions. For example, in a library management system, an off-the-shelf database system may be employed to manage the holdings of the library. The holdings are defined, and the interface to the DBMS is defined by the language of the DBMS. In a KBS, the problem domain is defined, but the specific problems are not. Instead concentration focuses on defining the knowledge that the system will require in order to address a general set of problems.

These differences require a different approach to the development of knowledge-based systems. In a KBS, the developers have to understand the problem domain that will support a credible solution set. In order to create the domain, knowledge engineers collect, or extract, and order knowledge (for example, the ordering of, and rules associated with, developing chemical compounds).

To expedite the building of knowledge-based systems, a number of kernel systems have been developed. These kernel systems are shells—they contain the inference engine (logical processing functions or search mechanism) and knowledge representation schemas but do not have a specific knowledge base. The software or knowledge engineer will select a kernel, in the same way that the database management system was selected to support the library system. In a simple scenario, a kernel system such as KES™ is selected. (KES is a trademark of Software Architecture & Engineering, Inc.) Rules are then developed based on a specific problem domain and a user interface created. If an off-the-shelf kernel is not used, the inference engine must be developed, a costly enterprise that has in the past made the application of knowledge-based systems difficult and time-consuming.

Knowledge-based systems affect software development in two ways:

- Improving the software development and management process.
- Changing traditional software engineering techniques.

The major impact that building knowledge-based systems has had on traditional software development models is the iterative approach in developing the system. A KBS development can be thought of as a trial-and-error process in which domain knowledge is continually added to the knowledge base, the system is exercised, new data are added, and so on. In traditional systems, the requirements to be met are defined at the beginning of the development, then allocated to the functional parts of the system. In a KBS, the requirements are completely different—the user may know the specific interface desired, but extraction of processing rules is a continuing and iterative process. In effect, the process is like a series of incremental prototypes. Instead of specific requirements being identified, the characteristics of the problem domain are identified. Instead of requirements and beginning design being decomposed, the concepts for representing the knowledge are explored, and an appropriate knowledge representation schema selected. Instead of the system being designed for coding, the design is oriented toward the structure that will be used to organize the knowledge. The implementation, instead of the coding of the design, is the formulation of the rules that embody the specific knowledge and expertise of the problem domain. This process is highly iterative (Figure 12-2).

Because this process does not fit neatly into existing models for software development, it causes problems for software managers who do not understand the differences involved. The development of a KBS may be only a part of a larger system, and management may try to superimpose the existing development process on the KBS development. Some say that the two cannot coexist. If the dynamics of the development are understood, however, the development model used can be tailored to accommodate KBS development.

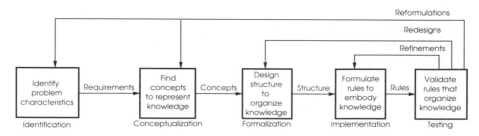

Figure 12-2   Evolutionary process of knowledge system development

Source: Stuart C. Shapiro (ed.), *Encyclopedia of Artificial Intelligence,* Volume 1, New York: John Wiley & Sons, 1987, p. 295. Copyright © 1987 Wiley. Reprinted by permission.

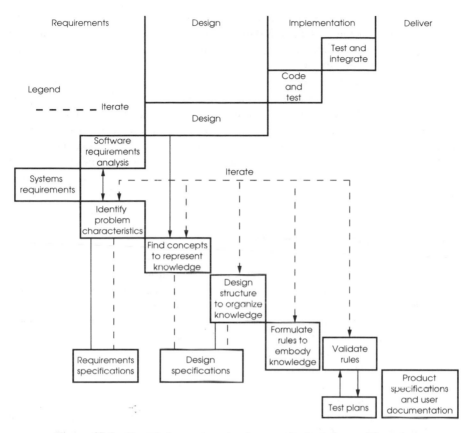

Figure 12-3 Knowledge-system development in the software life cycle

Figure 12-3 shows how the development process may be integrated into the incremental model. The trick is to modify documentation requirements to be compatible with the KBS development process. A modified software requirements specification can be used to record problem characteristics. A modified design document can be used to define concepts to represent knowledge and record the design of the knowledge representation structure. The testing documents will have to be modified in order to validate the rules.

Eventually new software management techniques and development models will evolve for knowledge-based systems. In the meantime, managers should be aware that, as with all development projects, KBS development must progress through requirements analysis, design, test, and integration to ensure that they meet user requirements.

A second area of interest is the use of knowledge-based techniques to improve the development of software. There is hope that these techniques can dramatically improve the productivity of software development. Techniques are being investigated for automatic programming. These techniques include synthesis of code from formal input-output specifications and from a natural language dialogue with the user. They rely on the use of formal specifications from which code can be automatically generated. Although there is interest and exploratory work in these techniques, it will be some time before they become of general use in the software management environment.

One of the most interesting techniques is in the capture of development knowledge for a specific applications environment. Today's documentation does not capture all the knowledge relating to a development. For example, design decisions may be made on various alternative design approaches. Usually the resulting design is documented, but the rationale for its selection is not. This knowledge is lost. If this knowledge is captured, the development process might be improved. Then, with a KBS containing this knowledge, the tool can be applied to provide expert advice on development.

12.2   REUSE AND STANDARDIZATION

As noted throughout the book, the topics of automation, reuse, and standardization have permeated most software improvement strategies within the acquisition community. The reasons for this emphasis are obvious. First, the software work load is increasing as systems get bigger and more complex. Without improvements in productivity, the amount of work that can be accomplished by the software work force in most organizations will not be adequate to meet the growing demand. Next, customers are demanding reduced software cost and improved quality. New and better ways of developing solutions to user problems need to be employed to accommodate these demands. Automation and reuse represent two complementary ways to improve productivity and customer satisfaction. Finally, increased standardization is needed to implement the improvement strategies. Standardized development environments need to be employed along with standard methods, languages, and tools to achieve the levels of productivity demanded by the marketplace.

12.2.1   Automation

Automation is being pursued to tool the life cycle processes for generating software so that engineers and programmers can do their jobs quicker and better. Considerable improvement has been made in this area as integrated collections of tools called software engineering or development environments (see Section 4.2.3) have been introduced for a variety of interconnected hardware platforms (networks containing personal computers, work stations, minicomputers, and mainframes).

The introduction of automation poses a dilemma for the buyer and seller. Both want to see improvements in productivity through automation, but they may take different approaches toward accomplishing this goal. The reasons for this divergence are simple. They may have invested in the past in equipment that may constrain their options (for example, one may be an IBM house while the other may be tied to Digital Equipment Corporation). That may have devised processes based on methods and languages that tie them to specific vendors (for example, an

Ada object-oriented design approach that uses Booch charts as the representation of choice for design and Ada as the language of choice for development). As a consequence, their methods may differ and each may use different tools and platforms. This divergence often leads to problems when the buyer transfers the seller's software into other organizations for life cycle support. Unless the tooling is specified as a deliverable, maintenance of the delivered product is often difficult and costly outside the seller's organization. Past experience suggests that the costs of maintenance can be reduced by using competitive market forces to keep the life cycle support organization lean. It is to the buyer's advantage, therefore, to establish ownership of the tooling or license to transfer it to another organization. The seller may confront a similar situation when subcontracting work. The seller may want to force the subcontractors to use a common set of tools and equipment.

In recent years, it has become common for the buyer to specify an environment. One of the following approaches is used to get the seller to agree to use a standard software engineering environment:

1. *Government or buyer-furnished equipment.* The buyer supplies the seller with the software tools and equipment to be used for developing and maintaining the software. This approach is seldom used because the buyer assumes liability for any problems that occur as a result of nonperformance. The buyer must also pay someone to keep the environment up-to-date. This presents a problem when the elements that make up the environment are in a state of flux.

2. *Interface requirements.* The buyer requires the seller to provide the software products (such as, designs, code, documentation) in a form compatible with the environment the buyer plans to use for life cycle support. The buyer avoids the liability and costs associated with dictating to the seller the exact products to use. The choice of the specific equipment and tools is left to the seller.

3. *Newly developed software.* The buyer requires the seller to develop, deliver, and transfer a software engineering environment as part of the acquisition. This is the most costly but least risky option as the buyer places total responsibility for equipment and tool selection in the hands of the seller.

Automation should be encouraged by the buyer. Independent of the option selected, the seller should be motivated to employ the best tools and equipment available. Incentives for automation can be provided contractually through value engineering and other programs that permit the buyer and the seller to share the resulting cost savings.

12.2.2 Reuse

The use of modern software languages like Ada and C++ has made software reuse practical. These languages can actually be used along with object-oriented methods and tools as a packaging technology to create libraries containing many different types of software artifacts (for example, code, designs, tests) that can be reused across builds, projects, and organizations. Reuse has not been practical in the past because packaging of software components was done in an ad hoc manner.

Implementing a reuse program requires long-term investments. The infrastructure present in most organizations must be changed so that policies, procedures, and practices encourage software engineers to develop and reuse existing software artifacts. Environments must be augmented with library systems that permit users to find components that fulfil their needs. These components must be of high quality and under configuration control. Otherwise, potential users won't trust them. In addition, some form of incentive needs to be offered to motivate people to use what already exists. Incentives may take the form of personnel policies that use degree of reuse achieved as a way to rate individual performance.

Again, the introduction of reuse in a project poses a dilemma to both the buyer and the seller. Both want to extract the benefits of a reuse program, but neither wants to pay for it. It takes considerable effort to design and develop reusable artifacts, and it requires money and effort to operate and stock a reuse library. Buyers and sellers are reluctant to invest the time and capital necessary to set up a reuse program.

There are several incentives for reuse. The first is an appeal to market forces. The buyer pressures the seller to invest in a reuse program that will eventually reduce seller costs and enhance competitiveness. The buyer encourages companies to develop salable reusable artifacts for incorporation into reuse libraries. Environment vendors are pressured to provide needed library capabilities off-the-shelf as part of their wares. A minimum exposure tack is followed in the effort to stimulate a commercial base for addressing buyer concerns. Yet such an approach suffers from the fact that the buyer surrenders much control.

As an alternative, the buyer and the seller can enter into a sort of partnership where incentives are used to stimulate one to satisfy the desires of the other. For example, the following incentive plan could be used by the buyer to reward the seller for reducing cost through reuse:

- *Award or incentive fee.* The buyer could use fees to reward the seller for achieving high levels of reuse. Of course, measures and criteria for administering fee payments will have to be established. In addition, incentives to keep a lid on costs will also have to be negotiated to minimize the buyer's exposure.
- *Value-engineering change.* The buyer could evaluate each reuse opportunity and share the savings with the seller on a negotiated basis using the concept of a value-engineering change. Each such change would be evaluated on its merits and approved when it would result in cost savings for the project.
- *Direct versus indirect allowances.* The buyer could reward the seller for reuse by making costs (such as for training) that are normally overhead expenses charged direct to the contract. Of course, administrative provisions for the award would have to be worked out in advance along with limits on the amounts to be paid when certain levels of reuse were indeed achieved.

- *Outright payments*. The buyer could pay the seller some nomimal amount each time an artifact was placed in a reuse library. Afterwards, the seller would receive some form of royalty payment each time the artifact was used by someone else.

Independent of the approach employed, the seller should be motivated by the contract to reduce cost by reusing off-the-shelf artifacts in software deliverables. Incentives similar to those listed need to be invoked contractually to financially reward the seller when reuse goals are achieved. The seller then needs to put into place internal incentives to motivate staff to make the reuse program work.

12.2.3 Standardization

The success of both the automation and reuse innovations discussed previously depends on the use of standards. Such standards present frameworks from which improvements in software productivity and quality evolve. In the case of automa-tion, standardization in the areas of platforms, networks, methods, database struc tures, and languages should be agreed upon prior to the unfolding of the strategy. Typically, some form of open-architecture standard is agreed to so that the system environment will be standardized no matter what hardware vendors are selected to provide platforms, communications devices, and peripherals. As an example, a company could adopt the Unix operating system, X-Windows, the Ada program-ming language, the ORACLE database manager, and the TCP/IP protocol as stan-dards so that the human/machine interface implemented would seem the same to users independent of the equipment selected for integration into the system.

In the case of reuse, other forms of standardization are needed. Software methods need to support the implementation of reuse artifacts. Standards for each artifact must be devised so that their representations (for example, design represented in the form of PDL), content (for example, form and style used for the code), and quality are uniform. Users of these artifacts must be able to depend on them, or the artifacts will not be reused. Finally, standards for the reuse library need to be developed so that access, operation, and maintenance can be supported as artifacts are inserted and withdrawn.

Standardization is a tricky game. Too much of it inhibits innovation and limits flexibility. Too little of it creates confusion and results in chaos. Balance is needed to prevent standards from tying the hands of those that have to implement them.

12.3 VERIFICATION AND VALIDATION

The process of verification and validation, as described in Chapter 6 (under Inde-pendent Verification and Validation), is being advocated as integral to the software development process. The difference between IV&V and V&V lies strictly in the word "independent." The concept is to promote V&V as a normal function of the development process. As currently described, V&V is an independent view of the engineering process. That is, the V&V function inspects the engineering process by providing an impartial view of the development. V&V is defined as "planning and performing all the reviews and audits (verification) and testing (validation) to be conducted throughout the software life cycle (SLC) to ensure that all requirements are satisfied" [IEEE, 1989].

In order to implement this function (or process, if one accepts the IEEE definition), V&V will have to be integrated into the life cycle development model. Fortunately, the IEEE draft standard P1074 provides guidance on how this may be accomplished [IEEE, 1989].

The V&V function will also have to be integrated into the seller organization. Most organizations do not include a V&V function. In a paper published in *IEEE Software*, four different approaches to integrating V&V into the organizational project environment are suggested [Wallace, 1989]:

1. Independent
2. Embedded in the systems engineering group
3. Embedded in the software quality assurance group
4. Embedded in the user group

The first, independent, is synonymous with IV&V as described in Section 6.6. This implies that the V&V function is totally independent of the project organization, either as an independent V&V supplier or as an independent function within the contractor organization.

The second, embedded in the systems engineering group, implies that the V&V group supports the project as shown in Figure 12-4. Thus V&V becomes more of a functional discipline as opposed to an organizational entity. The strong point of this approach is that the project organization has better control of the function, and V&V will reinforce project capabilities. The disadvantage, naturally, is the cost of a new functional entity.

The third, embedded in the software quality assurance function, is probably a poor choice due to the intrinsic conflict between the traditional role of QA in the project and the engineering approach of V&V. V&V could easily become more of an audit and inspection function and therefore an adjunct to the QA force. That, of course, is not all bad since QA functions often suffer from a lack of resources and emphasis. Over time, the QA function, redefined to incorporate a V&V function, could acquire the engineering experience and techniques necessary to become effective.

The last, user V&V, is identical to IV&V with the user responsible for the function. This concept has been advocated for some time. Its main argument is that the user is in the best position to verify and validate the system because the user must ultimately live with it. When the user assumes maintenance and support, user involvement in V&V increases their understanding of the system. This in turn facilitates the work of maintenance and support. V&V is not intended, however, to be a learning experience for the user. That is a task better left to the training program.

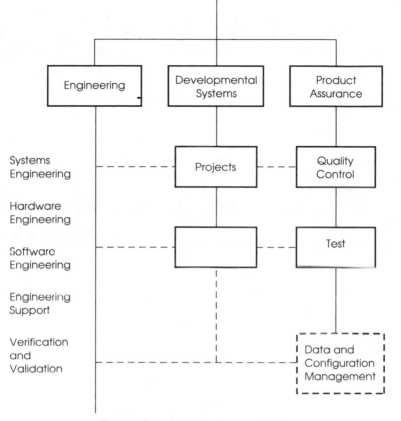

Figure 12-4   V&V in the organization

Another problem with a user V&V role is that most user organizations do not have the experienced personnel needed to adequately perform the function. In most cases the user is forced to seek support, usually from a V&V supplier. Thus the user supplants the buyer for contractually managing the V&V function, creating a schism in acquisition management. With the support of the buyer and seller, the user should participate in operational testing as a part of the system test team or as the lead organization for conducting operational testing.

The greatest difficulty with accepting this new thrust for a traditional V&V project role is the lack of guidance and procedures on how V&V relates to and interfaces with the project development team are described [Wallace, 1989]. Adding V&V will increase the overall cost of the development effort. Therefore, the same considerations for its application (see Chapter 6) are in order. The role of V&V may become more established, particularly in large contractor organizations and on large projects. The issues of integrating it into the project environment, when to apply it, and responsibility for its implementation will have to be addressed.

The most significant observation to be made is this: there is more emphasis being placed on V&V as a discipline. Thus the buyer and seller will have to understand the discipline and its application, both from a functional and an organizational viewpoint. To end on a positive note, V&V is certainly a concept whose time has come—it remains to be seen just how it will be integrated into the buyer/seller environment.

REFERENCES

[IEEE, 1989], *IEEE Draft Standard P1074/D4, Standard for Software Life Cycle Processes*, New York: The Institute of Electrical and Electronic Engineering Inc., August 8.

[Wallace, 1989] D. R. Wallace and R. U. Fujii, "Software Verification and Validation: An Overview," *IEEE Software*, Vol. 6, No. 3, IEEE Computer Society, Los Alamitos, CA, May, pp. 10–17.

Functional Road Map

Area	Defined	SOW	Buyer	Seller	Mentioned
Configuration management	*2.3.3	*4.3.3	6.3	7.7	8.1.4
Quality assurance	*Ch. 10 2.3.4	*4.3.4		7.6.2 7.8	8.1.5
Reviews and audits	*7.6 2.3.2	*4.3.5.3	6.4.1	*7.6	8.2.2 10.2.4
Testing	2.2.4 2.2.5	*4.3.5.2	*6.4.4 6.4.5 6.4.6.7		8.1.7
Requirements management		*4.2.1	*6.2.1		1.4
Indicators	*2.3.5	*4.3.5.4	*6.4.6	7.5	*9.6 10.4
Data rights	*11.6				5.2.4 11.7
Risk	3.2.2		*6.2.3	*7.9	
Documentation	*2.3.1	*4.3.1 4.3.2	6.4.6.8		8.1.3

* Indicates more substantive treatment

IEEE Software Engineering Standards Third Edition

ANSI/IEEE Std 728 1983 *Glossary of Software Engineering Terminology*

ANSI/IEEE Std 730-1984 *Software Quality Assurance Plans*

ANSI/IEEE Std 828-1983 *Software Configuration Management Plans*

ANSI/IEEE Std 829-1983 *Software Test Documentation*

ANSI/IEEE Std 830-1984 *Software Requirements Specifications*

ANSI/IEEE Std 982.1-1988 *Standard Dictionary of Measures to Produce Reliable Software*

ANSI/IEEE Std 982.1-1988 *Guide for the Use of IEEE Standard Dictionary of Measures to Produce Reliable Software (IEEE Std 982.1-1988)*

ANSI/IEEE Std 983-1986 *Software Quality Assurance Planning*

ANSI/IEEE Std 990-1987 *Ada As a Program Design Language*

ANSI/IEEE Std 1002-1987 *Taxonomy for Software Engineering Standards*

ANSI/IEEE Std 1008-1987 *Software Unit Testing*

ANSI/IEEE Std 1012-1986 *Software Verification and Validation Plans*

ANSI/IEEE Std 1016-1987 *Software Test Descriptions*

ANSI/IEEE Std 1028-1988 *Standard for Software Reviews and Audits*

ANSI/IEEE Std 1042-1987 *Guide to Software Configuration Management*

ANSI/IEEE Std 1058.1-1987 *Standard for Software Project Management Plans*

ANSI/IEEE Std 1063-1987 *Standard for Software User Documentation*

(Copies of approved ANSI/IEEE Standards may be obtained from The IEEE Computer Society, Order Department, 10662 Los Vaqueros Circle, Los Alamitos, CA 90720, 1-800-272-6657.)

Federal Acquisition Regulation

GENERAL STRUCTURE OF THE FAR

Subchapter A—General

Part 1—Federal acquisition regulations system
Part 2—Definitions of words and terms
Part 3—Improper business practices and personal conflicts of interest
Part 4—Administrative matters

Subchapter B—Competition and Acquisition Planning

Part 5—Publicizing contract actions
Part 6—Competition requirements
Part 7—Acquisition planning
Part 8—Required sources of supplies and services
Part 9—Contractor qualification
Part 10—Specifications, standards and other purchase descriptions
Part 11—Acquisition and distribution of commercial products
Part 12—Contract delivery or performance

Subchapter C—Contracting Methods and Contract Types

Part 13—Small purchase and other simplified purchase procedures
Part 14—Sealed bids
Part 15—Contracting by negotiation

Subchapter H—Clauses and Forms

BIBLIOGRAPHY

Agresti, W. W. *Tutorial: New Paradigms for Software Development.* New York: IEEE Computer Society Press, 1986.

Arthur, L. J. *Measuring Programmer Productivity and Software Quality.* New York: Wiley, 1985.

Arthur, L. J. *Software Evolution: The Software Maintenance Challenge.* New York: Wiley, 1988.

Augustine, N. R. *Augustine's Laws.* New York: AIAA, 1984.

Barr, C. T., E. D. Callender and M. J. Steinbacker. "Life-Cycle Management & Documentation Concepts for the Space Station Program." *Proceedings of the (COMPSTAN) Computer Standards Conference,* Washington, DC, March 21–23, 1988.

Beizer, B. *Software Systems Testing and Quality Assurance.* New York: Van Nostrand Reinhold, 1984.

Bersoff, E. H., V. D. Henderson and S. G. Siegel. *Software Configuration Management.* Englewood Cliffs, NJ: Prentice Hall, 1980.

Block, B. *The Politics of Projects.* New York: Yourdon Press, 1983.

Boehm, B. W. "A Spiral Model of Software Development and Enhancement." *Computer,* Vol. 21, No. 5, Los Alamitos, CA: IEEE Computer Society, May 1988, pp. 61–72.

Boehm, B. W. "Improving Software Productivity." *Computer,* Vol. 20, No. 9, Los Alamitos, CA: IEEE Computer Society, September 1987, pp. 43–57.

Boehm, B. W. *Software Engineering Economics.* Englewood Cliffs, NJ: Prentice Hall, 1981.

Boehm, B. W. *Tutorial: Software Risk Management.* New York: IEEE Computer Society Press, April 1988.

Booch, G. *Software Engineering with Ada,* 2nd ed. Redwood City, CA: Benjamin-Cummings, 1987.

Bowen, T. P., G. B. Wigle and J. T. Tsai. *Specification of Software Quality Attributes, RADC-TR-85-37, Vol. 1–3.* Boeing Aerospace Company, 1985.

Brennan, J. R., and S. A. Burton. "Warranties: Concept to Implementation." *Proceedings Annual Reliability and Maintainability Symposium,* 1989, pp. 1–7.

Brooks, F. P. "No Silver Bullet: Essence and Accidents of Software Engineering." *Computer,* Vol. 20, No. 4, Los Alamitos, CA: IEEE Computer Society, April 1987, pp. 10–19.

Brooks, F. P. *The Mythical Man-Month: Essays on Software Engineering.* Reading, MA: Addison-Wesley, 1975.

Bryan, W. L., and S. G. Siegel. *Software Products Assurance: Techniques for Reducing Software Risk.* New York: Elsevier, 1987.

Buckley, F. J. *Implementing Software Engineering Practices.* New York: Wiley, 1989.

Burrill, C. W., and Leon W. Ellsworth. *Modern Project Management.* Burrill-Ellsworth Associates, NJ: 1980.

Callender, E. D., et al. "NASA Space Station Standards for Information System Documentation." *Proceedings of the IEEE COMPASS 87,* Washington, DC: July 1987.

Carver, D. L. "Acceptable Legal Standards for Software." *IEEE Software,* Vol. 5, No. 3, Los Alamitos, CA: IEEE Computer Society, May 1988, pp. 87–93.

Chow, T. S. *Tutorial: Software Quality Assurance—A Practical Approach.* Los Alamitos, CA: IEEE Computer Society Press, 1985.

Comptroller General of the United States. *Contracting For Computer Software Development—Serious Problems Require Management Attention to Avoid Wasting Additional Millions.* U.S. Government Accounting Office, FGMSD-80-4, Washington, DC, November 9, 1979.

Conte, S. D., H. E. Dunsmore and V. Y. Shen. *Software Engineering Metrics and Models.* Menlo Park, CA: Benjamin-Cummings, 1986.

Cooper, F. L., III. *Law and the Software Marketer.* Englewood Cliffs, NJ: Prentice Hall, 1988.

Cooper, J. D., and M. J. Fisher. *Software Quality Management.* New York: Petrocelli, 1979.

Cusumano, M. A. "The Software Factory: A Historical Interpretation." *IEEE Software,* Vol. 6, No. 2, Los Alamitos, CA: IEEE Computer Society, March 1989, pp. 23–30.

Dart, S. A., R. J. Ellison, P. H. Feiler and N. Haberman. "Software Development Environments." *Computer,* Vol. 20, No. 11, Los Alamitos, CA: IEEE Computer Society, November 1987, pp. 18–28.

Deasy, K., and A. C. Martin. "Seeking the Balance between Government and Industry Interests in Software Acquisition." *Rutgers Computer and Technology Law Journal,* Vol. 14, No. 1, 1988.

Defense Systems Management College. *System Engineering Guide.* Fort Belvoir, VA, 1983.

DeMarco, T. *Controlling Software Projects.* New York: Yourdon Press, 1986.

DeMarco, T. *Structured Analysis and System Specification.* Englewood Cliffs, NJ: Prentice Hall, 1979.

DeMarco, T., and T. Lister. *Peopleware: Productive Projects and Teams.* New York: Dorset House, 1987.

DeMillo, R. A., W. M. McCracken, R. J. Martin and J. F. Passafiume. *Software Testing and Evaluation: A Report*. Menlo Park, CA: Benjamin-Cummings, 1987.

Deming, W. E. *Out of the Crisis*. Cambridge, MA: MIT Center for Advanced Engineering Study, 1986.

Deming, W. E. *Quality, Productivity and Competitive Position*. Cambridge, MA: MIT Center for Advanced Engineering Study, 1982.

Department of the Air Force. *Air Force Systems Command Software Management Indicators, AFSCP 800-43*. Andrews Air Force Base, MD, January 31, 1986.

Department of the Air Force. *Air Force Systems Command Software Quality Indicators, AFSCP 800-14*. Andrews Air Force Base, MD, January 20, 1987.

Department of the Air Force. *Government Contract Law*, 6th ed. March 1979.

Department of the Air Force. *Weapons System Warranties, Air Force Regulation 800-47*. May 17, 1988.

Department of the Army. *Procurement Law*. Pamphlet No. 27-153, January 1976.

Department of Defense. *Draft Total Quality Management Guide*. DOD 5000.51-G, August 23, 1989.

Department of Defense. *Federal Acquisition Regulations*. February 1987.

Department of Defense. *Transitioning from Development to Production—Solving the Risk Equation*. DOD Manual 4245.7, September 1985.

Department of Defense Standard 1703. Software Development Standards, May 1987.

Department of Defense Standard 2167A. Defense System Software Development, February 29, 1988.

Department of Defense Standard 2168. Defense System Software Quality Program, August 1, 1979.

Department of the Navy. *Defense Contracts Management for Technical Personnel*. 1983.

Dunn, R., and R. Ullman. *Quality Assurance for Computer Software*. New York: McGraw-Hill, 1982.

Edmunds, R. A. *The Prentice Hall Guide to Expert Systems*. Englewood Cliffs, NJ: Prentice Hall, 1988.

Evans, M. W. *The Software Factory*. New York: Wiley, 1989.

Evans, M. W., and J. Marciniak. *Software Quality Assurance and Management*. New York: Wiley, 1987.

Evans, M. W., P. Piazza and J. B. Dolkas. *Principles of Productive Software Management*. New York: Wiley, 1983.

Fairley, R. E. *Software Engineering*. New York: McGraw-Hill, 1985.

Fox, J. M. *Software and Its Development*. Englewood Cliffs, NJ: Prentice Hall, 1982.

Freedman, D. P., and G. M. Weinberg. *Handbook of Walkthroughs, Inspections, and Formal Reviews*, 3rd ed. Boston: Little, Brown, 1982.

Gevarter, W. B. *An Overview of Expert Systems, NBSIR 82-2505*. Washington, DC: U.S. Department of Commerce, May 1982.

Gevarter, W. B. "The Nature and Evaluation of Commercial Expert System Building Tools." *Computer*, Vol. 20, No. 5, Los Alamitos, CA: IEEE Computer Society, May 1987, pp. 24–41.

Goel, A. L. *An Experimental Investigation into Software Reliability*. Rome Air Development Center Technical Report: RADCTR-88-213, October 1988.

Grady, R. B., and D. L. Caswell. *Software Metrics: Establishing a Company-wide Program.* Englewood Cliffs, NJ: Prentice Hall, 1987.

Hoare, C. A. R. "Programming: Sorcery or Science?" *IEEE Software,* Vol. 1, No. 2, Los Alamitos, CA: IEEE Computer Society, April 1988, pp. 5–16.

Humphrey, W. S. *Managing the Software Process.* Reading, MA: Addison-Wesley, 1989.

Humphrey, W. S., and D. H. Kitson. *Preliminary Report on Conducting SEI-Assisted Assessments of Software Engineering Capability, Technical Report CMU/SEI-87-TR-16.* Pittsburgh, PA: Software Engineering Institute, July 1987.

Humphrey, W. S., and W. L. Sweet. *A Method for Assessing the Software Engineering Capability of Contractors, Technical Report CMU/SEI-87-TR-23.* Pittsburgh, PA: Software Engineering Institute, September 1987.

IEEE. *ANSI/IEEE Std 729-1983, IEEE Standard Glossary of Software Engineering Terminology.* New York: The Institute of Electrical and Electronic Engineers, Inc., 1983.

IEEE. *ANSI/IEEE Std 1058.1-1987, Standard for Software Project Management Plans.* New York: The Institute of Electrical and Electronic Engineers, Inc., 1987.

IEEE. *IEEE Draft Standard P-1061/D20, Standard for a Software Quality Metrics Methodology.* Los Alamitos, CA: IEEE Computer Society, September 1, 1989.

IEEE. *IEEE Draft Standard P1074/D4, Standard for Software Life Cycle Processes.* New York: The Institute of Electrical and Electronic Engineers, Inc., August 8, 1989.

IEEE Computer Society. "Tools—Making Reuse a Reality." *IEEE Software,* Vol. 4, No. 4, Los Alamitos, CA: IEEE Computer Society, July 1987.

Jordan, P. W., K. S. Keller, R. W. Tucker and D. Vogel. "Software Storming: Combining Rapid Prototyping and Knowledge Engineering." *Computer,* Vol. 22, No. 5, Los Alamitos, CA: IEEE Computer Society, May 1989, pp. 39–48.

Kidder, T. *Soul of a New Machine.* New York: Avon 1982.

Londeix, B. *Cost Estimation for Software Development.* Reading, MA: Addison-Wesley, 1987.

Lugi, "Software Evolution Through Rapid Prototyping." *Computer,* Vol. 22, No. 5, Los Alamitos, CA: IEEE Computer Society, May 1989, pp. 13–25.

Marine, G. E. "Integrating Software Quality Metrics with Software QA." *Quality Progress,* November 1988, pp. 38–43.

McClure, C. *CASE is Software Automation.* Englewood Cliffs, NJ: Prentice Hall, 1989.

McCorduck, P. *Machines Who Think.* San Francisco, CA: Freeman, 1979.

Metzger, P. W. *Managing a Programming Project,* 2nd ed. Englewood Cliffs, NJ: Prentice Hall, 1981.

Meyer, N. D., and M. E. Boone. *The Information Edge.* New York: McGraw-Hill, 1986.

Miyamoto, M. *A Book of Five Rings.* New York: Bantam, 1982.

Musa, J. D. "Tools for Measuring Software Reliability." *IEEE Spectrum,* Vol. 26, No. 2, New York, Feb. 1989, pp. 39–42.

Musa, J. D., A. Iannino and K. Okumoto. *Software Reliability: Measurement, Prediction, Application.* New York: McGraw-Hill, 1987.

NASA Software Management Assurance Plan (SMAP). Information System Life-Cycle Documentation Standards, Release 4.3, February 28, 1989.

Page-Jones, M. *Practical Project Management: Restoring Quality to DP Projects and Systems*. New York: Dorset House, 1985.

Peters, T., and N. Austin. *Passion for Excellence*. New York: Random House, 1985.

Peters, T. J., and R. H. Waterman. *In Search of Excellence*. New York: Harper & Row, 1982.

Presson, E. *Software Test Handbook*. RADC-TR-84-53, Vol. 1–2, Boeing Aerospace Company, March 1984.

Pressman, R. S. *Making Software Engineering Happen*. Englewood Cliffs, NJ: Prentice Hall, 1988.

Pressman, R. S. *Software Engineering: A Practitioner's Approach, 2nd ed.* New York: McGraw-Hill, 1987.

Radatz, J. W. *Analysis of IV&V Data (R:SED-81319)*. San Pedro, CA: Logicon, Inc., 1981.

Reifer, D. J. "Ada's Impact: A Quantitative Assessment." *Proceedings ACM SIGAda International Conference*, December 1987.

Reifer, D. J. "Contracting for Software Quality Assurance." *Proceedings 13th Hawaii International Conference on System Science*, Honolulu, 1980

Reifer, D. J. *Final Report: Findings of Reuse Survey Task*. RCI-TN-410A, August 30, 1989.

Reifer, D. J. *Final Report: Recommendations of the Reuse Taxonomy Development Task*. RCI-TN-418A, September 14, 1989.

Reifer, D. J. *Tutorial: Software Management, 3rd ed.* New York: IEEE Computer Society Press, 1986.

Reifer, D. J. "Workstation/APSE Productivity Study Results," *Proceedings of TRIAda '89*, October 1989.

Reifer, D. J., R. W. Knudson and J. Smith. *Final Report: Software Quality Survey*, American Society of Quality Control. November 20, 1987.

Royce, W. W. "Managing the Development of Large Software Systems: Concepts and Techniques." *Proc. WESCON*, August 1970. Also available in *Proc. ICSE 9*, Computer Society Press, 1987.

Samuelson, P. *Toward a Reform of the Defense Department Software Acquisition Policy, Technical Report CMU/SEI-86-TR-1*. Pittsburgh, PA: Software Engineering Institute, 1986.

Samuelson, P., and K. Deasy. *Intellectual Property Protection for Software*. Curriculum Module SEI-CM-14-2.0, Software Engineering Institute, Carnegie Mellon University, Pittsburgh, PA, 1989.

Schlender, Brenton R. "How to Break the Software Logjam." *Fortune*, Vol. 120, New York, September 25, 1989, pp. 100–112.

Schultz, H. P. *Software Management Metrics, Technical Report ESD-TR-88-001*. Bedford, MA: The MITRE Corporation, May 1988.

Schwartz, K. D., "DOD Hopes Quality Control Can Save Time, Money." *Government Computer News*, January 8, 1990, p. 40.

Taylor, W. A. *What Every Engineer Should Know About Artificial Intelligence*. Cambridge, MA: MIT Press, 1988.

Thayer, R. T. *Tutorial: Software Engineering Project Management.* Los Alamitos, CA: IEEE Computer Society Press, 1988.

U.S.A.F. *Draft Air Force Systems Command/Air Force Logistics Command Pamphlet, Software Risk Abatement.* AFSC/AFLC Pamphlet 800-45, February 11, 1988.

Weinberg, G. M. *Understanding the Professional Programmer.* New York: Dorset House, 1988.

Winston, P. H. *Artificial Intelligence.* Reading, MA: Addison-Wesley, 1977.

Wrubel, R. "Restructuring the Pentagon." *Financial World,* November 14, 1989, pp. 57–60.

Yourdon, E. *Managing the System Life Cycle: A Software Development Methodology Overview,* 2nd ed. Englewood Cliffs, NJ: Prentice Hall, 1988.

Yourdon, E. *Structured Walkthroughs,* 4th ed. Englewood Cliffs, NJ: Prentice Hall, 1988.

INDEX